Private Equity Financing in Infrastructure and Real Estate

Josephine Gemson · Thillai Rajan A.

Private Equity Financing in Infrastructure and Real Estate

Impact, Strategies, and Value Addition

Springer

Josephine Gemson
King's University College at Western University
London, ON, Canada

Thillai Rajan A.
Department of Management Studies
Centre for Research on Start-ups and Risk Financing
Indian Institute of Technology Madras
Chennai, Tamil Nadu, India

ISBN 978-981-16-1633-4 ISBN 978-981-16-1634-1 (eBook)
https://doi.org/10.1007/978-981-16-1634-1

This Springer imprint is published by the registered company Springer Nature Singapore Pte Ltd.
The registered company address is: 152 Beach Road, #21-01/04 Gateway East, Singapore 189721, Singapore

Foreword

"Build a better mousetrap," the American philosopher Ralph Waldo Emerson said (at least according to legend), "and the world will beat a path to your doorstep." The recent history of private capital illustrates the wisdom of this two-century-old adage.

While wealthy individuals have been providing funds to entrepreneurs at least since the time of Hammurabi in ancient Babylon, the modern private capital industry did not originate until after World War II. In 1946, General Georges Doriot—Harvard Business School professor, architect of the U.S. Army's supply chain in Europe during the War and subsequent founder of the INSEAD business school—launched American Research & Development. ARD was by most accounts the first formalized private capital fund: It sought to invest in private entities, using money raised from institutional as well as individual investors. Its immortality was assured by its US$70 thousand investment in Digital Equipment Corporation, which turned into more than 500 times that amount.

Doriot's success attracted many imitators. First came funds dedicated to venture capital in the 1950s and 1960s, then leveraged buyout specialists in the late 1970s and early 1980s. These were followed by private capital funds undertaking mezzanine, growth, fund-of-fund, secondary and many other flavors of investment. Soon, financiers realized that the private capital model could work effectively in other asset classes as well.

While institutions and families had long invested in real estate, many of these deals were done through direct transactions or publicly traded real estate investment trusts. Many credit Sam Zell with forming the first real estate private capital fund, Zell-Merrill I, which was raised in 1988. In establishing this fund, modeled directly after buyout funds of the day, Zell was motivated by the excessively leveraged transactions that characterized the deals of the day. He correctly anticipated that there would be ample chances for an "opportunistic" fund that could swoop in and buy distressed properties once the market collapsed.

Zell was soon joined by others: first Goldman Sachs and the Whitehall funds, and then a plethora of others. These included dedicated real estate investment groups (for instance, AEW, Colony, Lone Star and Starwood), investment bank-affiliated funds (CSFB and Lehman soon joined Goldman in sponsoring funds) and buyout groups that crossed over to offer products (Angelo Gordon Apollo, Blackstone and Cerberus, to name a few). And just like corporate investing evolved from undifferentiated funds undertaking a wide variety of investments to many specialists, the early generalist real estate funds splintered into groups undertaking a wide variety of projects, from "core plus" to infrastructure. Doriot's initial mousetrap, over the course of a few decades, had taken on many more forms and grown far more substantial than he could have ever imagined!

This book examines this evolution, focusing on funds investing in real estate and infrastructure. While these groups have many resemblances to their cousins undertaking venture capital and leveraged buyouts, they also faced distinctive challenges when it came to evaluating, structuring, governing and exiting investments. The authors articulate the special features associated with these critically important deals, globally but also in some cases with an India-specific focus. The issues are indeed fascinating ones, which the book does a terrific job of putting into a broader context.

January 8, 2023

Josh Lerner
Harvard Business School
Boston, Massachusetts, USA

Preface

You see, but you do not observe.
—Sir Arthur Conan Doyle, A Scandal in Bohemia

While the world faced a black swan event in early 2020 in the form of the COVID-19 pandemic, it was feared that its extreme rarity and severe impact worldwide would create dire economic and financial market consequences. However, after hitting a few (many) bumps (hard) along the way, it became "the new normal" to adapt to calamitous situations. This "new normal" paved the way, eventually, for normal-ish sort of activities—working from home, online synchronous education, food delivered to our door, groceries picked up, doctor on call without having to visit the hospital, and the like—activities which could not have been thought possible even at the beginning of the decade.

On that note, we ask the question, What is infrastructure?

In the opening class on infrastructure finance, we start by asking this question. While the students may find it difficult to define or explain what infrastructure is, they are mostly comfortable to state what their perception of infrastructure is by citing an example. This leads us to believe that infrastructure belongs to that set of topics, where *"one knows it when they see it"*.[1]

Academic literature has also acknowledged the fact that one of the most remarkable aspects of infrastructure is how little one really thinks about it.[2] Infrastructure has been traditionally classified into two categories: physical infrastructure—comprising roads, bridges, power plants and so on, and social infrastructure—comprising schools, hospitals, public libraries and so on. More recently, in practice or policy-making, there has been a tendency to associate the term infrastructure with specific sort of projects and even institutions. For example, in a policy conference where the then Prime Minister of India, Dr. Manmohan Singh spoke, institutions

[1] This phrase was made popular by the US Justice Potter Stewart in 1964 when he attempted to define obscenity.

[2] Gerencser and Hamiliton (2011).

such as stock exchanges, regulatory agencies, banks and so on were considered as economic infrastructure.

In this book, we restrict our discussion to largely physical infrastructure. Access to physical infrastructure plays a very important role in enhancing the quality of life. Several studies have also highlighted the direct relationship between infrastructure and economic growth (e.g. Aschaeur, 1989). There are numerous examples of countries embarking on large infrastructure projects to stimulate economic growth in their economies. While the common man may not think too much about infrastructure unless it is absent or stops working, it is perhaps one of the foremost items on the agenda of many governments. Taken together, the governments of the USA, Canada, Australia, UK, Russia, China, India and France (just to name a few) have pledged to invest a mind boggling US$4.9 trillion in infrastructure over the next decade. The sheer intensity of the amounts should certainly draw attention into infrastructure.

Infrastructure projects are, in general, capital intensive. The dominant model of infrastructure creation in the modern world has been by the public sector or the government. However, since the 1990s, changes in the political and economic paradigm have led to increased private sector ownership and participation in infrastructure projects. For example, The Canada Investment Bank (CIB), established under the Canada Infrastructure Bank Act in 2017, actively seeks investment and participation from public, private and institutional investors for its US$35 billion projects.[3] The Chair of Canada Infrastructure Bank, Micheal Sabia, said,

"One of the defining features of the Canada Infrastructure Bank is attracting private investment to new infrastructure. Every dollar of public investment in these initiatives is intended to attract additional dollars from private and institutional investors". [4]

Among the various reasons for the shift toward private sector participation, two stand out: (i) augmenting government resources with private sector capital and (ii) bringing private sector efficiencies into the infrastructure sector.

Private sector infrastructure projects were characterized by significant proportion of debt funding (from banks and term-lending institutions), with the equity component coming from the private sector project developers. However, with the scale of projects increasing, the developers were unable to meet the entire equity requirement for the project. In addition, many developers sought liquidity for their previous investments, so that they had the capital for the future projects. This led to the emergence of a new breed of investors, viz. private equity (PE), who began to invest in the equity and equity-based securities in infrastructure projects.

While PE has been in existence for decades, primarily as Venture Capital for Technology investments, Buyout Funds for Mergers and Acquisitions and so on, the incidence of PE investing in infrastructure projects is new. This prompted us to write this book.

---

[3] https://www.pbo-dpb.gc.ca/en/blog/news/BLOG-2021-015--canada-infrastructure-bank--banque-infrastructure-canada#_ftn1.

[4] https://pm.gc.ca/en/news/news-releases/2020/10/01/prime-minister-announces-infrastructure-plan-create-jobs-and-grow.

PE may not have been something that you and I discuss at the dinner table, perhaps, until Taylor Swift dragged PE into her fights over music rights.[5] Suddenly, PE was all everyone talked about although it had by then had quietly but surely developed from an alternate asset class into an asset class it its own right.

PE has been most famously known for its mind-boggling deals like the acquisition of RJR Nabisco in 1989, which was the inspiration for the successful book and movie "Barbarians at the Gate", the acquisition of Hilton for US$26 billion at the height of the real estate bubble in 2007, and the US$48 billion acquisition of TXU—the largest electric utility of Texas between 2005 and 2007, which failed so spectacularly in 2014, causing even America's most famous investor Warren Buffet to lose nearly US$900 million in the process.

Since the late 90s, PE investors had begun their investment forays into the infrastructure sector. What started as a trickle, soon grew significantly. In 2006, the value of infrastructure deals backed by PE investors was about US$73 billion, whereas in 1988, it had been just 2 percent of the same. About US$50 billion–US$100 billion annually is raised globally by PE firms for infrastructure investing. In February 2022, Brookfield Asset Management announced that they were seeking to raise US$25 billion for their fifth flagship infrastructure fund, while their fourth fund of US$20 billion had already committed 75 percent of its capital for investment.[6] Brookfield Asset Management is a Canadian multinational company, one among the many alternate investment management firms worldwide.

Parallel to the infrastructure sector, the real estate sector has also been getting the attention of PE investors. Both these sectors have several common features: (1) large upfront investments, mostly in construction-related activities; (2) long asset lives, with the post-construction subsequent maintenance expenditures only a fraction of the initial upfront investment; (3) tangible and physical nature of the assets created; and (4) importance of these sectors in stimulating economic growth through the consumption of primary materials such as cement and steel as well as for employment creation. Therefore, while conceptualizing the scope of this book, we decided to include the real estate sector, along with infrastructure to broaden the insights. Well, another reason is also the dominance of the real estate sector over infrastructure sector. PE investment flows into real estate, at the rate of US$100–US$150 billion annually has been almost thrice the amount in infrastructure.

Both infrastructure and real estate are an integral part of the economy ultimately promoting a better standard of living and an enhanced quality of life. While real estate houses the world's population, their work, their leisure and everything in between, infrastructure links the physical systems providing connectivity and enables them to function efficiently. Infrastructure has often been rightly referred to as the backbone of a nation, providing physical structures for an economy to function, survive and thrive.

---

[5] https://www.nytimes.com/2019/11/24/business/taylor-swift-carlyle-scooter-braun.html.

[6] https://financialpost.com/investing/brookfield-to-target-25-billion-for-biggest-infrastructure-fund.

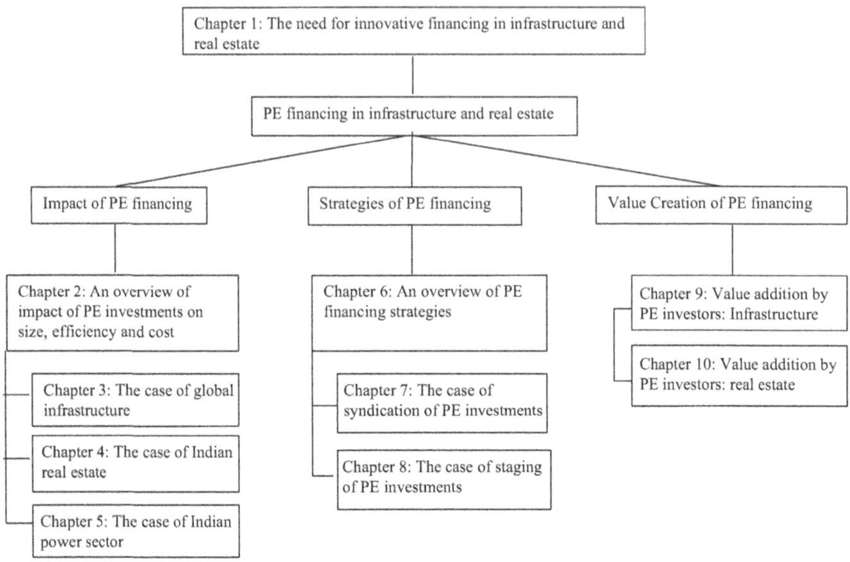

Fig. 1 Structure of this book

It is in this context that this book presents almost a decade's worth of scholarly inquiry into PE investments into infrastructure and real estate. This book examines such investments through various facets—the impact of PE on the infrastructure sector and the real estate sector, the various strategies used by these investors when they invest, and the value created.

A schematic structure of the book is given in Fig. 1. We start with an introductory chapter where we discuss the need and relevance for innovative financing in infrastructure and real estate sectors. We infer PE financing to be an innovative financing mechanism in these two sectors, which sets the context for the subsequent chapters of the text.

The remainder of the text is divided into three broad sections. The first section, comprising four chapters, delves into the impact of PE investments, with specific emphasis on project size. A short overview for the section sets the context for the three main chapters in the section. The first of those chapters (Chap. 3 of the book) analyzes PE investments in worldwide infrastructure deals and estimates the quantitative impact of the PE presence in infrastructure projects. While PE is known for large capital sizes and the use of extensive leverage, this study compares these qualities among infrastructure projects. It also examines the determinants of PE investments in infrastructure projects and explores the extent of PE financing in developed versus developing and emerging economies. The second of those chapters (Chap. 4 of the text) looks at the impact of PE in the Indian real estate. The third chapter in the section (Chap. 5 of the text) explores the case of PE in the Indian power sector.

The second section examines the financing strategies of PE investments. While there are several investment strategies used by PE investors, we examine the following two often seen strategies: staging and syndication. A brief overview of staging and syndication is presented in Chap. 6. Chapter 7 presents an analysis of PE syndication in infrastructure projects. It explores the choice for, the drivers of and the extent of syndication in PE investments. Chapter 8 examines the choice for, the motives behind and the determinants of PE staging in the infrastructure sector. Though the chapters on syndication and staging are predominantly based on the data of infrastructure projects, we believe the findings would be applicable for the real estate sector too.

The third section explores the value creation of PE financing. An important differentiating feature of PE investments as compared to other funding sources is the active involvement of the investors in monitoring and value addition in their portfolio investments. Therefore, a book like this would not be complete if value addition made by PE investors was not discussed. The final two chapters help us to address this objective. Using a combination of in-depth interviews and secondary data analysis, we highlight how PE investors create value in infrastructure (Chap. 9) and real estate (Chap. 10) sectors.

This book will prove useful to a variety of readers, from scholars in academia and beyond, to practitioners and policy-makers, and those who are directly or indirectly invested in infrastructure and real estate. The implications could be harnessed into best practices for these investment sectors, which long-standing and new investors will value as they continue to evaluate their investment objectives.

As authors, we have been privileged to be involved in this timely topic and encourage such relevant conversation. Our work has benefitted from people who contributed directly and indirectly to our studies—in the form of researchers, discussants, and reviewers. This book would not have been possible without the wholehearted support of our families and loved ones. We wish to thank our editors at Springer—Nupoor Singh, Fermine Shaly, and Lokeshwaran Manickavasagam—for bringing this project to publication. Last but not least, we would also like to thank our colleagues, students and scholars for being a part of our research journey.

Thillai Rajan began his research on this topic as a Fulbright-Nehru Senior Research Scholar at the Harvard Kennedy School, Harvard University. The financial support from the Fulbright Foundation and the collaboration with Prof. Gomez Ibanez and Prof. Akash Deep of Harvard Kennedy School have been a tremendous help in shaping his scholarly enquiry during the initial days. Thillai Rajan gratefully acknowledges the financial support from the Fulbright Foundation, and Prof. Akash Deep and Prof. Gomez Ibanez for the time spent in innumerable discussions on this subject. The Mossaver Rahmani Centre for Business and Government at the Harvard Kennedy School hosted Prof. Thillai Rajan during his stay and visit to the HKS, for which he is very grateful.

Josephine delved into PE in infrastructure during her Ph.D. days—as a research scholar under the tutelage of Thillai Rajan. It was during her time at the Indian Institute of Technology Madras (IIT-M) when she began researching on this topic and continues to do so even today. Josephine gratefully acknowledges the financial support from the King's Research Grants at King's University College at Western University for sections of this book.

London, Canada Josephine Gemson
Chennai, India Thillai Rajan A.

Contents

About the Authors

Josephine Gemson is currently Associate Professor at the School of Management, Economics and Mathematics at King's University College at Western University, Canada. She received her graduate degree in Finance from the University of Strathclyde, Glasgow, UK and her PhD from the Indian Institute of Technology (IIT) Madras, India. Her research interests include corporate finance, private equity, and project and infrastructure finance, and she has published her work regularly in noteworthy journals including the *Quarterly Review of Economics and Finance, Venture Capital, Utilities Policy, Journal of Private Equity, Journal of Structured Finance, and Public Works Management & Policy*. She teaches finance, economics, and accounting, and has experience teaching at the undergraduate, MBA, and executive-MBA levels in various countries.

Thillai Rajan A. is Professor of Finance at the Indian Institute of Technology Madras, Chennai, and a Founder of YNOS Venture Engine. He also heads the Centre for Research on Start-ups and Risk Financing at the Indian Institute of Technology Madras. A past Associate at the Mossavar-Rahmani Centre for Business and Government, Harvard Kennedy School, Harvard University, his teaching and research areas include corporate finance, project and infrastructure finance, public private partnerships and venture capital. He obtained his PhD from the Indian Institute of Management Bangalore and has received international research grants from organizations such as DFID, 3iE, and AusAID. His research has been published regularly in various journals, most notable among them being *Utilities Policy, Venture Capital, Energy Policy, Journal of Private Equity, ASCE Journal of Construction Engineering and Management, Development Policy Review, and The Journal of Development Effectiveness*. From 2009 to 2018 he edited the annual India Venture Capital and Private Equity Report series.

Chapter 1
The Need for Innovative Financing

When the winds of change blow, some people build walls and others build windmills.
—An ancient Chinese proverb

1.1 Introduction

On April 14, 2022, during the holy period of Lent and Ramadan alike, news broke out in the financial world that the Italian billionaire Benetton family had teamed up with the Blackstone Group, a flagship PE firm, to bid for the infrastructure group Atlantia, an Italian industrial company that operated motorways and airports.[1] The move to take Atlantia private was thought to be part of the Benetton's plan to reinvent Atlantia, after the company experienced a few setbacks, including the sale of Autostrade, following the deadly Genoa bridge collapse in 2018. The buyer consortium (PE Blackstone group and Benetton holding company Edizione) was said to have offered Atlantia investors €23 a share in cash, a move that saw the stock rising as much as 5.8 percent in Milan. Consequently, the deal valued the company's equity at €19 billion, and reportedly was the largest public-to-private transaction for a European listed company. Such deals highlighted the fervent PE activity and trends in infrastructure

[1] https://www.bloomberg.com/news/articles/2022-04-14/benettons-blackstone-offer-to-buy-atlantia-for-eu23-per-share, https://pitchbook.com/news/articles/largest-take-private-europe-blackstone-benetton-atlantia (accessed 15 Apr 2022).

Some sections of this chapter are based on the journal papers titled "Impact of private equity investments in infrastructure projects" which appeared in Utilities Policy, 2012, https://doi.org/10.1016/j.jup.2011.12.001, "What Do PE Investors Seek From Syndication Partners? Evidence From the Infrastructure Sector" which appeared in Public Works and Management Policy, 2015, https://doi.org/10.1177/1087724X15613095, and "A new perspective on private equity stage financing: Evidence from investments in infrastructure" which appeared in *Venture Capital: An International Journal of Entrepreneurial Finance.* 17(4), 299–325, https://doi.org/10.1080/13691066.2015.1052193.

J. Gemson and Thillai Rajan A., *Private Equity Financing in Infrastructure and Real Estate*, https://doi.org/10.1007/978-981-16-1634-1_1

and real estate, despite the uncertainties caused by the looming COVID-19 pandemic, soaring energy prices and geopolitical volatility.

Gangavaram Port is an all-weather, multipurpose port located in the town of Vishakapatnam in the South Indian state of Andhra Pradesh. This was the deepest Indian port and, at a depth of 21 m, it could handle Super Cape size vessels of up to 200,000 DWT—cargo groups including coal, iron-ore, fertilizer, limestone, bauxite, raw sugar, project cargo, alumina and steel products. It was a Greenfield project in one of the world's emerging economies—India. The construction of this port began in December 2005. In 2007, the US-based private equity group Warburg Pincus took a 31.5 percent stake in the project. The port was set up on schedule and began operations in July 2009. In 2018, it handled an annual cargo tonnage of 18.04 million tons. Subsequently, Warburg Pincus signaled its interest to sell its stake in this port. Warburg Pincus, continuing its stint in India's burgeoning investments in and development of infrastructure, had since shown interest in CleanMax Solar (in one of the largest overseas investments in Indian rooftop solar space up to US$100 million), in acquiring Air India (India's international airline services), in investing in healthcare in India, and in logistics and building warehouses.[2]

On June 8, 2022, Bain Capital closed a US$2 billion "special situations fund" for the Asia–Pacific Region to cover various asset types but with a focus on real estate.[3] For Bain Capital, an American private investment firm specializing in PE and VC among other forms of investing, this fund was the second of its type in Asia, with the first valued at US$1 billion. Barnaby Lyons, one of the firm's managing directors acknowledged that real estate, financial services, and aviation sectors across Asia had been key areas for Bain's special situations deal making and would remain a focus for the second fund.

Investments such as these underline the interest of PE firms in the infrastructure sector and the real estate sector the world over. Infrastructure facilities, which were once developed, financed and operated by the public authorities have gradually moved toward private sector development and financing. Since the early 80s, private-sector financing of infrastructure projects have experienced a dramatic revival (Brealey et al., 1996). The advent of PE investment in infrastructure is another step in the trajectory of private financing of infrastructure. With more deals, PE has begun to gain spotlight as an investment tool to provide capital to infrastructure projects (Lorenzo, 1996). While real estate has been predominantly financed by the private sector for a long time, the advent of PE more or less coincided in both infrastructure and real estate. From a modest start in the 80's, the trickle of PE money into infrastructure and real estate soon grew to large proportions, and several billion-dollar funds dedicated to core sector financing came into existence. From about US$5 billion in 1980, total PE investments grew to the tune of about US$200 billion by 2003, translating to a CAGR of 17.4 percent. In line with the overall trend, PE investments in real estate

[2] https://www.livemint.com/topic/warburg-pincus.

[3] https://pe-insights.com/news/2022/06/08/bain-capital-closes-2-billion-asia-special-situations-fund/ (accessed 09 Jun 2022).

witnessed steep growth. As per Preqin,[4] there has been a gradual rise in logistic Private Equity Real Estate (PERE) deals during 2009–19, with 207 deals in 2019 with an aggregate value of US$32 billion.

1.2 Infrastructure and Real Estate: Creating the Setting

1.2.1 What Constitutes Infrastructure and Real Estate?

Infrastructure plays a very important role in ensuring a high quality of life in the modern world. Infrastructure and real estate, because of the tight interlinkages with economic growth, are also called the backbone of a nation. It is with infrastructure that regions are able to function effectively, yet one of the most remarkable aspects of infrastructure is how little one really thinks about it.[5]

Lewis (2008) provided a well-rounded discussion into the origins and meaning of infrastructure.[6] While this term has been around from the 1870s (in France at least from 1875, and in England at least from 1887), its meaning includes the underlying foundations or basic framework—such as a system or organization, the permanent installations required for military purposes, and the system of public works of a country, state or region, including the resources required for an activity. If this covers a large dimension, it would perhaps be comforting to note that infrastructure is much easier to recognize than to define. For example, physical infrastructure is broadly composed of physical improvements such as roads, railways, airports, seaports and their corresponding improvements such as tunnels, bridges, canals and others—all constituting transport infrastructure; electricity, gas, pipelines, telecommunications, water distribution, sewerage and their improvements such as transmission, distribution, treatment plants and others—all constituting utilities; energy—power plants, oil and gas pipelines, wind, water, solar, geothermal, alternative forms and others; and oil and gas and improvements such as services, exploration and others. The Handbook of Research on Economic, Financial, and Industrial Impacts on Infrastructure Development defines infrastructure as "*the basic physical structures required for an economy to function and survive, such as transportation networks, a power grid and sewerage disposal systems*".

While other forms of infrastructure such as social infrastructure—health care, education, recreation and others exist, the physical infrastructure described above is the most common to recognize.

[4] 2020 Preqin Global Real Estate Report, https://www.preqin.com/data/real-estate (accessed on 09.06.2022).

[5] Gerencser and Hamiliton (2011).

[6] https://hakpaksak.wordpress.com/2008/09/22/the-etymology-of-infrastructure-and-the-infrastructure-of-the-internet/ (accessed 07 June 2022).

The Reserve Bank of India (RBI)[7] defined infrastructure as "*developing, or developing and operating, or developing, operating and maintaining an infrastructure facility in energy, logistics and transportation, telecom, urban and industrial infrastructure, agro processing, construction for storage of agro products, schools and hospitals, pipelines for oil, petroleum and gas, water and sanitation*". This definition includes both physical and social infrastructure services and makes an all-encompassing claim on development, operations and maintenance on the various systems of infrastructure.

The Indian Infrastructure Report, 1996, defined infrastructure as "*the physical framework of facilities through which goods and services are provided to the public*". In this assessment of infrastructure, the public is introduced in infrastructure and is held in association with it. While infrastructure is viewed as perhaps the life blood of an economy, the people in the economy are the end users of the same whose use of these systems will ultimately define the purpose and existence of infrastructure. Physical infrastructure facilities are developed for the use and benefit of the people, and ultimately a country. It facilitates rapid and easy human and material movement across a country; in addition to improving connectivity and stepping up access to goods, skills, services and employment opportunity.

Like infrastructure which works behind the scenes, the real estate sector too forms an integral part of a country's economy. It houses the country's people and provides location facilities for all businesses—primary, secondary, and tertiary. Real estate can simply be considered as land—and any physical property and improvements affixed to the land, including but not limited to houses, buildings, landscaping, fencing and wells.

As per Banister and Berechman (2000), based on Kay (1993), infrastructure activities [and real estate activities] are considered to have the following characteristics:

(1) They are networks with commonalities; and involve delivery systems and there are substantial interactions in the provision of services of these activities to individual customers.
(2) They form a small but indispensable part of the total cost of the wide range of products in which they are used. Thus, the losses which result from failure of these services are often very large compared to the basic cost of service provision.
(3) They can be thought of as substantial elements of natural monopoly. Competitive provision of the infrastructure and real estate itself is very costly, often prohibitively so. This need not exclude competition in the use of the same.
(4) Capital costs of infrastructure and real estate are generally large as against the running costs.
(5) The sunk costs of establishing infrastructure and real estate are substantial: A high proportion of the total cost of the service is irrevocably incurred before the service is offered.

[7] RBI Circular dated November 30, 2007 (DBOD No. BP.BC.52/21.04.048/2007-08).

1.2.2 Investments in Infrastructure and Real Estate

There are many meanings to what constitutes infrastructure and real estate investment. Gramlich (1994) regarded infrastructure capital as large capital-intensive natural monopolies such as highways, other transportation facilities, water and sewer lines, and communications systems. Recently, the activities regarded as infrastructure investment include:

- Energy (power generation and supply)
- Transport (toll roads, light rail systems, bridges and tunnels)
- Water (sewerage, wastewater treatment and water supply)
- Telecommunications (telephones)
- Social infrastructure (hospitals, prisons, courts, museums, schools and government accommodation)

Real estate investments broadly include the following types of investments.

- Real physical property
- Real estate investment trusts
- Real estate limited partnerships
- Mortgage investment entity
- Syndicated mortgage investments.

In a series of papers in 1989, Aschauer (1989a, 1989b, 1989c) used econometric estimations to highlight the relationship between infrastructure investment and productivity in the USA and other developed countries, thus establishing the importance of infrastructure. Subsequent literature and research that followed showed close linkages between the presence of adequate infrastructure and an improved quality of life (Aschauer, 1990; Baily et al., 1993; Duffy-Deno & Eberts, 1991; Eisner, 1991). Research in the 1990s also provided evidence that under favorable conditions, infrastructure investments were shown to contribute to economic growth and poverty reduction at both the macro- and microlevel (Aschauer, 1989a, 1989b, 1989c; Sanchez-Robles 1998). Aschauer (1989a, 1989b, 1989c, 1990), Munnell (1990), Morrison and Schwartz (1992) and Nadiri and Mamueas (1994) concluded that (public) capital in infrastructure contributed importantly to output and economic growth. The World Bank found larger effects of infrastructure on economic growth (Timilsina et al., 2021).

While academic studies underlined the importance of infrastructure and its direct relationship with improving productivity, studies by the World Bank (1994) and Hulten (1994) also found that differences in the use of infrastructure (relating to the quality and quantity) accounted for 25 percent of the growth differential in East Africa between 1970 and 1990, and for more than 40 percent of the growth differential between high-income and low-income countries over the same period. A major part of the per capita output gap that developed between Latin America and East Asia over the 1980s and 1990s was attributed to inadequate investment in infrastructure (Calderon and Severn, 2003; Rioja, 2003).

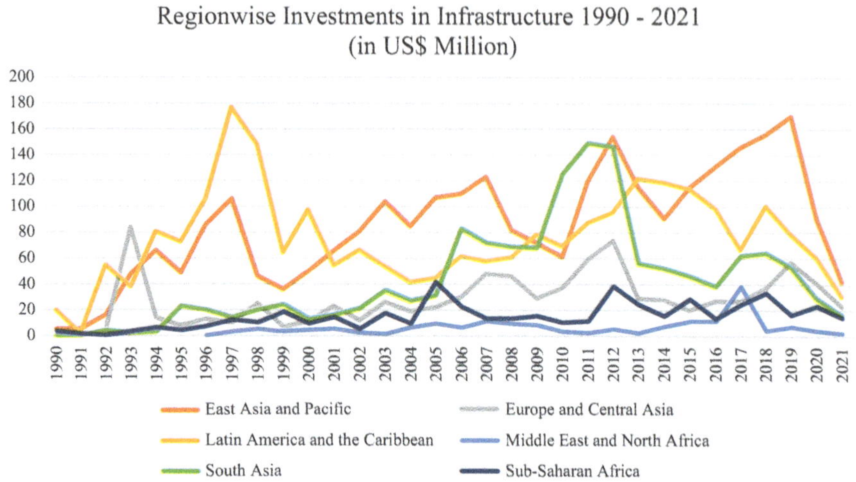

Fig. 1.1 Infrastructure investments regionwise, 1990–2021. *Source* Infrastructure investments (including private investments) in energy (electricity and natural gas), transport (airports, ports, railways, roads) and utilities (water and sewerage, and waste). Sourced from World Bank, private participation in infrastructure project database (http://ppi.worldbank.org) and compiled by authors

> In terms of job creation, every billion dollars invested in physical infrastructure creates 47,000 new jobs.
>
> Bernie Sanders, United States Senator.

Although governments worldwide acknowledged the benefits of an able infrastructure, in practice however, governments of various countries have been voicing their inability and unwillingness to provide large sums of money to fund infrastructure projects (Macomber, 2011). They started reducing their investments in infrastructure to reduce debt levels and contain taxation (Grimsey and Lewis, 2002). Governments have also been liberalizing infrastructure financing to include private participants and encouraging the private sector to invest in infrastructure (Kingcombe, 2011); with the twin objectives of job creation and improving economic performance (Chan et al., 2009). The private sector has responded enthusiastically, and there has been increased participation by the private sector in infrastructure development and financing since the 2000.[8]

Figure 1.1 presents the regionwise investments in infrastructure during 1990–2021. These include investments from the respective governments as well as the private developers and investors.

Figure 1.1 depicts investments in energy, telecom, transport and water and sanitation with private participation. The private sector participation into infrastructure consists of investments through PE and public–private partnerships (PPPs). Private

[8] It is to be noted that private sector has been playing a dominant role in infrastructure construction, operation and maintenance, since the governments have traditionally procured these services from private sector through contracting. The change that occurred in the 2000s has been that private

sector investment commitments to infrastructure totaled approximately US$62 billion between 1990 and 2002 (Silva et al., 2006). In 2006, the value of infrastructure deals backed by PE investors was approximately US$73 billion or 50 percent of the total value of such deals, a figure significantly higher than in 1988 when PE firms represented only 2 percent of this value.

Despite huge investments into infrastructure, the annual requirements for infrastructure have been steadily increasing. In 2003, Griffith-Fay and Yepes concluded that an annual spending of 3 percent of Latin America's GDP, viz. an estimated US$71 billion, was needed for new infrastructure investment and maintenance, compared with actual infrastructure spending of 2 percent of GDP, viz. around US$47 billion, in 2005 (Kingombe, 2011; Griffith-Jones & Ocampo, 2008). This left the region with an infrastructure financing gap of approximately US$24 billion. The OECD report of 2007 concluded that the global infrastructure investment requirements for transport, electricity generation, transmission and distribution, water and telecommunications would be about US$57–67 trillion by 2030. Griffith-Jones and Ocampo (2008) stated that the estimated financing gap between what was invested in the Asia–Pacific region (around US$48 billion) and what is needed (US$228 billion) is around US$180 billion every year. India has a shortfall of about US$150 billion–US$190 billion in capital available for infrastructure projects (McKinsey and Company, 2008). Thillai Rajan (2010) estimated that global investment requirements for infrastructure over the next 20 years stands anywhere between US$25 trillion–US$40 trillion.

Requirements for infrastructure development had been steadily rising and stood at about US$4 trillion annually in 2011. The OECD estimated that US$53 trillion of investment, equivalent to an annual 2.5 percent of global GDP was needed to meet the demand over the coming decades.[9] However, governments of various countries have been voicing their inability to invest large sums of capital into infrastructure to curb excessive deficit funding. It can therefore be concluded that private investments will play a key role in infrastructure development in the future. Among the different sources of private capital, PE is a very significant and important one. The OECD opines that privatizations would increase efficiency and reduce public funding requirements. Though PE funding in infrastructure might not be as large as that of loan capital from financial institutions, as a source of equity capital, they have a very important role, including attracting loan funding. PE investments into infrastructure are expected to have a robust growth going by the interest shown in the initial years. PE infrastructure market had grown by a staggering 429 percent during 2007–09, according to the London-based database group, Private Equity Intelligence Ltd (Preqin). In 2009, Preqin estimated that a total of US$34.9 billion was raised by 18 funds, up from US$6.6 billion raised in 2005 by 11 funds.

Table 1.1 presents the infrastructure funding needs and gap in the major infrastructure sectors worldwide.

---

sector has also been involved as a developer and investor in infrastructure, activities which were earlier seen as the domain of the public sector.

[9] https://www.oecd.org/newsroom/massiveinfrastructureinvestmentneededtomeetfuturedemandsaysoecd.htm#:~:text=The%20OECD%20estimates%20USD%2053,and%20key%20rail%20routes%20alone.

Table 1.1 Efficiency and funding gaps in the major infrastructure sectors

Description	Energy sector (power and oil and gas) (US$ billion per annum)	Transport sector (US$ billion per annum)	Water and utilities (water, waste and recycling) (US$ billion per annum)	Total (US$ billion per annum)
Infrastructure spending needs	−40.8	−18.2	−21.9	−80.9
Existing spending	11.6	16.2	7.6	35.4
Efficiency gap	6	3.8	2.9	12.7
Gain from raising capital execution	0.2	1.3	0.2	1.7
Gain from eliminating operational inefficiencies	3.4	2.4	1	6.8
Gain from tariff cost recovery	2.3	0.1	1.8	4.2
Potential for reallocation	n.a	n.a	n.a	0
Funding gap	−23.2	1.9	−11.4	−32.7

Source Briceno-Garmendia et al. (2010) quoted in Foster and Briceno-Garmendia (2010)

Table 1.2 presents conclusions of various studies in the past decade with findings highlighting the infrastructure requirements and gaps.

"Take-privates [PE] will be a standout theme in 2022. Pricing is favorable, dry powder[10] sits at record levels, and the heightened risk of a European recession means further volatility is on the horizon."

—PitchBook EMEA senior analyst Dominick Mondesir

(https://pitchbook.com/news/articles/largest-take-private-europe-blackstone-benetton-atlantia, accessed 15 Apr 2022)

Increasing investments by PE funds into infrastructure warrants an increasing demand to study these investments and the consequences of the same. Large increases of PE investment into infrastructure are certainly worth considering, given the fact

[10] Dry powder refers to cash reserves kept on hand, usually by PE firms, to cover any future obligations such as the purchase of assets, and fund acquisitions.

Table 1.2 Conclusions of various studies in the past decade with findings highlighting the infrastructure requirements and gaps

Paper	Year	Region	Conclusion
Griffith-Fay and Yepes	2003	Latin America	An annual spending of 3 percent of Latin America's GDP, around US$71 billion, was needed for new infrastructure investment and maintenance, compared with actual infrastructure spending of 2 percent of GDP, around US$47 billion
Malone	2005	Australia	A cumulative shortfall of about AUD 25 billion in infrastructure, due to declining government investment levels since the 1980s
OECD	2007	Global	the global infrastructure investment requirements for transport, electricity generation, transmission and distribution, water and telecommunications would be about US$57–67 trillion by 2030
Griffith-Jones and Ocampo	2008	Asia Pacific Region	The estimated financing gap between what was invested in the Asia–Pacific region (around US$48 billion) and what is needed (US$228 billion) is around US$180 billion every year
Asian Development Bank	2009	Asia	US$8 trillion is needed to sustain and implement the development of the Asian macro region
Thillai Rajan	2010	Global	The global investment requirements for infrastructure over the next 20 years stands anywhere between US$25 trillion–US$40 trillion
European Commission	2011	Europe	Europe will need between Euro 1.5 trillion and Euro 2 trillion of infrastructure investments by 2020
Society of Civil Engineers	2013	USA	Total infrastructure financing gap is US$1.7 trillion, with an additional US$3.6 trillion needed by 2020
McKinsey	2013	Global	The global infrastructure investment requirements would be about US$71 trillion by 2030

Source Compiled by authors

that infrastructure as an investment sector did not feature on the PE radar until the late 80s.

1.3 Characteristics of Infrastructure and Real Estate Investments

Investing in and developing infrastructure assets and real estate demands a different set of skills due to specific features and significant characteristics that differentiate them from standard manufacturing, expansion and modernization projects. Both infrastructure and real estate projects are large projects (also having long lives) and are structured differently from conventional corporate finance projects.

(i) **Large projects**

Large projects are those which cost US$500 million or more (Esty, 2004) and have their own set of risk characteristics. Most infrastructure projects and real estate projects fall into this category. The increasing size of projects in recent years has resulted in a new category of projects, the mega infrastructure projects, which have been dominating the narrative globally. Mega implies the size of tasks involved in developing, planning, and managing projects of the magnitude (Flyvbjerg et al., 2003). The US Federal Highway Administration defined mega projects as major infrastructure projects that cost more than US$1 billion. What differentiates large and mega projects from smaller projects is the quantum of capital at stake, the technical requirements, and its complexity (Bruzelius et al., 2002), the span of geographic and disciplinary boundaries, and the environmental and social effects of such projects (Ralf, 1993; Esty, 2004).

Mega Projects—The New Administrative Capital in Egypt, Africa

Egypt is constructing a New Administrative Capital about 28 miles (45 km) east of Cairo. Started in 2015, this US$58 billion project is designed to be a hub for government and the finance industry. This new city will house the Iconic Tower, Africa's soon-to-be tallest building and can house 6.5 million people. A US$4 billion, 100-km monorail project is also on-going, which will connect Cairo and the new city.

David Sims, author of Egypt's Desert Dreams, a book on development projects, said the backing of Egypt's presidency and military made the project "too big to fail".

https://www.reuters.com/article/us-egypt-new-capital/egypts-new-desert-capital-faces-delays-as-it-battles-for-funds-idUSKCN1SJ10I (accessed 15 Apr 2022).

Large monies at stake have a cascading effect on the ability and incentives of the owners and managers to make careful, value-enhancing investment and financing decisions (Esty, 2004). They have the ability because large projects require at least 1–5 years to structure; they have the incentive because significantly more money is at stake—both their personal wealth and their professional reputations are in the line of fire as well as substantial amounts of capital from other investors.

Large projects also have magnified costs—which arise from costly capital market imperfections. These imperfections—agency conflicts, asymmetric information and so on—impose "deadweight" financing costs on firms (Esty, 2004). For example, an agency conflict that causes a deadweight cost of 5 percent of asset value is worth only US$1 million in a US$20 million investment, but is worth US$100 million in a US$2 billion investment. Facing a potential loss in value of US$100 million, capital providers are required to willingly undertake costly actions.

Finally, asset size has a particularly important effect on an investor's incentive and ability to finance new investment. Asset size affects the investor's willingness to bear risk. Smaller sized investments bring out risk-seeking behavior, while larger sized investments tend to bring out risk-averse behavior. Kalecki (1937) suggested two reasons for the increasing marginal risk with investment size. The first was the fact that the greater the investment, the more was the wealth position of the investor endangered in the event of an unsuccessful business. The second reason making the marginal risk rise with the size of investment was the danger of "illiquidity". Infrastructure assets with features of site specificity and asset specificity (Williamson, 1983) are considered more illiquid than other asset classes.

(ii) **Project finance structure**

Infrastructure projects are commonly structured on a project finance basis (Esty, 2004; Gatti, 2008) and real estate projects can be structured in this way too. Project finance involves the creation of a legally independent project entity, known as a special-purpose vehicle (SPV) to manage and run the infrastructure asset. Park and Chang (2013) opine that there are many benefits to project finance conceptually, including its standalone economic and legal nature, access to significant levels of non-recourse or limited recourse debt based on expected cash flows, customizable risk allocations and asset specific governance systems. This makes project companies standalone entities, and there is an organizational decision to finance assets separately rather than jointly, which is the case with corporate-finance investment (Esty, 2004).

The project finance structure is financed with equity from one or more sponsors and a high percentage of debt (debt-to-total capitalization ratio of 70 percent compared to 35 percent for public companies). Leverage values in infrastructure and real estate projects can vary from 10–30:90–70 (Finnerty, 1996). Nevitt and Fabozzi (2000) argue that the main benefit of the project finance structure would be the possibility to generate higher returns through the use of a higher degree of leverage that may not be possible in a regular commercial financing.

Esty (2004) opines that the project finance structure helps in the reduction of agency conflicts inside project companies by creating an asset-specific governance system. Large, tangible asset projects with high cash flow potential are prone to agency conflicts that could destroy value (Jensen and Meckling, 1976), while the asset specificity can lead to costly hold-up agency conflicts (Williamson, 1985). The project finance structure can reduce agency costs between ownership and management by lessening cash flow problems and avert opportunistic behaviors (Park and Chang, 2013).

Further, these projects have very comprehensive contracts (Brealey et al., 1996). For example, when the US$3.6 billion financing for the Baku–Tbilisi–Ceyhan pipeline closed in February 2004, it required 208 finance documents and 17,000 signatures from 78 parties (Pope, 2004).

Typical infrastructure projects have lifetimes of 5–40 years (Mor and Sehrawat, 2006). Spending decisions and associated cash outlays occur sequentially over the construction time or gestation period which is roughly about 4–8 years. Thus, the construction period takes "time to build", and the project yields no cash return until it is completed (Majd and Pindyck, 1985). The construction period is characterized by high initial investments (Gramlich, 1994) which create specific infrastructure assets. These infrastructure assets, after becoming operational produce cash flows which are used to restore the investment by repaying the debt contracted and remunerate the capital invested at a rate consistent with the degree of risk inherent in the project. This property makes the deal non-recourse in nature (Brealey et al., 1996) where each periods' gross revenues, such as toll receipts, help first pay the operating and maintenance expenses, then capital expenditures, debt services, and finally, dividends to equity investors. Figure 1.2 shows the timeline of a typical infrastructure project designed under project finance, highlighting the nature and changing characteristics of risks at different points in the lifetime of the infrastructure asset.

The phases of the infrastructure project also have very distinct risk profiles[11] and impact the future outcomes in different ways. Some of the risks faced at different phases of the infrastructure project are described below (Gatti, 2008).

(a) **Precompletion phase risk**

This phase involves planning and building the infrastructure project and lasts till the start of project operations. It is characterized by a concentration of industrial risks, for most part. These risks should be very carefully assessed because they emerge at the outset of the project, before the initiative actually begins to generate positive cash flows.

Activity planning risk arises from the project management logic—where the timing and resources for the various activities that are linked in a process leads to a certain result within a preset time frame. The logical links among the various activities are vital in order to complete construction of asset at times fixed and start functioning. Delays in completing one activity can have major repercussions on subsequent activities.

[11] Thomas et al. (2006) mention the main elements of project risk management to include the identification, the measurement é assessment and the process of prioritizing and responding to various project risks.

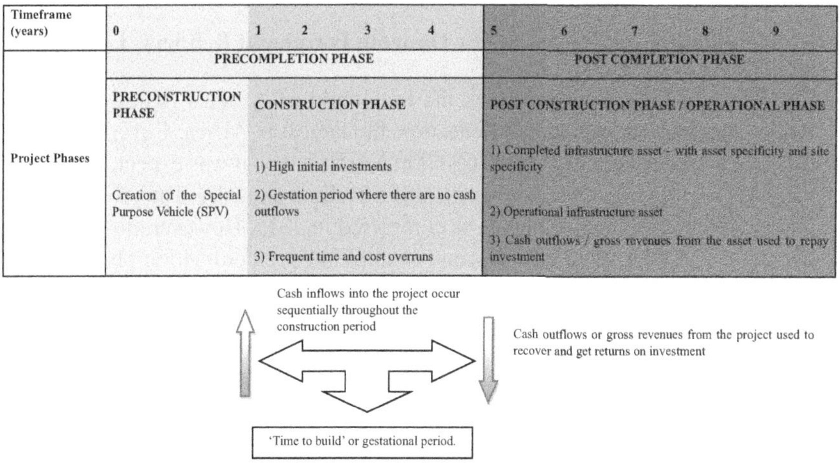

Classification of risks (Sourced from Gatti, 2008)

Pre-completion phase risks	Post completion phase risks	Risks common to pre-completion and post completion phases
Activity planning risk	Supply risk	Interest rate risk
Technological risk	Operational risk	Exchange risk
Construction risk	Market risk	Inflation risk
		Credit / counterparty risk
		Environmental risk
		Regulatory risk
		Political risk
		Legal risk

Fig. 1.2 Timeline of a typical infrastructure project highlighting the various risks faced at different phases. *Source* Gatti, 2008, adapted and modified by authors

The risk is, in fact, the structure on which the SPV depends to generate cash flows during the operation phase may not be available. For example, if the construction completion time does not coincide with the start of the testing time, it can lead to a sizable increase in costs.

The construction of an asset sometimes requires the use of innovative technology which may not be fully understood by the contractor. Mostly, the contractor of the project decides on the most suitable technology for the project. However, it is not uncommon for a contractor to find that the technological choice for the project had already been made upstream by other sponsors (Gatti, 2008). When the contractor and technology supplier do not concur on ideas, technology risks can arise. Technology risk is an emerging risk which relies on innovation and investment in technology and can sometimes prove very difficult for infrastructure projects.

Pre-completion Phase Risk—The Dangote Petroleum Refinery, Lagos, Africa

The Dangote Petroleum Refinery, the brainchild of Africa's richest person, Akilo Dangote, was scheduled to become the largest in Africa. Covering over 2635 ha with capacity to process 650,000 barrels a day, it was expected create a market for Nigerian crude oil worth US$11 billion annually. The project was announced in 2013, scheduled to be completed in 2016. However, this project has been rich with strife, and a prime example of pre-completion phase risk. Beginning with the move of the proposed site to Lekki in Lagos, the project has been fraught with environmental concerns, targeted by protestors, and delayed due to staffing reductions because of the need for social distancing due to the COVID'19 pandemic. The refinery which was estimated to cost US$19 billion was scheduled to begin production in 2019. However, as a result of these initial delays, and it was expected to begin production only by late 2022.

https://www.reuters.com/world/africa/dangote-complete-nigerian-oil-refinery-q4-executive-2022-04-04/, https://www.theafricareport.com/29913/nigerias-dangote-still-expects-refinery-to-be-running-early-2021/ (accessed 15 Apr 2022).

Innovative Technology—Konza Technological City, Kenya, Africa

Konza Technological City, a flagship project of Kenya 2030 Vision, is expected to become home to Kenya's burgeoning tech scene. The "smart city" is expected to be integrated with an urban information and communication technology (ICT) network that supports delivery of connected urban services and allows for efficient management of those services on a large scale. It is expected to offer four key city services: infrastructure services (including transportation, utilities, public safety, and environment), citizen services (including access and participation), city services (including city information, planning, and development), and business services (including supportive services for local commerce).

Although this project has raised more than US$800 million in funding, progress on this project was slower than expected.

https://konza.go.ke/, https://www.cnn.com/2021/01/14/africa/gallery/africa-infrastructure-projects-hnk-spc-intl/index.html (accessed 15 Apr 2022).

Construction risk or completion risk refers to the fact that the project may not be completed or the construction may be delayed. Some examples of construction risk relate to:

- Non-completion or delayed completion due to force majeure
- Completion with cost overruns
- Delayed completion
- Completion with performance deficiency

In a project finance transaction, construction risk is rarely allotted to the SPV or its lenders. As a result, the contractors or even the sponsors are required to assume this risk.

(b) **Postcompletion phase risk**

The chief risks in the postcompletion phase include the performance of the plant as compared to project and industry standards, including the supply of output, and the sale of the product or service. Performances that fall short of the agreed standards could lead to a reduction in cash flows generated by the project during its economic life. Lower than expected cash flows dull the sheen of the project as they translate into lower internal rates of return, affect non-recourse financing and affect the lenders and sponsors ability to get repaid.

Post Completion Phase Risk—The Felipe Ángeles International Airport, Mexico City, Mexico

In March 2022, the Felipe Ángeles International Airport, north of Mexico City, was inaugurated. Constructed at a price of US$13 billion, it was intended to be a hub for Latin America. The airport is located about 30 miles from Mexico City. However, the roads leading to it were incomplete at the time of the airport opening and the unfinished rail line linking the airport to the capital was not expected to open until 2023 making it challenging for transit passengers who will land in Felipe Ángeles and then take the long journey to the current international airport for a connecting flight abroad. Further, Mexican carriers were not yet able to fly from Felipe Ángeles to the United States after the Federal Aviation Administration downgraded its air safety rating for Mexico last year. Air industry experts have also warned that the mountains surrounding Felipe Ángeles could make takeoff and landing dangerous.

https://www.nytimes.com/2022/03/25/world/americas/mexico-international-airport.html (accessed 15 Apr 2022)

(c) **Risks found in both the pre- and postcompletion phase**

These types of risks occur systematically during the life of the project, though with differing intensity depending on the phase in the lifecycle of the project. Some of the salient risks are described below:

- **Interest rate risk** arises if there is an unexpected increase in the benchmark rate to which the cost of financing is indexed. This can then cause an increase in the value of the investments and thus reduce the amount of funds present in the project.
- **Exchange rate risk** occurs when a company's cash flows—and therefore profits and income—are stated in a different currency and are affected because of changes in exchange rate between that currency and the currency of the home country.
- **Inflation risk** arises when the cost dynamic is subject to a sudden acceleration that cannot be transferred to a corresponding increase in revenues. Inflation risk is captured by the decline in purchasing power and affects most contracts between the SPVs and their commercial counterparties since they are based on revision mechanisms for rates or installments based on the behavior of a given price index.
- **Credit risk or counterparty risk** is inherent in the parties who enter contracts with the SPV. For this purpose, the creditworthiness of the various parties including the contractor, the product buyer, the input supplier and the plant operator is carefully assessed by the financiers of the project to establish their financial soundness.
- **Environmental risk** refers to any undesirable and adverse impacts (or even the threat of the same) the infrastructure asset could have on the environment encompassing the project. Examples of environmental risks include construction of an asset which can damage the surrounding environment, change in laws that result in a requirement to change building variants thereby increasing investment costs, and public opposition to projects with major environmental impact are some environmental risks.
- **Regulatory risks** are caused by inefficiency in public administration or the complexity of bureaucratic procedures. They include the following:

  - The permits needed to start the project are delayed or cancelled
  - The basic concessions for the project are unexpectedly renegotiated
  - The core concession for the project is revoked or the project is nationalized.
  - If delays are the result of specific political intent to block the initiative, this situation would be similar to political risk.

- **Political risk** includes a lack of government stability, a change in government and so on, which could impact the project negatively, especially if the new administration does not share the same views as the previous one. Political risks are especially visible in developing countries, where legal structures are not well defined, governments are politically unstable, and there is little experience of private capital investments in strategic sectors.

Political Risk—The Bengaluru International Airport, Bengaluru, India

During the construction of the Bengaluru International Airport, an international airport in Bengaluru, India, there were 17 changes in political heads in the central government, along with corresponding changes in the civil aviation, and state government during the construction period between 1994 and 2006. Only in 2 instances were the heads of the Central Government, Ministry of Civil Aviation, and State Government from the same political party. This caused innumerable problems and delays in the construction of the project (Thillai Rajan & Gemson, 2011).

- **Legal risk** ascertains whether the commercial law of the host country offers contract enforceability should problems emerge during the construction or post-completion phases. In addition to the degree of economic development in a country, it also involves a series of other factors such as a country's independence of the judiciary and autonomy of institutions.

While all the risks identified can be managed appropriately, what is important is to recognize the presence of these risks and put in place appropriate risk mitigation mechanisms to safeguard the project and its operations.

1.4 Is Private Equity Equipped to Handle Infrastructure Investment?

Infrastructure and real estate projects also have a higher degree of risk and uncertain returns to the equity investor, such as PE, in comparison with other projects (Gramlich, 1994).

PE firms normally do not make large-sized investments in projects. Average investments by PE firms in deals in information technology worldwide was US$10.08 million between 1990 and 2009 while average investments by PE firms in deals in medical, health and life sciences worldwide was US$8.51 million between 1990 and 2009. In comparison, average investment by PE firms in deals in infrastructure worldwide was US$27.21 million between 1990 and 2009 (Securities Data Corporation database, calculated by authors).

Long construction times and gestation periods are unfavorable to PE firms, who usually invest with funds that have predetermined, finite lives of 7–10 years after which the partnerships are liquidated and the proceeds distributed to partners (Black & Gilson, 1998). According to Venture Economics (1988), the average holding period (time elapsed between the initial investment and the return of capital) for an investment was 4.9 years. During the lifetime of a fund too, the proceeds from investments in firms are distributed to limited partners as realized. A fund's performance record, which is based on completed investments, is the fund's principal tool for persuading capital providers to invest in the manager's next limited partnerships. It is also in the best interest of the PE fund to exit old investments in order to free up managerial resources before launching a new fund (Cumming & MacIntosh, 2001). Thus, the importance of timely returns is imperative for the success of the PE fund and the reputation of the PE firm too. For this purpose, PE firms need to show great prescience choosing projects—infrastructure or real estate, as timely completion and success of the project is pertinent for the success of the PE firm.

Further, due to the nature of their capital, PE is at the "bottom bucket" (Page et al., 2010) of the cash flow waterfall, receiving incomes only after payment to all other investors. The cash flow waterfall is presented in Fig. 1.3. Equity usually has little ability to lay further claims on the infrastructure project. Thus, PE firms will need to invest in infrastructure projects that pay out adequate returns to enhance their reputation and strengthen their ability to raise future funds.

These risk factors cause uncertainty over the project and to the PE investors in the project. Finally, PE investors in infrastructure are "purely financial" investors and normally do not share any product market relationships with the infrastructure project (Gemson et al., 2012); unlike other sponsor investors in infrastructure projects such as construction companies, equipment suppliers, maintenance agencies, operating agencies or even the host government. They invest capital to seek substantial returns on their investment (Gatti, 2008). Thus, it becomes necessary for PE firms to safeguard their investments in the projects they invest in. They are thus required to shift

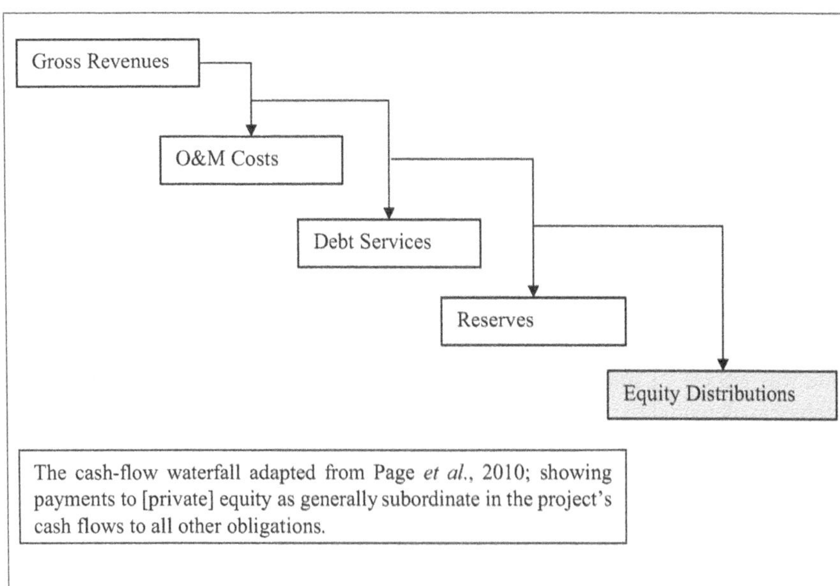

Fig. 1.3 Cash flow waterfall. *Source* Page et al. (2010), adapted and modified by authors

away from rigid procedures and make investment assessments under uncertainty using various strategies. The goal is to make decisions that manage the risks that arise from uncertainty while simultaneously enabling the pursuit of opportunities (Mikaelian et al., 2008).

Although the impact of PE in infrastructure and real estate has been tremendous, it nevertheless has remained a nascent field [accounting for only about 10 percent of the total private transactions in 2006]. Both infrastructure and real estate projects are considered extremely risky and uncertain and project failures in the form of time and cost overruns occur with alarming frequency. Literature support for PE in such projects has been largely incomplete with conflicting evidence at the least. Governments have been keen to attract private investors to benefit from the value created by these private participations. We believe that PE investment flow in infrastructure and real estate is an important financial innovation that has strong implications for the development of these sectors. The text explains how such private investments, more specifically PE, has been able to contribute to the development of infrastructure and real estate sectors.

References

Aschaeur, D. A. (1989a). Is public expenditure productive? *Journal of Monetary Economics, 23*(2), 177–200.

Aschaeur, D. A. (1989b). Public investment and productivity growth in the group of seven. *Economic Perspectives, 13*(5), 17–25.

Aschaeur, D. A. (1989c). Does public capital crowd out private capital? *Journal of Monetary Economics, 24*(2), 171–188.

Aschauer, D.A. (1990). Why is infrastructure important? In A. H. Munnell (Ed.), *Is there a shortfall in public capital investment*? (pp. 21–50).

Bailey, M. L., Burtless, G., & Litan, R. E. (1993). *Growth with equity: Economic policy making for the next century*. Brookings Institution.

Banister, D., & Berechman, J. (2000). *Transport investment and economic development*. Routledge.

Black, S. B., & Gilson, R. J. (1998). Venture capital and the structure of capital markets: Bank versus stock markets. *Journal of Financial Economics, 47*(3), 243–277.

Brealey, R. A., Cooper, I. A., & Habib, M. A. (1996). Using project finance to fund infrastructure investments. *Journal of Applied Corporate Finance, 9*(3), 25–38.

Bruzelius, N., Flyvbjerg, B., & Rothengatter, W. (2002). Big decisions, big risks. Improving accountability in mega projects. *Transport Policy, 9*, 143–154.

Calderon, C., & Serven, L. (2003). The output costs of Latin America's infrastructure gap. In The World Bank (Ed.), *The limits of stabilization: Infrastructure, public deficits and growth in Latin America*. World Bank

Chan, C., Forwood, D., Roper, H., & Sayers, C. (2009). *Public infrastructure financing: An international perspective*. Productivity Commission Staff Working Paper, March 2009.

Cumming, D. J., & MacIntosh, J. G. (2001). Venture capital investment duration in Canada and the United States. *Journal of Multinational Financial Management, 11*, 445–463.

Duffy-Deno, K. T., & Eberts, R. W. (1991). Public infrastructure and regional economic development: A simultaneous equations approach. *Journal of Urban Economics, 30*(3), 329–343.

Eisner, R. (1991). Infrastructure and regional economic performance. *New England Economic Review, Federal Reserve Bank of Boston, 1991*, 47–58.

Esty, B. C. (2004). Why study large projects? An introduction to research on project finance. *European Financial Management, 10*(2), 213–224.

Finnerty, J. D. (1996). *Project financing: Asset-based financial engineering.* Wiley and Sons, Inc.

Foster, V., & Briceño-Garmendia, C. (2010). *Africa's infrastructure: A time for Transformation* (p. 2010). World Bank.

Flyvbjerg, B., Holm, M., & Buhl, S. (2003). How common and large are cost overruns in transport infrastructure projects? *Transport Reviews, 23*(1), 71–88.

Gatti, S. (2008). *Project finance in theory and practice: Designing, structuring, and financing private and public projects.* Academic Press Advanced Finance Series.

Gemson, J., Gautami, K. V., & Thillai Rajan, A. (2012). Impact of private equity investments in infrastructure projects. *Utilities Policy, 21*, 59–65.

Gerencser, M., & Hamiliton, B. A. (2011). Re-imagining infrastructure. *Journal of Applied Corporate Finance, 23*(3), 18–29.

Gramlich, E. M. (1994). Infrastructure investment: A review essay. *Journal of Economic Literature, 32*, 1176–1196.

Griffith-Jones, S., & Ocampo, J. A. (2008). *Sovereign wealth funds: A developing country perspective.* Paper presented at Sovereign Wealth Funds workshop, 18 February, London.

Grimsey, D., & Lewis, M. K. (2002). Evaluating the risks of public private partnerships for infrastructure projects. *International Journal of Project Management, 20*, 107–118.

Hulten, C. R. (1994). *Infrastructure capital and economic growth: How well you may use it may be more important than how much you have.* NBER Working Paper 5847, December 1994.

Jensen, M.C., & Meckling, (1976). Can the corporation survive? Center for research in government policy and business Working Paper No. 76-4, University of Rochester, Rochester, NY 1976.

Kalecki, M. (1937). The principle of increasing risk. *Economica, New Series, 4*(16), 440–447.

Kay, J. (1993). Efficiency and private capital in the provision of infrastructure. In *Infrastructure policies for the 1990s* (pp 55–74). OECD

Kingcombe, K. M. (2011). *Mapping the new infrastructure financing landscape.* Research Note, Overseas Development Institute, U.K.

Lewis. (2008). https://hakpaksak.wordpress.com/2008/09/22/the-etymology-of-infrastructure-and-the-infrastructure-of-the-internet/. Accessed 07 June 2022

Lorenzo, W. (1996). The advent of private equity in Latin America. *The Columbia Journal of World Business, 31*(1), 60–68.

Macomber, J. (2011). The role of finance and private investment in developing sustainable cities. *Journal of Applied Corporate Finance, 23*(3), 64–74.

Majd, S., & Pindyck, R. S. (1985). *Time to build, option value and investment decisions.* National Bureau of Economic Research, Working Paper No 1654, NBER Working Paper Series.

McKinsey and Company Building India (2008). *Financing and investing in infrastructure*, Financial Services Practice, 2008.

Mikaelian, T., Rhodes, D. H., Nightingale, D. J., Hastings, D. E. (2008). Managing uncertainty in socio-technical enterprises using a real options framework. In *Proceedings of 6th Conference on Systems Engineering Research*, Los Angeles, CA.

Mor, N., & Sehrawat, S. (2006). *Sources of infrastructure finance.* Working Paper Series, Institute for Financial Management and Research, Centre for Development Finance.

Morrison, C. J., & Schwartz, A. E. (1992). *State infrastructure and productive performance.* Working Paper No. 3981, National Bureau of Economic Research.

Munnell, A. (1990). Why has productivity growth declined? Productivity and public investment. *New England Economic Review*, 3–22.

Nadiri, M. I., & Mamueas, T. P. (1994). The effects of public infrastructure and R&D capital on the cost structure and performance of US manufacturing industries. *The Review of Economics and Statistics, 1994*, 22–36.

Nevitt, P. K., & Fabozzi, F. J. (2000). *Project financing*(7th ed.). Euromonry Books, London, UK.

Page, S. N., Ankner, W., Jones, C., & Fetterman, R. (2008). The risks and rewards of private equity in infrastructure. *Public Works Management & Policy, 13*(2), 100–113.

Park, A., & Chang, C.-Y. (2013). Impacts of construction events on the project equity value of the Channel Tunnel project. *Construction Management and Economics, 31*(3), 223-237. https://doi.org/10.1080/01446193.2012.76171
Pope, H. (2004). Caspian pipeline financing solidifies U.S. policy, *Wall Street Journal*, A13.
Ralf C. Buckley (1993). How accurate are environmental impact predictions?. *Ambio, 20*, 3–4
Rioja, F. K. (2003). The penalties of inefficient infrastructure. *Review of Development Economics, 7*(1), 127–137.
Sánchez-Robles, B. (1998). Infrastructure investment and growth: Some empirical evidence. *Contemporary Economic Policy, XV, I*(1), 98–109.
Silva, L. C., Estache, A., & Jarvela, S. (2006). Is debt replacing equity in regulated privatized infrastructure in developing countries? *Utilities Policy, 14*, 90–102.
Thillai Rajan, A. (2010). *Private equity in infrastructure: Does it help?* Working Paper Series, Harvard University and Indian Institute of Technology Madras.
Thillai Rajan, A., & Gemson, J. (2011). Financial closure of Bengaluru International Airport Limited. *Emerald Emerging Markets Case Studies Collection., 1*(4), 1–22.
Thomas, A. V., Kalidindi, S. N., & Ganesh, L. S. (2006). Modelling and assessment of critical risks in BOT road projects. *Construction Management and Economics, 24*(4), 407–424.
Timilsina, G., Stern, D. I., & Das, D. K. (2021). How much does physical infrastructure contribute to economic growth? An empirical analysis. Policy Research Working Paper 9888.
Venture Economics Venture capital performance. (1988). *Review of the financial performance of venture capital partnerships*. Venture Economics Inc.
Williamson, O. E. (1983). Credible commitments: Using hostages to support exchange. *American Economic Review, 73*, 526.
Williamson, O. E. (1985). *The economic institutions of capitalism*. The Free Press.
World Bank. (1994). *World development report: Infrastructure for development*. Oxford University Press.

Chapter 2
An Overview of the Impact of PE Investments on Size, Efficiency, and Cost

You and I come by road or rail, but economists travel on infrastructure.
—Margaret Thatcher

The infrastructure and real estate sectors are invariably viewed as being owned by the state, the development of which is primarily the responsibility of the government and is financed with public funds. Various country governments enter into funding agreements with different regions (states/provinces) for the purpose of developing and supporting strategic projects in infrastructure and real estate. For example, the Office of Infrastructure in Canada (also known as Infrastructure Canada) was created as a federal department in 2002 and continues as a department of the Government of Canada responsible for federal public infrastructure policy. Through the Government of Canada plan, the Government of Canada leads the creation, development and maintenance of infrastructure facilities. From its inception in 2016, over CAD 180 billion has been invested in various projects to support public transit, trade, development of communities and social spaces, and social and green programs. In India, the Secretariat for Infrastructure in the Planning Commission initiates policies for infrastructure development and the Ministry of Housing and Urban Affairs is largely responsible for various aspects in real estate. The central government allocates funds for infrastructure through the Union Budget. The latest budget (2022–23) had a massive impetus on the development of infrastructure and real estate including affordable housing projects, road projects and renewable energy projects.

Despite committing large sums of money to infrastructure and real estate projects, the capital available to fill the infrastructure and real estate requirements is not sufficient. Country governments have actively and publicly sought the assistance of private capital for such projects. For example, in Australia, the recent Review of Partnerships Victoria Provided Infrastructure: Final Report to the Treasurer included a recommendation that the state "*should seek to pilot new financial and partnership structures…that combine the benefits of private sector risk taking with the Government's comparative advantage in securing funds*" (Fitzgerald, 2004, p. 35).[1]

[1] Fitzgerald (2004), Malone (2005)

J. Gemson and Thillai Rajan A., *Private Equity Financing in Infrastructure and Real Estate*, https://doi.org/10.1007/978-981-16-1634-1_2

Private investments in infrastructure and real estate projects are now steadily increasing. In 2017, 17 percent of the total investments into infrastructure and 305 projects were from predominantly private sources. A total of 9848 PE deals were clocked in the real estate sector in 2019, and 2020 saw a slight decline to 5797 PE deals.[2] These numbers are set to increase given the various government initiatives such as public–private partnerships (PPPs) and other forms of PPIs to expand the options for infrastructure and real estate development and financing. PE, as a private source of capital for infrastructure and real estate projects, has also seen a persistent growth.

This section (Chaps. 3–5) examines the impact of PE investments in infrastructure and real estate.

The case of global infrastructure

Chapter 3 examines the impact of PE investments on size, efficiency and cost of capital in infrastructure projects. Using worldwide data, we attempt to quantify the impact of the PE presence on infrastructure projects. While PE is known for large capital sizes, and the use of extensive leverage, this study compares these qualities among infrastructure projects. It also examines the determinants of PE investments in infrastructure projects and explores the extent of PE financing in developed versus developing/emerging economies.

The case of Indian real estate

Chapter 4 examines the impact of PE investments in the real estate sector. Using project-level and investment-level data in India, we examine the impact that such investments have on the real estate sector. The real estate sector is usually regulated by various country or state and province laws in the country where it is housed, and is characterized by relative lack of liquidity, large lot sizes, high transaction costs and heterogeneity. This study provides a comparative analysis of PE investments across projects, PE investor types and fund types. While this study is set in India, the best practices and insights gained by this study are applicable for developing/emerging economies.

The case of the Indian power sector

Given the need for investment capital, governments, especially in developing countries, liberalized the power generation sector to private investment, which has, in recent years, attracted sizable investments from the same. Chapter 5 explores the impact of PE investments in the power sector in an emerging economy, i.e., India. We do this by comparing private sector power projects that had PE investment vis-à-vis those that did not have any PE investment, and examine PE impact on key parameters including cost (unit capacity cost) and time (project commissioning time). The results showed that PE investment was associated with a significant, but opposite effect on unit capacity costs and project commissioning time. The results of this study indicate

[2] *2021 Preqin Global Real Estate Report* (Retrieved from https://www.preqin.com/data/real-estate on 08.06.2022).

that new sources of private capital such as PE can help to capture additional benefits that may not be possible with conventional private sector investment.

References

Fitzgerald, P. (2004). *Review of partnerships Victoria provided infrastructure: Final report to the treasurer*. Growth Solutions Group

Malone, N. (2005). The evolution of private financing of government infrastructure in Australia—2005 and beyond. *The Australian Economic Review, 38*(4), 420–430.

Chapter 3
The Case of Global Infrastructure

If you are going to achieve excellence in big things, you develop the habit in little matters. Excellence is not an exception. It is a prevailing attitude.
—Colin Powell

3.1 Introduction

Project finance is perhaps the most popular and suitable technique available to finance infrastructure projects. Project finance, also known as non-recourse financing, is the structured financing of a specific economic entity—the special-purpose vehicle (SPV), in this case the project company. Esty and Sesia (2005) defined project finance as "involves[involving] the creation of a legally independent project company financed with equity and non-recourse debt for the purpose of financing a single purpose capital asset, usually with a limited life".

This chapter is based on the journal paper titled "Impact of private equity investments in infrastructure projects" which appeared in Utilities Policy, 2012, https://doi.org/10.1016/j.jup.2011.12.001. Some sections of this chapter are based on the journal papers titled "Impact of private equity investments in infrastructure projects" which appeared in Utilities Policy, 2012, https://doi.org/10.1016/j.jup.2011.12.001, "What do PE investors seek from syndication partners? Evidence from the infrastructure sector" which appeared in Public Works and Management Policy, 2015, https://doi.org/10.1177/1087724X15613095, and "A new perspective on private equity stage financing: Evidence from investments in infrastructure" which appeared in *Venture Capital: An International Journal of Entrepreneurial Finance*. 17(4), 299–325, https://doi.org/10.1080/13691066.2015.1052193.

J. Gemson and Thillai Rajan A., *Private Equity Financing in Infrastructure and Real Estate*, https://doi.org/10.1007/978-981-16-1634-1_3

The Special Purpose Vehicle Behind the Channel Tunnel Project

The Channel Tunnel is the longest undersea tunnel in the world, with an undersea length of 38 kms. It is composed of three tunnels, each 50 kms in length and bored at an average of 40 m below the seabed. The Channel tunnel connects the United Kingdom (Kent, Folkestone) and France (Pas-de-Calais, Coquelles) with Eurotunnel Shuttles, Eurostar, and freight trains running on two monodirectional single-track tunnels.

The Channel Tunnel project was considered to be the largest and the second largest project financing in history, with financing stages of the project in 1987 and 1990 (Megginson, 2001).

The Channel Tunnel project was established in 1986 as a partnership between France Manche SA (France) and The Channel Tunnel Group Limited (UK) to build and operate the tunnel under a 55-year concession from the French and UK governments. This partnership was a subsidiary of Eurotunnel SA (France) and Eurotunnel PLC (UK), while Eurotunnel Finance SA (France) and Eurotunnel Limited (UK) were also subsidiaries with responsibilities for financing the project. Eurotunnel Developments SA (France) and Eurotunnel Developments Limited (UK) were also formed as subsidiaries to enter into joint venture agreements with third parties for the purposes of developing properties and businesses outside, but resulting from, the Eurotunnel system. The original capital of £47 million (Equity Offering 1) for Eurotunnel was provided by the promoters, which included five banks (National Westminster, Midland, Credit Lyonnais, Banque Nationale de Paris, and Banque Indo-Suez), and a 10-company consortium, Transmanche-Link (TML), which included five UK contractors (Balfour Beatty, Costain, Tarmac, Taylor Woodrow and Wimpey) and five French contractors (Bouygues, Demez, SAE, SGE and Spie Batignolles).

Sources:

- https://www.getlinkgroup.com/en/our-group/eurotunnel/channel-tunnel/ (accessed 22 May 2022)
- Park and Chang (2013) Impacts of construction events on the project equity value of the Channel Tunnel project, Construction Management and Economics, 31:3, 223–237, https://doi.org/10.1080/01446193.2012.761715

Financing for such projects is created by one or more sponsors using equity or mezzanine debt for which the lender considers cash flows as being the primary source of loan reimbursement, whereas assets represented only collateral. On the equity side, capital is provided by corporate sponsors and developers; on the debt side, capital is provided by bank syndicated loans.

The following represent some sources of capital used in project financing:

(1) Developmental loan—A developmental loan is essentially debt financing provided during a projects developmental period to a sponsor with insufficient resources.

(2) Subordinated loan—Subordinated loans, also called mezzanine financing or quasi-equity, is senior to equity capital but junior to senior debt and secured debt. They are usually used to cover over-runs during the construction stage.
(3) Senior debt—Senior debt comes from commercial banks and institutional lenders and are an obvious choice for financing needs of a project. Senior debt of project finance usually constitutes the largest portion of the financing. These loans usually formed least 50 percent of the capital needs.
(4) Host government—The host government can also be a direct or indirect source of financing. This is more evident in the emerging markets where the governments are usually eager to fund and support infrastructure projects.

This capital is usually provided by the sponsors who finance the infrastructure project. The sponsors of the project are mainly of four kinds. Given below are the sponsors who finance the project in infrastructure finance (Gatti, 2008):

(1) Industrial sponsors whose goals are to harness initiatives linked to the core business and who see the infrastructure project as relevant upstream or downstream integrates in some way as linked to their core business
(2) Contractors and suppliers whose goals are to develop, build or run plants and are interested in participating in the initiative by providing equity and subordinated debt
(3) Public sponsors—they can be central or state governments in the location of the project or state-owned enterprises linked directly or indirectly to their respective governments whose aims center on social welfare
(4) Purely financial investors, who sought profits from the venture.

Sponsors in the Bengaluru International Airport Limited

The Bengaluru International Airport Limited (BIAL) is India's first greenfield project constructed on a project finance basis. The total project cost of Rs. 14.11 billion was to have been met as follows: equity of Rs. 3260 million, out of which Rs. 850 million would be from AAI and GoK, with the remaining Rs. 2400 million would be from the JVP's. In addition, GoK would provide a state support of Rs. 3500 million. Commercial debt funding would contribute the remaining Rs. 7350 million for the project. The JVP included Larsen & Tubro Limited, Seimens AG, Unique Zurich AG. The venture capital arm of Seimens AG—Seimens Project Ventures—provided a capital contribution of 57 million Euros.

Debt was funded through four leading Indian financial institutions—SBI Capital Markets, ICICI, IL&FS, and IDFC.

Source:

Thillai Rajan, A. & Gemson, J. (2011). Financial closure of Bengaluru International Airport Limited. Emerald Emerging Markets Case Studies Collection., 1(4), 1–22.

Largest infrastructure funds in the global market as on Jan 1, 2022.

Fund name	Fund manager	Headquarters	Target size (US$, billion)	Region focus
ISQ Global Infrastructure Fund III	I Squared Capital	USA	12	Various
KKR Global Infrastructure Investors IV	KKR	USA	12	Various
Stonepeak Infrastructure Fund IV	Stonepeak Infrastructure Partners	USA	10	North America
Brookfield Global Transition Fund	Brookfield Asset Management	Canada	7.5	Various
TPG Rise Climate Fund	TPG	USA	7	North America
AMP Capital Infrastructure Debt Fund V	AMP Capital	Australia	5	Various
Partners Group Direct Infrastructure 2020	Partners Group	Switzerland	5	Various
Global Infrastructure Partners Emerging Markets Fund	Global Infrastructure Partners	USA	5	Various
AIP Infrastructure II	AIP Management	Denmark	4.55	Various
European Diversified Infrastructure Fund III (EDIF) Series Two	First Sentier Investors	Australia	3.98	Europe

Source https://www.infrastructureinvestor.com/funds-in-market/, accessed 13 Apr 2022

3.2 The Need for Innovation in Financing in Infrastructure

Infrastructure financing and development continues to be dominated by the public sector. While both project sponsorship—the number of projects being implemented—and the volume of infrastructure project investments are attributed to the public sector, private participation in infrastructure brings with it important and necessary advantages.

Acute financial risks in infrastructure projects add to the normal operating risk due to the lack of internal resources (Capizzi et al., 2010) available to these projects. The kind of financial risks attached to such projects arose generally from infrastructure project imperfections which boiled down to information asymmetry factors and transaction and agency costs and from the inadequacy and hesitancy of the existing financial systems to meeting the needs of these businesses.

Inadequacies arose primarily because existing financiers such as governments and banks lacked the necessary know-how to deal with challenges imposed by infrastructure projects—both in terms of structure and in terms of risk. The hesitancy was due to the fact that these capital providers thought it a gamble to invest huge amounts of capital to infrastructure projects. Infrastructure projects as large projects (which on an average cost US$500 million or more) require large initial outlays and capital requirements. Such large capital-intensive projects also required the money to be "locked into" the projects during the gestation period or construction time. The cascading effect of the risk of large projects hindered the inception, growth and development of infrastructure projects with traditional financers.

The project finance structure of infrastructure projects also caused a high degree of leverage in them. While debt levels of 70–90 percent were not uncommon in infrastructure projects, such high degrees of leverage tended to cause challenges between lenders and borrowers. Studies of the costs, benefits and risks involved in infrastructure projects concluded that failures in these projects occurred regularly.

In late 2018, the Ministry of Statistics and Programme Implementation, an organization that monitors large infrastructure projects in India, observed that out of 1452 projects above US$21.73 million (₹150 crores) each being monitored, about 363 infrastructure projects reported cost overruns reflecting 18.73 percent of the original cost and 375 projects reported time overruns of approximately 45.14 months.[1] Durydev et al. (2017) analyzed construction projects in Cambodia and found that although residential construction projects attract high proportions of investment, cost overruns occur with alarming regularity (CIDP, 2015; United Nations Development Programme [UNDP], 2009). Memon et al. (2011) and Azis et al. (2013) reviewed construction projects in Malaysia and found some reasons for cost overruns to be improper planning, lack of experience, information and communication mismanagement and lack of adequate financial management.

[1] https://economictimes.indiatimes.com/news/economy/infrastructure/363-infrastructure-projects-show-cost-overrun-of-over-rs-3-42-lakh-crore/articleshow/67815547.cms, accessed 25.07.2019.

The Case of Taoyuan International Airport

The Taoyuan International Airport (TIA) plays an important role in connecting local and international markets, given that Taiwan considers itself "The Hub of Asia" and is a gateway to the Asian region. Around 2015, Taoyuan International Airport Corporation (TIAC) embarked on an ambitious development plan to expand and transform its airport infrastructure by constructing a third terminal and a third runway. This was done as a response to the increased growth of passenger flights and freight traffic in the Asia Pacific region.

The proposed third runway was to run parallel to the two existing runways and separated from the existing northern runway to allow for independent operations. The project team AECOM, an infrastructure company with presence in over 50 countries, undertook extensive topographical and geotechnical (borehole) surveys to provide the technical basis for the subsequent engineering assessments, and conducted runway length analysis and separation studies to determine the optimal placement of the runway with the given land availability, obstacles, and airport boundary constraints. The government was in charge of procuring the land needed to construct the runway. The Civil Aeronautics Administration (CAA), in-charge of this process, was required to inform the owners of farmland whose properties are to be expropriated and all the residents within the Phase I Development Area of the Taoyuan Aerotropolis Project to attend preparatory meetings for the administrative hearings. This increased the number of people to be informed from 8000 to 20,000.

In January 2016, the Civil Aeronautics Administration issued an official statement saying that the decisions made by Legislative Yuan and Taoyuan City Government to expand the number of people eligible to attend the preparatory meetings for land expropriation hearings that caused a huge delay in the land acquisition process. This statement was in response to the Taoyuan Mayor Cheng Wen-tsan criticizing of the agency, criticizing the CAA for inefficiency and short-sightedness, and that he expected that given the way things were going, it would probably take at least 15 years just to finish an airport runway.

In a press conference in August 2020, Minister of Public Construction Wu Tse-cheng, was hopeful that the project would be completed by 2025, despite the ongoing pandemic and the proposals for a delay until 2030. The Ministry of Transportation conceded that the delay was motivated by lower traffic and concerns that the necessary acquisitions of land could not be wrapped up in time, while noting that in case of further expropriations and land acquisition, a new completion date would be agreed upon.

Sources:

https://aecom.com/projects/taoyuan-international-airport-runway-3-preliminary-planning-execution/ (Accessed 19 July, 2021).

https://www.taipeitimes.com/News/taiwan/archives/2016/01/29/2003638342 (Accessed 19 July, 2021).

https://www.taiwannews.com.tw/en/news/3994492 (Accessed 19 July, 2021).

Flyvbjerg et al. (2003) studied the cost side of transport infrastructure development in the USA and concluded that these projects did not perform as promised. Majority of the projects fell into cost escalations due to incorrect estimates of costs and benefits due to errors in analyses leading to misleading cost–benefit analyses. They found that cost overruns of 50–100 percent and revenue shortfalls of 20–70 percent were common. Moreover, the risks generated from misleading cost estimates were typically ignored or underplayed in infrastructure decision making, to the detriment of social and economic welfare. The authors concluded that these errors were due to the problem of misinformation, sometimes referred to as information asymmetry.

Imperfect or asymmetric information (Berger & Udell, 1995; Keasey & Watson, 1993) related to the ex-ante evaluation of the project and the entrepreneur and to the ex-post monitoring of performance (moral hazard). This could potentially lead to adverse selection (Chan et al., 2009), and increased agency costs (Capizzi et al., 2010). The problem of information asymmetry was rampant in infrastructure projects where the parties involved in the project can possess different sets of information concerning the project—its financial viability, demand characteristics, rules of state, workings of governments, concessions available and the like.

Information asymmetries were important in theory but difficult to identify in practice (Karlan & Zinman, 2009). Information asymmetry is a major hurdle to allocative efficiency, and the financing vehicle may help address this problem (Chan et al., 2009). Traditionally, the degree of information asymmetry may be reduced through two mechanisms: the provision of collateral as part of the debt contract and/[or] the development of a close working relationship between the lender and the borrower (Binks & Ennew, 1996). Since infrastructure projects are already highly leveraged, a good working relationship between lenders and borrowers is sought after, in an attempt to reduce project information asymmetry. Thus, knowledgeable lenders are in demand, for in addition to being sources for financing for infrastructure projects, they would also work toward reducing asymmetries between lenders and borrowers. Gerencser and Hamiliton (2011) held that infrastructure financing is composed not just of innovation, engineering and construction, but also of finance, management and planning. It reflected a synergy of action between a variety of stakeholders from the market economy and in government at various levels.

The Heritage House and the Road Project

A 121-year-old heritage house that stood in the way of a massive road and bridge repair on Wharncliffe Road South, London, Ontario, Canada made headlines in Canada in early 2018 when its owner refused to allow the property to be relocated across the street, in a road project which was intended to remove the traffic bottleneck which was slowing drivers and causing collisions on one of the city's major north–south corridors.

While city engineers concluded that the land acquisition was necessary for successful completion of the project, the owner argued there should be room to add another lane under the current rail bridge, which was more than 94 years old.

City staff and politicians were willing to spend an extra half million dollars to move the house in an attempt to preserve its heritage features and keep its historic neighbourhood, an accommodation considered to be more than generous, by many, which was rejected by the owner.

https://torontosun.com/news/provincial/london-ont-eyes-500gs-move-of-womans-heritage-house-for-road-repair, accessed 13 Apr 2022.

In this regard, more and more attention is being devoted toward PE, a private financer, as a means of overcoming all these hurdles. New institutional economic theory and finance theory suggested that specialized financial intermediaries like PE are able to reduce some of these information asymmetries effectively (Engel & Stiebale, 2009).

3.3 PE Investments in Infrastructure

There are many ways in which PE investors invest in infrastructure projects. The first was through the creation of dedicated infrastructure funds. The parent PE investor or investors contributed capital to this infrastructure fund which was then invested in infrastructure projects. This model was followed by investors looking to create a versatile infrastructure investment portfolio. The second category was through direct investments by financial institutions into projects. This type of investment was used by institutions that are looking to diversify a particular portfolio. The third category was investments from sovereign wealth funds that made direct contributions to the infrastructure project.

Table 3.1 presents a summary of PE investment in infrastructure from 1990 to 2009.

PE in infrastructure has grown from a niche sector into a separate asset class. Several of the infrastructure funds launched during the 1990s have more than US$5 billion under management. More than 118 dedicated PE infrastructure funds with total commitments of US$119 billion have been set up during 2004–2008. About US$200 billion has been raised by specialist funds between 2006 and 2017, with at least the same again allocated by pension funds and other direct investors.[2] Twenty primarily focused on North America have closed since 2004 raising US$41.5 billion, with US$1.7 trillion being invested in infrastructure assets globally between 2010 and 2017.[3] In the UK alone, some 56 percent of water assets, all of UK's major airports, most ports, and all passenger rail rolling stock now sit within specialist investor vehicles. A total of 72 infrastructure funds were set up between 2006 and 2008 where 56 of them were bunched across four main world regions: USA, Europe, MENA countries and India. Approximately half of the new funds follow the PE model (Orr, 2009).

In a survey conducted by the Probitas Partners[4] in 2007 to gauge investor interest, opinions and perspectives on investing in infrastructure, the group found that most investors were extremely interested in investing in this sector. While more than 25 percent already had active infrastructure investment programs in place, over 52 percent confirmed that they were either actively considering infrastructure investing

Table 3.1 PE investment in infrastructure from 1990 to 2009

Description	1990–1994	1995–1999	2000–2004	2005–2009
Estimated PE investment in infrastructure (US$, billion)	0.89	2.41	9.54	19.31
Percentage growth rate over the previous period		171%	296%	102%
Percentage growth rate in total overall PE investment over the previous period		599%	107%	15%
Project finance investment in infrastructure that have PE investment (US$, billion)	9.91	25.78	43.2	159.62
Percentage growth rate over the previous period		160%	68%	270%
Percentage growth rate in project finance investment without PE over the previous period		396%	67%	19%

Source Securities Data Corporation, Venture Xpert (infrastructure includes investment in energy, transport and water and utilities)

[2] https://www.pwc.com/gx/en/industries/assets/pwc-giia-global-infrastructure-investment-2017-web.pdf, accessed 25.07.2019.

[3] https://www.pwc.com/gx/en/industries/assets/pwc-giia-global-infrastructure-investment-2017-web.pdf, accessed 25.07.2019.

[4] Probitas Partners is an independent provider of investment solutions to the institutional market based in USA and UK. This survey was conducted in Spring 2007 where 1,500 institutional investors were contacted and 114 responses were received from senior investment executives from Public & Corporate Pension Plans, Fund of Funds Managers, Family Offices, Endowments & Foundations, Consultants & Advisors, Insurance Companies and other agencies. Source: Investing in infrastructure funds, September 2007. Probitaspartners.com.

or would opportunistically do so in the future. 34 percent said they would increase allocations to infrastructure in the coming year. A majority of the respondents also stated that they would put infrastructure investments in their PE allocations.

The value of infrastructure deals backed by PE investors in 2006 was approximately US$73 billion or 50 percent of the total value of such deals, a figure significantly higher than in 1988 when PE firms represented only 2 percent of this value. Nevertheless, infrastructure PE remains a nascent field, accounting for only 10 percent of the total private transactions in 2006.

3.4 Research on PE Investments in Infrastructure

PE investors have invested in companies in all sectors of the economy (Hall, 2008). Initially developed to finance innovative hi-tech companies, the scope of industry sectors being financed by PE has increased to including infrastructure companies as well (Lorenzo, 1996). There are a number of reasons for PE investors to invest in infrastructure.

The first reason for PE investments in infrastructure is to allow for industry sector accessibility. The intense success of PE as VC in start-up companies has brought in a number of sectors under their radar—infrastructure included. Hall (2006) analyzed PE investments across utilities, energy, health care and other public infrastructure services. Discussing investment strategies of PE in infrastructure, the author mentioned four main categories by which PE invests—VC, buyouts, infrastructure funds and hedge funds. Focusing on the implications of the growth of PE in public services and utility companies in Europe, the author opined that PE funds have outperformed the stock market. He stated that however, profits of these funds were closely related to general economic trends and not independent of them as originally believed. Due to this, he was altogether not overly optimistic about the sustainability of PE returns in infrastructure.

The next reason for PE investments in infrastructure is to allow for region accessibility. PE firms were less active in developing countries and as late as 2005 they failed to make adequate profits, with an average return of only 3 percent in developing countries as compared with nearly 14 percent in the USA and 11 percent in Europe. PE firms invested US$10.5 billion in Asia in 2005. By comparison, PE firms invested only US$1 billion in Latin America and nothing at all in Africa, the Middle East or the CIS.

Orr and Kennedy (2008) highlighted recent trends of new players in global infrastructure. They concluded that PE investing in infrastructure was a definite trend driven by robust capital market activity and low interest rates. They also provided implications and strategies of the new trends in global infrastructure markets from the point of view of project sponsors, construction and engineering companies, pension funds, microlenders and multilateral organizations (Roundtable participants). They also underscored the role of multilateral development banks and suggested a "theory of plums" which was the idea that private buyers of infrastructure concessions often had greater knowledge about the true value of the concessions than did government sellers and that private buyers were therefore in a position to pick "plums."

Page et al. (2008) identified the various risks and rewards associated with PE investments in the infrastructure. They alleged that since PE holders were at the bottom bucket of the cash flow waterfall, they were likely to absorb project risks, especially demand risk. Analyzing private equity investment funds (PEIFs), the authors mentioned lower volatilities, diversification of portfolios and mitigation of inflation as benefits PE reaped with infrastructure investing. They concluded that PE funding could be effective if project duration issues are well understood, government sponsors agreed to reasonable regearing, novation and project development terms.

Masih et al. (2009) explored opportunistic and strategic infrastructure investment in emerging Asia. They believed that as the dynamic global investment unfolded, select investments in public–private infrastructure such as PE would become more attractive for long-term investors.

Orr (2009) analyzed the PPP model and was of the view that the success of the model heralded infrastructure as a new asset class, encouraging PE investors to invest actively in what he called "investable infrastructure". He concluded that PE style investment strategies added value by applying strategic management expertise, i.e., giving older assets a face-lift, expanding service capacity, bundling smaller assets, generating organic growth, initiating a rate-case review or moving assets to more efficient tax structures.

Chowdhury et al. (2009) discussed the growing role of Multilateral Development Finance Institutions (MDFIs) as investors in PE, and many ways to encourage new investment formats, new fund management practices and new risks and opportunities. Infrastructure investing was politically easier for MDFIs because infrastructure has been viewed as the natural responsibility of the public sector. MDFIs cited reasons for investing such as the positive multiplier effects, efficient capital deployment, political risk cover, deal flow agglomeration and encouragement of clean energy. An investment into a project by an MDFI gave credibility to the project and indicated positive developmental significance and good governance. Together, these signals served as a positive catalyst to mobilize even larger amounts of debt and equity capital from pension funds, sovereign funds and institutional investments.

Thillai Rajan (2010) is of the view that infrastructure assets were uncorrelated with other asset categories such as stocks and bonds and had superior risk-return trade-off. Further, these projects had steady and stable cash flows. Also, a reduction in investment in PE funds by pension funds and other long-term investors could have caused the PE funds to start investing in infrastructure.

Thillai Rajan et al. (2011) analyzed 173 PE investments in the Indian infrastructure sector on transactions in transport, power and telecom sectors between 2000 and 2010. They concluded that the transport sector consistently received PE investment over the years. However, the power sector, including investment in renewable energy, attracted the maximum amount of investment. Examination of the demography of deals indicated that specific regions or hubs in the country attracted PE investment in specific sectors, suggesting that PE investments were dominated by different sectors in different states. They also found that syndicated deals between foreign and domestic investors resulted in a much higher average investment compared to either foreign or domestic investors, suggesting that the presence of domestic investors provided a lot of comfort to the foreign investors, leading to higher investment.

Gemson et al. (2012) analyzed PE investments in 2821 infrastructure projects that were announced between 1990 and 2009. They found that projects with PE investment were larger when compared to projects that did not have PE investment, indicating that that PE investment helped in successfully financing larger projects. PE investment in infrastructure was also more frequently seen in developed countries as compared to developing countries. In developing countries, the number of sponsors was higher in projects with PE investment without any corresponding increase in project size, indicating that PE investors have helped in sharing the project risk among a larger group of investors, thereby reducing the risk faced by the individual sponsors.

3.5 Impact of PE Investments in Global Infrastructure

While a number of academic studies have analyzed PE investments in infrastructure, only a handful of them have examined the impact such investments have had. This section uses worldwide infrastructure projects between 1990 and 2009 to identity the impact of PE investments in physical infrastructure projects in the transport sector, energy sector and utilities sector.[5] A total of 2821 infrastructure projects were examined which were spread over 34 developed economies and 83 developing/emerging economies. The total nominal value of the project costs of these 2821 deals worked out to about US$1.43 trillion. A total of 349 projects (12.3 percent of the sample) had PE investments in them.

3.5.1 Projects with PE Investments: A Comparative Analysis

A comparative analysis[6] indicated that infrastructure projects that received PE funding (average project size US$649.6 million) were larger than those that did not receive PE funding (average project size US$474.7 million). These values were significant at a 99 percent significance level for the entire period 1990–2009. When the time period was broken down into 1990–2000 (period 1) and 2001–2009 (period 2), and mean values were compared, the results followed the same trend. However,

[5] Project level data was obtained from the Global Project Finance (GPF) database, provided by Venture Xpert. This GPF database provides details on projects that have successfully achieved financial closure on project financing basis. Project information available in the GPF database included sector, cost, gearing ratio, date of financial closure, type of private participation, and the sponsors of the project.

[6] The nonparametric Mann–Whitney U-test was used to test if there were any significant differences between such projects.

the difference was not significant in the former time period but significant at the latter time period. The inference that can be made from this result was that PE investors have become increasingly comfortable in investing in large infrastructure projects. While the mean cost of projects without PE has more or less remained at the same level between period 1 and period 2, the mean cost of projects with PE has increased by 253 percent in Period 2.

Comparative analysis was further extended into examining projects demographically. Projects in developed economies and developing/emerging economies were compared to examine trends of PE investments in infrastructure across demographics.

Figure 3.1 Panel A presents the comparative analysis of infrastructure projects in developed economies and Fig. 3.1 Panel B presents the comparative analysis of infrastructure projects developing/emerging economies

PE-invested projects were significantly larger than non-PE-invested ones in developed countries. These values were significant in period 2 and in the overall sample. An average PE-invested project was approximately 54 percent larger in the overall sample. When developing countries are considered, an interesting finding was that project sizes were not significantly different between the two categories. This is in contrast to the findings seen in the overall analysis as well as for developed countries. The reason behind this finding could be due to the reason that PE investment in infrastructure has been a more recent phenomenon, and the PE investors do not have the comfort yet to invest in large projects in developing countries between 1990 and 2009.

The last ten years, however, have noted significant increases of PE capital in developing economies. China, Indonesia, Russia, India and Bangladesh received more than half of the global commitments in 2017 while the emerging economies of Cambodia, Mongolia, the Philippines, Ghana, Jordan, Egypt, Turkey, Colombia, Brazil and Mexico recorded higher private investment commitments in infrastructure than public investment commitments, indicating the respective countries' seriousness in promoting private sector participation.

Examining only PE investments, the size of infrastructure projects in developed countries is higher in the overall analysis, but the difference is not statistically significant (Fig. 3.2). Taken together with the previous findings, this indicates that the average size of an infrastructure project in a developing country is higher, but it is not the case when we compare only projects that had PE investment. PE investors have more experience investing in developed countries, and that could be the reason why they are able to invest in larger projects in developed countries.

3.5.2 PE Investments: Debt Ratio

Next, the debt ratio is examined with respect to PE investments in infrastructure. Debt ratio is the percentage of debt capital used in financing the project. Presence of PE investment can provide an element of comfort to the project lenders for the following reason. A PE investor would have recourse only to the residual cash flows

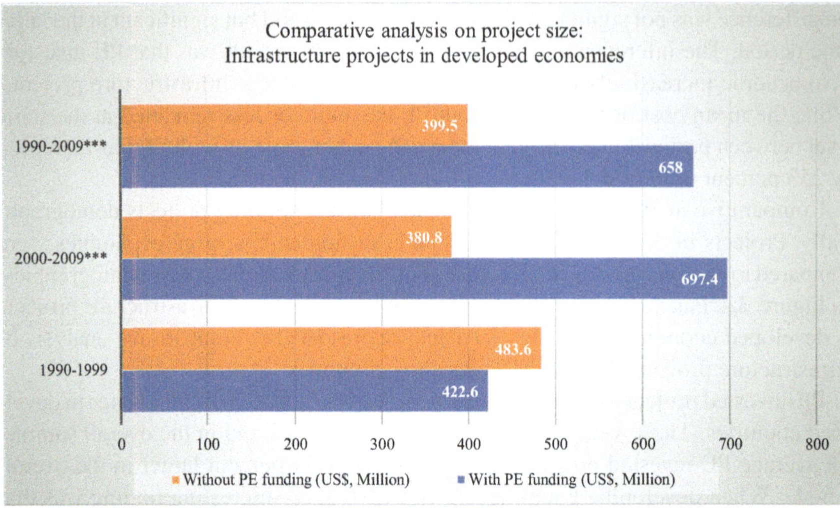

*** significant at 99% CI

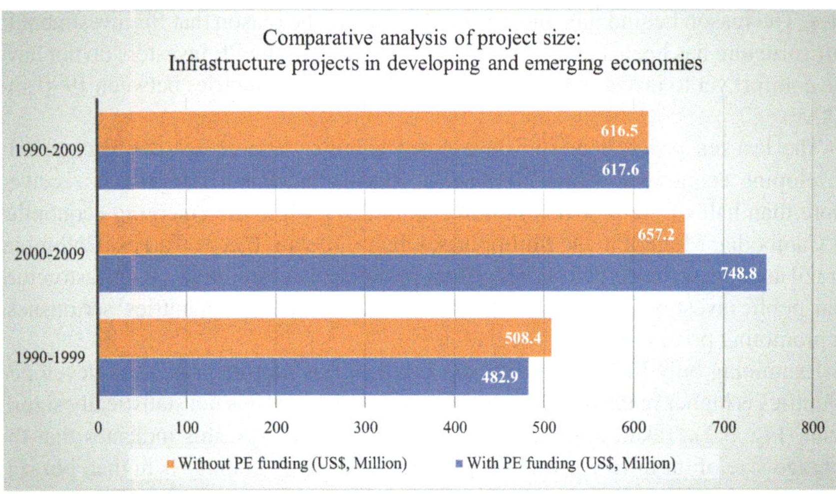

Fig. 3.1 Panel A: Comparative analysis: Infrastructure projects in developed economies. *** significant at 99% CI. Panel B: Comparative analysis: Infrastructure projects in developing and emerging economies
*** significant at 99% CI

after the lenders have been serviced unlike the other sponsors who can benefit from project contracts. Therefore, there is an incentive for the PE investor to monitor the other consortium sponsors to ensure that the project is successfully constructed, since the returns to PE investors would depend upon the successful completion of

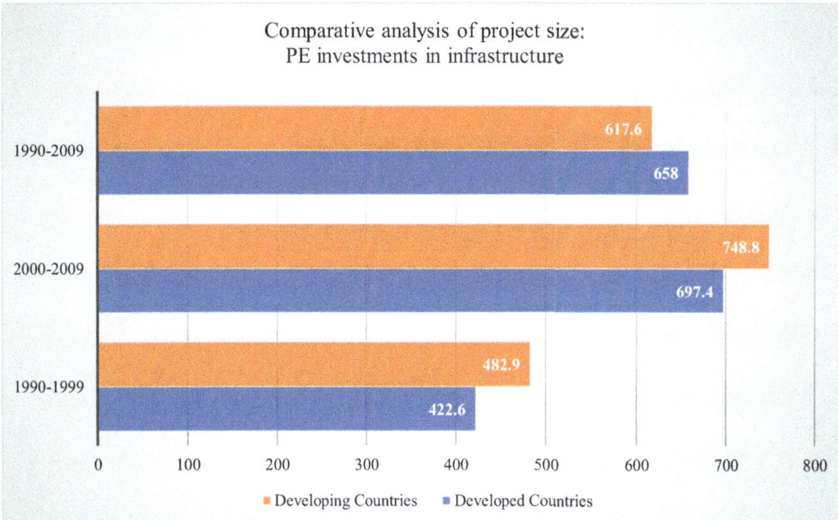

Fig. 3.2 Comparative analysis of PE investments in infrastructure based on project size
*** significant at 99% CI

the project. The argument is that the act of monitoring by PE investors to safeguard their investment indirectly benefit the lenders too.

Previous studies have indicated a negative relationship between project risks and debt ratio, i.e., as project costs increased, debt ratios became lower (Chemmanur & John, 1996). Given this background, debt ratios for projects with PE funding should be significantly lower than what is seen for projects without PE funding because project costs of PE-funded projects are higher. However, comparison of debt ratios indicated that there was no significant difference between the two sets of projects. This indicates that projects with PE funding are able to support higher levels of debt than what would have been possible otherwise.

When investments in developed countries are considered (Fig. 3.3, Panel A), the overall debt ratio indicated no significant difference between the two categories of projects. In developing economies, the debt ratio was not significantly different between the two types of projects in both the periods. However, in the overall analysis, the debt ratio of projects without PE investment is significantly higher than that of projects that had PE investment (Fig. 3.3, Panel B). The findings from the comparison of debt ratios in the two groups are on expected lines. Projects in developed countries are able to support higher debt levels as compared to projects in developing countries. The difference is also statistically significant (Fig. 3.4).

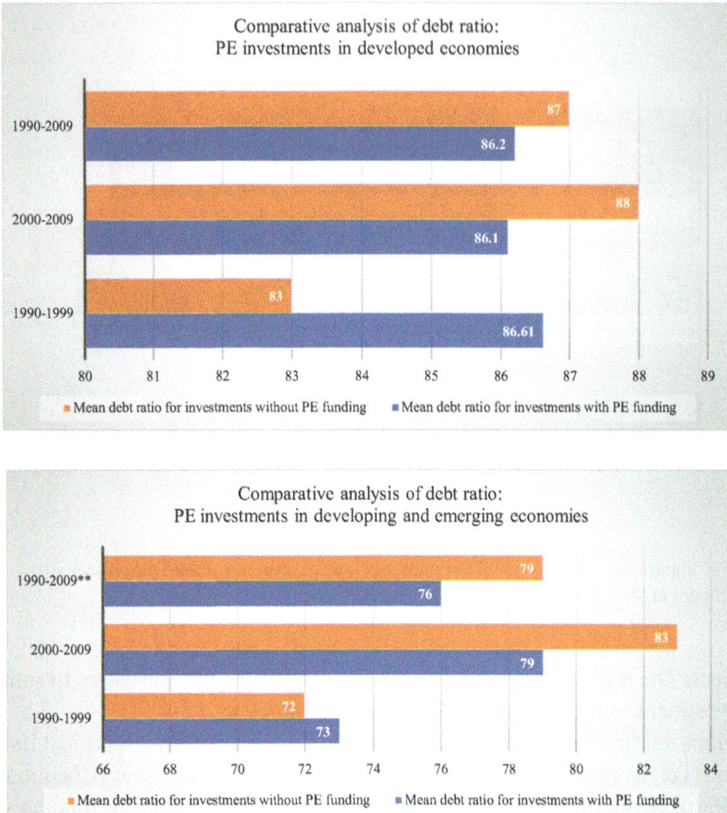

Fig. 3.3 Panel A: Comparative analysis of debt ratio: PE investments in developed economies. Panel B: Comparative analysis of debt ratio: PE investments in developing and emerging economies *** significant at 99% CI

3.5.3 *PE Investments: Number of Sponsors*

The next set of comparisons is with the number of sponsors in a project. The number of sponsors represents the main shareholders in the project. Analysis of the number of sponsors indicated that the average number of sponsors in a PE-funded project was higher than that of a project with no PE investment. The difference was statistically significant for both the periods (Fig. 3.6). This indicated that PE investors were not replacing existing investors but were bringing in additional investment capital. Since larger projects needed higher amounts of equity capital, PE investors could be seen as bringing in the additional equity, thereby relieving the financial burden on operational sponsors for more equity funding.

In developed countries too, the number of sponsor investors in PE-funded projects was significantly higher than non-PE-funded projects (Fig. 3.5, Panel A). Similarly,

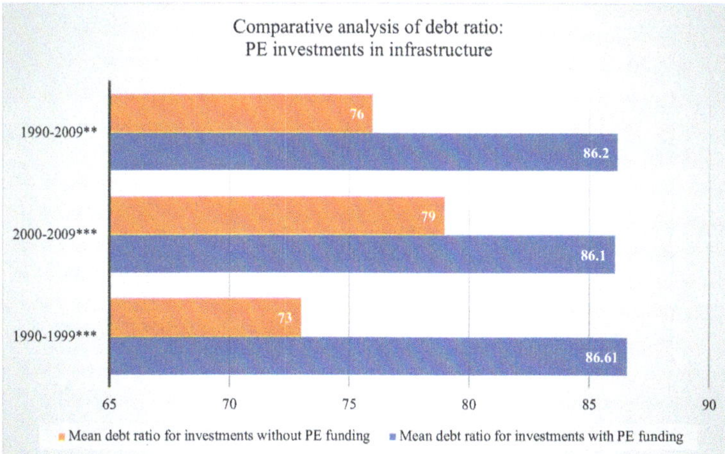

Fig. 3.4 Comparative analysis of PE investments in infrastructure based on debt ratio
*** significant at 99% CI

in developing countries, the number of sponsors in projects with PE investment was significantly higher (Fig. 3.5, Panel B). While the project sizes are not significantly different between the two categories of projects, number of sponsors in projects with PE investment is higher. This means that the average investment made by a sponsor in projects with PE investment is lower. This indicates that promoter sponsors of infrastructure projects in developing countries see PE investment not just as a source of capital, but as an opportunity to conserve their capital, and spread the project risk to larger group of investors.

The number of sponsors was higher in developing countries than in developed countries in both the time periods and the overall sample, indicating that the level of syndication is higher in developing countries. Given the higher level of uncertainty associated with implementing projects in developing countries, this result is also more or less on expected lines, as a higher level of syndication leads to a reduction in the risk assumed by the individual sponsors (Fig. 3.6).

3.6 Project Size and PE

The comparative analysis in the previous section indicated that infrastructure projects that had PE investment were significantly larger that those without PE investments. A total of 964 infrastructure projects between 2000 and 2009 were examined next to identify whether a relationship could be established between project size and the presence of PE investment. After controlling for other factors such as time, project sector (Oil and Gas, Power, Transport, Water and Petrochemicals), number of sponsors, and the risk level of the host country where the project is being implemented.

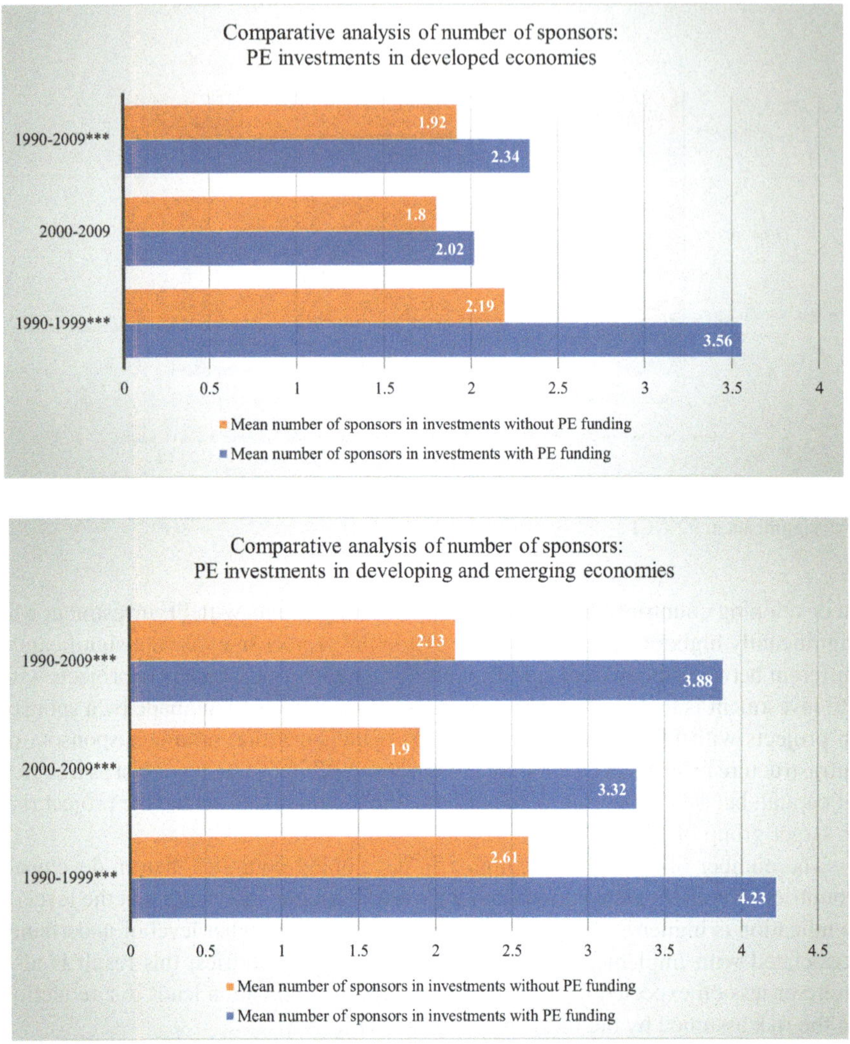

Fig. 3.5 Panel A: Comparative analysis of number of sponsors: PE investments in developed economies. Panel B: Comparative analysis of number of sponsors: PE investments in developing and emerging economies. *** significant at 99% CI

Such a test establishes the validity of the results of the comparative analysis as well as serves as a robustness check.

Equation 3.1 provides the regression model used in the analysis, and Table 3.2 provides details of the variables used in the regression equation.

$$\begin{aligned}\text{Log(COST)} &= \beta_0 + \beta_1(\text{PE}) + \beta_2(\text{OIL}) + \beta_3(\text{POWER}) + \beta_4(\text{TRANS}) \\ &\quad + \beta_5(\text{WATER}) + \beta_6(\text{BILOAN}) + \beta_7(\text{TGAP}) + \beta_8(\text{CONRISK}) \\ &\quad + \beta_9(\text{PRIVLEVEL}) + \beta_{10}(\text{SPONS}) + \varepsilon \end{aligned} \tag{3.1}$$

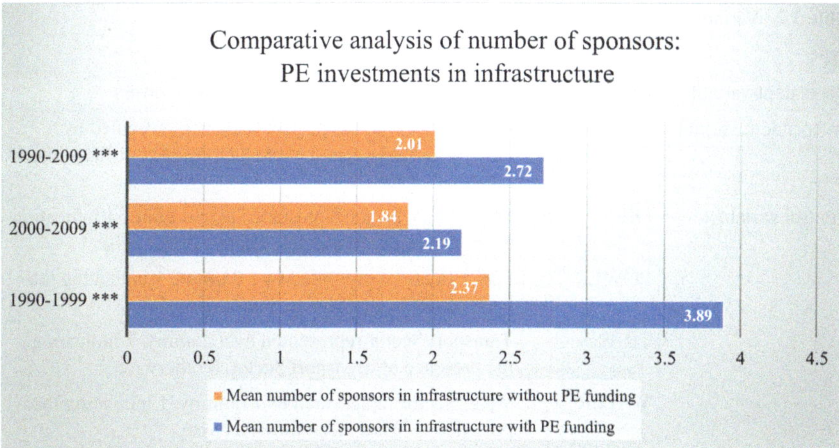

Fig. 3.6 Comparative analysis of PE investments in infrastructure based on number of sponsors. *** significant at 99% CI

The model can be explained as follows: Project cost has been taken to represent the project size, since bigger projects would mean a higher cost. This is the dependent variable or the explained variable in the regression. Given the wide variation in project costs, the log of project costs has been used in the regression model.

The independent variables or the explanatory variables are described as follows. In a project finance transaction, project design and parameters are finalized before it is financed, i.e., the quantum of investment required, and type of the investors is dependent on the project characteristics and not vice versa. Therefore, the presence of PE investor is considered as a lagging variable.

Some sectors are more capital intensive than others. For example, transport and conventional power projects generally have a higher cost as compared to water projects. To account for such sector-level differences, four dummy variables have been used to represent the five different sectors.[7] Since costs would also depend upon the year in which the project has been implemented, the regression model also includes a variable to capture the effect of time. To identify the influence of bilateral loans in financing infrastructure projects, a variable (BILOAN) has been included to account for such sources of financing. Risk levels of the host country also play a role, as the cost of financing becomes higher in countries with higher risk. CONRISK has been used as a variable to account for such country risks. The other variables used in the model are the level of privatization (PRIVLEVEL) and the number of sponsors (SPONS).

The results of the multiple regression (Fig 3.7) indicate that the coefficient of the PE variable is positive and statistically significant. This is in line with the findings the comparative analysis. This result indicates that PE investment plays a significant role in achieving financial closure of large projects. It can also mean that because of

[7] This also fulfills the degrees of freedom in dummy variable usage.

Table 3.2 Variables used for multivariate regression analyses

Type	Variable	Description
Dependent variable	COST	The log of the project cost (in nominal terms)
Independent variable	PE	PE investment in the project. This is represented by a dummy variable, 1 indicating the presence of PE in the project, 0 otherwise
Control variables	OIL	Oil and Gas Sector represented by a dummy, 1 indicating the presence of Oil and Gas Sector, 0 otherwise
	POWER	Power Sector represented by a dummy, 1 indicating the presence of Power Sector, 0 otherwise
	TRANS	Transport Sector represented by a dummy, 1 indicating the presence of Transport Sector, 0 otherwise
	WATER	Water Sector represented by a dummy, 1 indicating the presence of Water Sector, 0 otherwise
	BILOAN	The presence of Bilateral Loan in the project. This is represented by a dummy, 1 indicating the presence of bilateral loan in the project, 0 otherwise
	TGAP	Represents the difference in time between the year the project was announced and 2010. Range is from 1–10. If projects were announced in 2000, it will correspond to a value of 10. This variable is taken to account for time
	CONRISK	Contains country ratings that are taken on a scale from 1 to 100, 100 representing most secure and 1 being the least. These ratings have been sourced from "Euromoney" and are available for calculation with the authors, on request
	PRIVLEVEL	The level of privatization is perceived ordinal assignment on a scale of 1 to 5 for projects with varying degrees of privatization. 1 is assumed to be the lowest degree of privatization and 5 the highest. The values are indicated in Annexure A
	SPONS	The number of sponsors in the infrastructure deal

access to newer sources of finance such as PE, it has been possible to successfully achieve financial closure of larger projects than what has been possible previously.

The coefficients of other variables that are statistically significant are on expected lines. For example, coefficients for dummy variables POWER, TRANS and WATER are significant and are negative. The coefficients indicate that transport projects have a higher cost, followed by power and water, which is how one would have anticipated it to be. BILOAN is statistically significant, and interestingly has a negative coefficient. This means that bilateral loans are more often provided for smaller private sector infrastructure projects as compared to larger projects.

The coefficient on time is positive and significant. This interestingly indicates that in the later years of the sample, project costs have decreased since the value of TGAP reduces with time. PRIVLEVEL has a positive impact on costs, which is again on expected lines. Projects that are being privatized are assumed to be in the

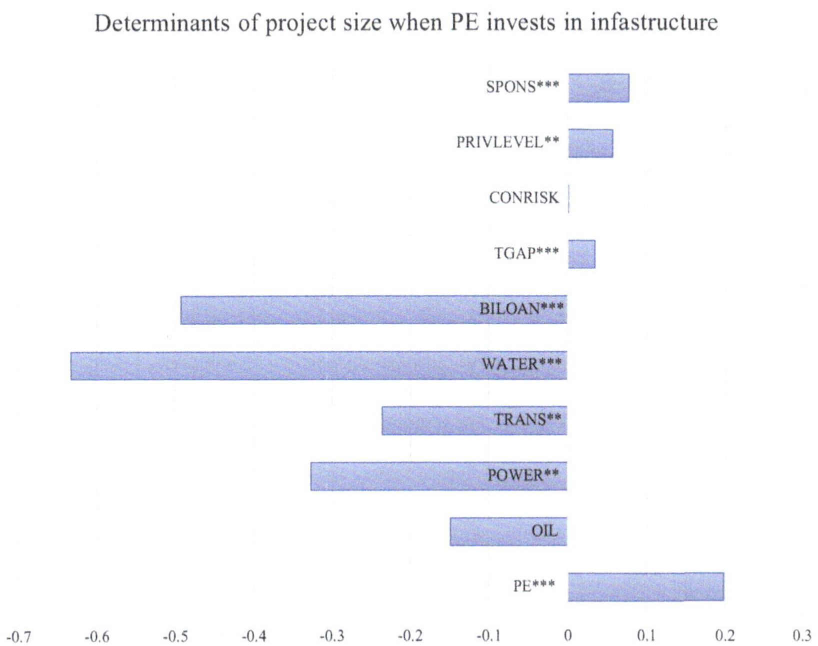

Fig. 3.7 Multiple linear regression to examine the determinants of project cost
*** significant at 99% ** significant at 95%

operation phase, and therefore might be valued higher. The coefficient of SPONS is also positive and statistically significant. As the project cost increases, more sponsors might be needed to fulfill the equity contribution.

3.7 Determinants of Private Equity Investments

The last section examined the determinants that led to PE investments in infrastructure and whether it is possible to predict if a particular infrastructure project in, say, the oil and gas industry, power industry, transport industry or water industry, would attract PE funding based on the inherent characteristics of the project (PRIVLEVEL, CONRISK, and BILOAN). Logistic regression was used, the dependent variable being a dependent dummy variable coded as 1 if the project had PE funding and zero otherwise. The variables used in this analysis are presented in Table 3.3. The model estimated is presented in the Eq. 3.2:

Table 3.3 Variables used in the analysis to examine the determinants of PE investments

Type	Variable	Description
Dependent variable	PE	PE investment in the project. This is represented by a dummy variable, 1 indicating the presence of PE in the project, 0 otherwise
Independent variables	OIL	Oil and gas sector represented by a dummy, 1 indicating the presence of Oil and Gas Sector, 0 otherwise
	POWER	Power Sector represented by a dummy, 1 indicating the presence of Power Sector, 0 otherwise
	TRANS	Transport Sector represented by a dummy, 1 indicating the presence of Transport Sector, 0 otherwise
	WATER	Water Sector represented by a dummy, 1 indicating the presence of Water Sector, 0 otherwise
	BILOAN	The presence of bilateral loan in the project. This is represented by a dummy, 1 indicating the presence of bilateral loan in the project, 0 otherwise
	TGAP	Represents the difference in time between the year the project was announced and 2010. Range is from 1 to 10. If projects were announced in 2000, it will correspond to a value of 10. This variable is taken to account for time
	CONRISK	Contains country ratings that are taken on a scale from 1 to 100, 100 representing most secure and 1 being the least. These ratings have been sourced from "Euromoney" and are available for calculation with the authors, on request
	PRIVLEVEL	The level of privatization is perceived ordinal assignment on a scale of 1–5 for projects with varying degrees of privatization. 1 is assumed to be the lowest degree of privatization and 5 the highest. The values are indicated in Annexure A
	SPONS	The number of sponsors in the infrastructure deal

$$
\begin{aligned}
z = {} & \beta_0 + \beta_1(\mathrm{OIL}) + \beta_2(\mathrm{POWER}) + \beta_3(\mathrm{TRANS}) \\
& + \beta_4(\mathrm{WATER}) + \beta_5(\mathrm{BILOAN}) + \beta_6(\mathrm{TGAP}) + \beta_7(\mathrm{CONRISK}) \\
& + \beta_8(\mathrm{PRIVLEVEL}) + \beta_9(\mathrm{SPONS}) + \varepsilon
\end{aligned} \tag{3.2}
$$

The sample used to estimate the PE investment choice model was the same as that used for the multiple regression analysis in the previous section. A total of 964 infrastructure deals which were financed in a project finance basis were examined, of which 117 were PE-invested deals and 847 were non-PE-invested ones. Given the binary nature of the dependent variable, a logistic regression was used.[8]

[8] A logistic regression is a specialized regression which is used when the dependant variable takes binary (0 or 1) values. In this regression, a value 1 was assigned to infrastructure deals that have PE, and a value 0 was assigned to deals that do not have PE investments.

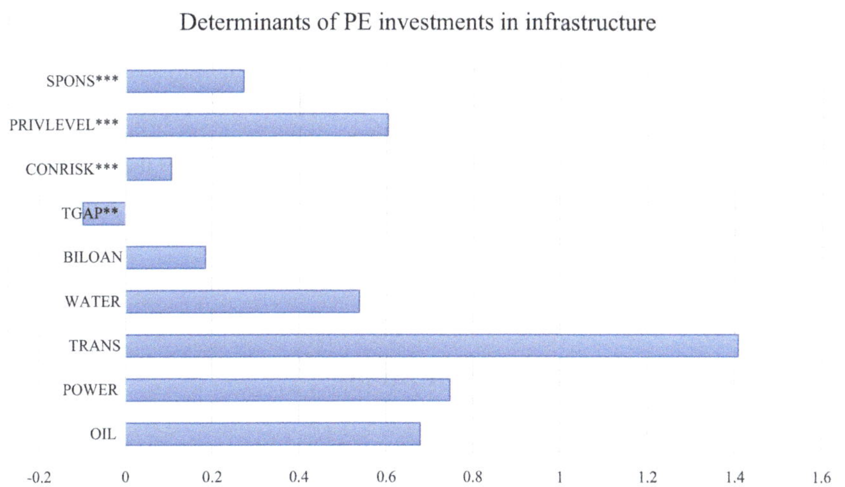

Fig. 3.8 Determinants of PE investments in infrastructure
*** significant at 99% CI, ** significant at 95% CI

Figure 3.8 reports the log likelihood ratio index for the log regression model. This index could be interpreted as a pseudo-R^2 for linear regressions and thus provides information about the explanatory power of the model being estimated. The explanatory power of the model could be evaluated by examining the likelihood ratio index which is 23.2 percent.

The logistic regression results for the estimation model are by and large on expected lines. They reveal that the variables TGAP, CONRISK, PRIVLEVEL and SPONS significantly influenced PE preferences for investing in a project.

None of the sectors significantly increased the probability of PE investing in the infrastructure sector. Although all the four sectors had positive coefficients, they were not significant in the model. On an average, transport sector had the highest cost and water sector the least. These results confirm the expected trends, as transport projects are comparatively larger than water and water related projects.

TGAP negatively and significantly increased the likelihood of PE investments in infrastructure which indicates that PE investments have been improving in recent years in infrastructure (smaller values correspond to years closer to 2009). This is positive news for the infrastructure industry as it indicates the willingness of PE investors to invest in infrastructure projects.

CONRISK positively and significantly influenced the choice of PE investments in infrastructure. The positive coefficient of the country risk variable implied the preference of PE investors to invest in developed countries (larger value) as compared to developing countries. PE investors are able to influence mature markets and create more value in them, hence their preference to invest there.

The variable PRIVLEVEL also positively and significantly influenced the decision of the PE investor to invest in infrastructure. A higher value entailed a higher degree of privatization and implies more flexibility in decision making for private sponsors, which seems to stand favorable from the PE investors point of view.

SPONS also positively and significantly influenced the decision of PE to invest in infrastructure projects—the more the number of sponsors, the higher the probability that PE would invest in the project. This implies that the projects which PE investors tend to target have larger costs and higher risks, i.e., there is presence of more syndication in an attempt to reduce risk.

3.8 Discussion and Policy Implications

The study provides some insights for policy makers and regulators interested in pursuing PE funding for infrastructure projects. This analysis was conducted at a global level to identify the impact of access to PE on infrastructure projects. As countries around the world begin to consider private sources of financing for public infrastructure projects, it becomes important for policy makers to consider PE as additional source of private financing. This analysis suggests that PE as an investor can provide significant benefits to the infrastructure project. PE investors are sophisticated investors who are able to sidestep bureaucratic signoffs and provided the much-needed value added capital to cash starved projects.

This study shows that PE is emerging as a new source of financing infrastructure projects between 1990 and 2009. When respective governments opened up the infrastructure sector to private investors, PE has responded enthusiastically by investing in them. Relatively new to investing in infrastructure, PE is now seen to invest in larger projects as compared to non-PE investors. According to Preqin, PE firms raised US$68.2 billion in the first three quarters of 2019, up 18 percent over the same period in 2017, surpassing the US$66.2 billion in all of 2016.[9]

The results of the analysis from 2000 to 2009 demonstrate that the trends of PE in developing countries are slightly different from those in developed countries. In developed countries, PE-funded projects were significantly larger than non-PE-funded ones. However, in recent times, emerging economies are witnessing larger inflows of PE capital into their infrastructure projects.

The multivariate regression shows a positive significant relationship between project size and the presence of PE. Sectorwise analysis although not significant shows the transport sector with the highest value thereby illustrating that transport projects are costlier than power projects and water projects. However, further analysis will be needed to substantiate the positive negative coefficient of the presence of bilateral loan. In this study, it indicates that larger projects do not support bilateral

---

[9] https://www.wsj.com/articles/investment-in-infrastructure-is-booming-despite-lack-of-progress-on-trumps-pledges-1538920801, accsessed 28.07.2019.

funding. The logistic regression reveals that country risk plays a positive significant role suggesting that PE investors prefer to invest in developed countries when compared to developing ones.

Thus, from a policy perspective, especially for developing countries, favorable environments and policies need to be created to encourage PE investments in infrastructure. Developing countries who need able infrastructure and do not have the resources to fund them will find it very beneficial to encourage PE investors. Increasing PE investment activity can also serve as a "signal" by encouraging independent oversight in project governance and attracting other private sources of capital thereby increasing the investment pool and capital availability for developing countries. This can be reassuring to lenders who provide large amounts of capital to infrastructure projects. Further benefits of PE investments include helping develop bigger projects than what is currently being pursued and reap significant advantages thereby providing means to create more Greenfield projects. It is vital therefore, in the interests of developing countries to focus of creating conducive environments to encourage PE investors in infrastructure.

3.9 Conclusion

This study quantifies the impact of the presence of PE investments on infrastructure projects. Focus is given to three parameters—the size of the project, the debt ratios handled by them and the number of sponsors in the project. A comparative analysis of projects that received PE funding to those that did not reveals that projects which received PE funding had larger average project size and more number of sponsor investors than those projects that did not receive PE funding. Controlling for project cost, they were also able to support higher debt ratios. The same results held ground in developed countries where PE-invested projects with non-PE-invested projects were compared. However, the results were reversed in developing countries, which showed no significant change in project sizes between PE-invested average project sizes and non-PE-invested ones. PE-invested projects also had lower debt ratios but more number of sponsors. This implied that PE is not able to influence developing markets as much as they can for developed markets in the early 2000s. PE investors were also unable to support high debt ratios in these markets. These results were reaffirmed when PE investments were compared with developed and developing countries and the average project size was found to be larger in developed countries. Further, PE was able to support larger debt ratios with significantly lower number of sponsors.

Multivariate regression analysis to ascertain if project size influenced PE investments confirmed that this hypothesis was indeed true. Further, year of investment, project structure and number of sponsors also influenced project size along with the various infrastructure sectors. The presence of bilateral loan negatively influenced the project size which indicated that smaller projects drew bilateral loans more than larger ones. Further, country risk did not significantly influence project size.

A logistic regression to estimate the probability of PE investing in an infrastructure project indicated that project cost, country risk, project structure and number of sponsors positively increased the probability of PE investments in infrastructure. Negative influence of year of investment suggested that PE invested in more recent projects.

Thus, an overall comparison between PE-invested projects and non-PE-invested ones in developed and developing countries highlighted significant differences in the patterns of investment. In developed countries, PE investors invested in larger projects and supported larger debt ratios when compared to non-PE investors. However, perhaps due to unfamiliarity of developing markets, they did not show any marked investments characteristics that differentiated them from non-PE investors. In addition, they could not sustain high debt ratios, but had significantly lower debt ratios than non-PE-invested projects. Also, they had significantly more number of sponsors (81.6 percent) as compared to projects without PE funding that indicated their penchant to increase syndicate size in an attempt to "spread out" risks.

References

Azis, M., Rahman, A., & Karim, A. (2013). Modeling causes of cost overrun in large construction projects with partial least square-SEM approach: Contractor's perspective. *Research Journal of Applied Sciences, Engineering and Technology, 5*(6), 1963–1972.

Berger, A. N., & Udell, G. F. (1995). Relationship lending and lines of credit in small firm finance. *The Journal of Business, 68*(3), 351–381.

Binks, M. R., & Ennew, C. T. (1996). Growing firms and credit constraint. *Small Business Economics, 8*(1), 17–25.

Capizzi, V., Giovannini, R., & Pesic, V. (2010). Determinants and effects of venture capital and private equity investments on Italian SMEs: Evidence from Italian puzzle. In *Midwest Finance Association Conference 2010*, February 2010, Las Vegas.

Chan, C., Forwood, D., Roper, H., & Sayers, C. (2009). *Public infrastructure financing: An international perspective*. Productivity Commission Staff Working Paper, March 2009.

Chemmanur, T., & John, K. (1996). Optimal incorporation, structure of debt contracts, and limited-recourse project financing. *Journal of Financial Intermediation, 5*(4), 372–408.

Chowdhury, A., Orr, R. J., & Settel, D. (2009). Multilaterals and infrastructure funds: A new era. *Journal of Structured Finance, 14*(4), 68–74.

Council for the development of Cambodia. 2015. Cambodia Industrial Development Policy 2015 - 2022. https://eurocham-cambodia.org/uploads/6a5ac-h.e.-mr.-sok-chenda-sophea-presentation.pdf. Accessed July 28, 2019.

Durdyev, S., Omarov, M., Ismail, S., & Lim, M. (2017). Significant contributors to cost overruns in construction projects in Cambodia. *Cogent Engineering, 4*, https://doi.org/10.1080/23311916.2017.1383638

Engel D., & Stiebale, J. (2009). *Private equity, investment and financial constraints—Firm-level evidence for France and the United Kingdom*. Ruhr Economic Papers 0126, Rheinisch-Westfälisches Institut für Wirtschaftsforschung, Ruhr-Universität Bochum, Universität Dortmund, Universität Duisburg-Essen.

Esty, B. C., & Sesia Jr., A. (2005). *An overview of project finance–2004 update*. Harvard Business School Case #205-065.

Flyvbjerg, B., Holm, M., & Buhl, S. (2003). How common and large are cost overruns in transport infrastructure projects? *Transport Reviews, 23*(1), 71–88.

Gatti, S. (2008). *Project finance in theory and practice: Designing, structuring, and financing private and public projects*. Academic Press Advanced Finance Series.

Gemson, J., Gautami, K. V., & Thillai Rajan, A. (2012). Impact of private equity investments in infrastructure projects. *Utilities Policy., 21*, 59–65.

Gerencser, M., & Hamiliton, B. A. (2011). Re-imagining infrastructure. *Journal of Applied Corporate Finance, 23*(3), 18–29.

Hall, D. (2006). *Private equity and infrastructure funds in public services and utilities*. Discussion Paper, London: University of Greenwich

Hall, D. (2008) Private equity and employment—The Davos/WEF/Harvard study. http://www.psiru.org/reports/2008-02-PE-WEF.doc. Accessed November 11, 2012.

Karlan, D., & Zinman, J. (2009). Observing unobservables: Identifying information asymmetries with a consumer credit field experiment. *Econometrica, 77*(6), 1993–2008.

Keasy, K., & Watson, R. (1993). *Small firm management*. Blackwell.

Lorenzo, W. (1996). The advent of private equity in Latin America. *The Columbia Journal of World Business, 31*(1), 60–68.

Masih, R., Adams, A., & Weddle, S. (2009). *Pillars of a new paradigm—Emerging Asia infrastructure*. Global Strategic Research, JP Morgan Asset Management. www.jpmorgan.com/insight. Accessed April 7, 2011.

Megginson, W. L. (2001). Towards a global model of venture capital? *Journal of Applied Corporate Finance, 16*(1), 89–107.

Memon, A.H., Abdul Rahman, I., & Abdul Aziz, A. A. (2011). Preliminary study on causative factors leading to construction cost overrun. *International Journal of Sustainable Construction Engineering and Technology, 2*(1), 57-71.

Orr, R. J. (2009). *Pensions and infrastructure: The path to common ground*. Collaboratory for Research on Global Projects, Stanford, California.

Orr, R. J., & Kennedy, J. R. (2008). Highlights of recent trends in global infrastructure: New players and revised game rules. *Transnational Corporations, 17*, 99–133.

Page, S. N., Ankner, W., Jones, C., & Fetterman, R. (2008). The risks and rewards of private equity in infrastructure. *Public Works Management & Policy, 13*(2), 100–113.

Park, A., & Chang, C.-Y. (2013). Impacts of construction events on the project equity value of the Channel Tunnel project. *Construction Management and Economics, 31*(3), 223-237. https://doi.org/10.1080/01446193.2012.76171

Thillai Rajan, A. (2010). *Private equity in infrastructure: Does it help?* Working Paper Series, Harvard University and Indian Institute of Technology Madras.

Thillai Rajan, A., Doshi, M., & Gemson, J. (2011). *Fueling growth and economic development: An analysis of private equity investments in real estate and infrastructure*. India venture capital and private equity report, Indian Institute of Technology, Madras.

Thillai Rajan, A., & Gemson, J. (2011). Financial closure of Bengaluru International Airport Limited. *Emerald Emerging Markets Case Studies Collection, 1*(4), 1–22.

United Nations Development Program. 2009. https://www.undp.org/cambodia/publications/annual-report-2010-0. Accessed July 28, 2019.

Chapter 4
The Case of Indian Real Estate

The best investment on Earth is earth.
—Louis Glickman

4.1 Introduction

Capital requirements for real estate are classified into four main categories, namely land acquisition, project development, construction, and sales and marketing. Land acquisition is the process of acquiring land and may include the process of securing entitlements, such as zoning and land use rights. Project development, also called property development, encompasses activities which get the land ready for the construction stage. This can include organizing for development activities, such as architecture and engineering services, land development activities such as subdivision of land, converting the land into parcels, etc. The construction is the building of the real estate, while the sales and marketing refer to the selling of the land and real estate to suitable buyers. Of these, land acquisition and construction account for the majority of the capital needs, and it is no secret that a sizable amount of capital is necessary in this business. The real estate sector is also rife with regulations based on the regions where the real estate is located. For example, property laws in Canada govern the rights and responsibilities of those who use and dispose land in the country, and Canadian real estate laws are mostly governed by provincial statutes such as requiring disclosure statements and financial details. This can cause constraints for developers, especially with regard to mobilizing capital.

This chapter is based on the journal paper titled "Private equity investment and real estate development. Evidence from residential projects in India." which appeared in Journal of Financial Management of Property and Construction Vol. 19 No. 3, 2014 pp. 202–225. https://doi.org/10.1108/JFMPC-02-2014-0001

J. Gemson and Thillai Rajan A., *Private Equity Financing in Infrastructure and Real Estate*, https://doi.org/10.1007/978-981-16-1634-1_4

4.2 The Real Estate Sector in India

The real estate sector is an integral component of India's economy. It houses one of the world's most populous country—a nation of 1.2 billion people and provides location facilities for all businesses. It is a robust employment generator, second only to the agriculture sector in India and is expected to reach US$1 trillion by 2035. The steep growth in the real estate sector—residential, commercial, and retail—are due to the continued growth of nuclear families, rapid urbanization, and rising household income.

The Indian real estate sector was ranked 20th among the top global markets for real estate development in 2012, with investments worth US$3.46 billion (₹190 billion) in the same year (Cushman & Wakefield, 2012). The Global Real Estate Transparency Index ranking improved to 34 in 2019 due to a betterment in regulatory reforms, better market data and green initiatives,[1] encouraging a growth in the demand for Indian real estate. Further, India's cost advantage, availability of skilled labour and low climate risk make the country an attractive setting in the Asia Pacific region as a potential industry hub, directly and indirectly real estate.

The demand for data centers in India is expected to increase by 15–18 million square feet by 2025 across major Indian cities.[2] As per investment information and credit rating agency (ICRA) estimates, Indian firms are expected to raise more than US$48 billion (₹3.5 trillion) through infrastructure and real estate trusts in 2022, a 65 percent increase from 2021 values.[3]

4.3 PE in Real Estate

As a form of risk capital, PE is known to finance companies in a variety of situations—from innovative start-ups to mezzanine companies, and even large mature public companies. They do so by obtaining capital from arms-length investors, also known as limited partners, and manage this money in fiduciary capacity by investing in specific deals. In addition to seeking high returns, firms also aim to achieve portfolio diversification.

As a financial intermediary, PE is known to operate in situations where information asymmetry is particularly prevalent (Gompers & Lerner, 1999). The real estate market is a classic example of an industry with steep information asymmetry. The physical real estate market is characterized by relative lack of liquidity, large lot sizes and high transaction costs with properties that are locationally fixed and heterogeneous.

[1] https://www.jll.ca/en/trends-and-insights/research/global-real-estate-transparency-index, accessed 17 Apr 2022.

[2] https://economictimes.indiatimes.com/industry/services/property-/-cstruction/real-estate-demand-for-data-centres-set-to-rise-by-15-18-million-sq-ft-by-2025-says-report/articleshow/82966705.cms?from=mdr, accessed 17 Apr 2022.

[3] ibef.org/industry/indian-real-estate-industry-analysis-presentation, accessed 17 Apr 2022.

Further, the low transparency of this sector also adds to information asymmetry (Georgiev et al., 2003).

Despite such challenges, the real estate sector has emerged as a viable alternative for PE to balance their portfolio (Adair et al., 1999), the most obvious reason being that property is a long-term low-risk investment with potential for diversification (Rydin et al., 1990). Trends in PE investments in India (Q1 2022) in real estate showed that the PE investments in real estate increased to US$6.2 billion in 2021. Between January 2021 and September 2021, PE investment inflows into the real estate sector in India stood at US$3.3 billion. Among the other asset classes, the office and retail asset class gradually increased their share of investment in the sector, from 25 to 62 percent and 1 to 21 percent from 2015 to Q1 of 2022, respectively.[4] Foreign PE investors continued to be the largest contributor. They accounted for almost 97 percent of all equity investments in Indian real estate.[5]

The growing interest of PE in Indian real estate is therefore both relevant, and timely, with greater participation of foreign investors and the increasing size of developers. In this study, we address the limited research on real estate investments in India. Despite this sector growing rapidly and attracting huge sums of capital, research on real estate investments has been limited. This could be attributed to the lack of reliable data and the difficulty in collecting the same, because of the opacity associated with financial transactions in real estate (FICCI, 2013). Further, existing research on real estate is limited to country-level and investor-level characteristics. In this study, we use micro-level factors for richer insights and a more granular understanding. We begin with an examination of PE investment in the real estate sector in India.

PE, as a source of financing real estate, has increased in many developing countries (Ernst & Young, 2013), and therefore, insights can seemingly be expanded to developing/emerging economies. We compare projects with and without PE investment to understand the differences in investment patterns between different types of PE investors. We classify PE investors based on characteristics of domicile (domestic vs. foreign investors) and fund focus (dedicated real estate funds vs. general funds). Finally, we explore the factors that influence PE decision making in real estate projects.

We expect useful implications from this study. First, the emergence of PE as an important source of financing real estate can have important ramifications for the sector. It is important that such financing is obtained from the right type of PE fund. For practitioners such as policy makers and real estate developers, insights into investment patterns would shed light on preferences of the different types of funds. Finally, for real estate developers intending to harness the benefits of PE capital, an appreciation of what makes PE tick would prove useful in their pursuance of this strategy.

[4] Investments in Real Estate (Trends in Private Equity Investments in India Q1 2022), Knight Frank Real Estate Consultants.

[5] See Footnote 4.

Table 4.1 Snapshot of the sample of residential projects in India between 2005 and 2012

Region	Number of projects	Construction area (in Million Sqft)	Land area (in Million Sqft)	FSI	Total project cost (in ₹[6] Million)
North	89	104.854	192.581	2.00	403,794.2
South	226	262.854	280.557	1.96	664,519.1
East	14	21.122	19.150	1.66	34,050.0
West	115	144.715	123.731	4.26	867,987.9
Central	9	4.034	5.831	1.03	20,100.0
Total	453	537.579	621.850		1,990,451.2

Source EMIS, CRISIL, Venture Intelligence, compiled by authors
For details on region, please see 11: Appendix: Data sources & Methodologies

4.4 Analysis

Our sample consisted of a total of 453 projects in the residential real estate sector in India. A total land area of 621.8 million sqft was developed with a construction area of 537.579 million sqft. Table 4.1 presents a snapshot of our sample of residential real estate projects in India between 2005 and 2012 based on region.

An examination of Table 4.1 indicates that Southern India had the highest number of residential projects in the period in question with 226 projects. This was followed by Western India with 115 projects and closely by Northern India with 89 projects. The construction area in Southern India was 262.854 million sqft, 150 percent more than that of Northern India that had 104.854 million sqft. area. Western India had a construction area 144.715 million sqft, around 82 percent of that of South India. Eastern India saw 14 projects while Central India saw by far the fewest numbers of projects being developed (9) with a total of 4.034 million sqft of area being constructed.

Upon examining land area, South India continued to occupy top spot with 280.557 million sqft of land area developed, 45 percent more than that of North India and 126.7 percent more than that of Western India. Eastern India had a total of 19.15 million sqft of land area developed for residential projects while Central India saw by far the least development of land with 5.83 million sqft of land area developed. The Floor Space Index (FSI), which represents the use of space, is calculated as a ratio of land area by construction area. Western India had the highest FSI with 4.26 followed by North India with an FSI of 2. South, East and Central India had residential projects which represented similar use of space with 1.96, 1.66 and 1.03 respectively.

In terms of total project cost, Western India had the highest project cost with a total of ₹867,987.9 million. Western India houses Mumbai, the world's most expensive

[6] Rupee is the currency of India. At the time of doing this study, the exchange rate of the Indian Rupee was roughly 1US$ = 62 Indian Rupees (₹).

Table 4.2 Summary of residential real estate market, classified according to metro and non-metro cities

Region	Number of projects	Construction area (in Million Sqft)	Land area (in Million Sqft)	FSI	Total project cost (in ₹ Million)
Metro	309	408.119	334.194	2.57	1,340,090.0
Non-metro	144	129.460	287.656	1.79	650,361.2
Total	453	537.579	621.850		1,990,451.2

Source EMIS, CRISIL, venture intelligence, compiled by authors
For details on region/metro, non-metro cities, please see 11: Appendix: Data sources & Methodologies

city[7] and the world's 16th most expensive city for residential real estate. Frank Knight LLP, an international property consultancy firm, recorded that a prime residential property in Mumbai had a price tag of ₹57,000 per sqft. Mumbai is one of the four old metro cities in India and a strategically located port in Western India. The four old metro cities include Delhi, Mumbai (erstwhile Bombay), Kolkata (erstwhile Calcutta), and Chennai (erstwhile Madras). It is also the financial capital of India and the heart of Bollywood, the entertainment industry of India and one of the largest movie industries of the world, which perhaps explains the extremely high real estate prices.

Table 4.2 presents a summary of the residential real estate market classified according to metro and non-metro cities.

An examination of Table 4.2 indicates that metro cities had 114 percent more number of projects than non-metro cities. In terms of land area developed, metro cities saw only 16 percent more area being developed. However, metro cities had 215.24 percent more construction area. This suggests that there were more number of high-rise projects being undertaken in metro cities. Reasons for this include lack of developable land and increasing cost of real estate prices.

The total project cost in metro cities was also 106 percent more than that of non-metro cities. Generally, metro cities are larger and more expensive than non-metro cities, the major reason being a higher cost of living. However, the cost-by-construction ratio of metro cities in lower than that of non-metro cities.

4.5 Analysis of Trends of PE in Residential Real Estate in India

First, we examined the regionwise distribution of the sample. A large proportion of projects (about 50 percent of the sample) were in the metro cities located in South

[7] Based on a recent study conducted by Frank Knight LLP, an international property consultancy firm http://www.rediff.com/business/slide-show/slide-show-1-mumbai-is-the-worlds-most-expensive-city/20120416.htm#12, accessed 25.10.2013.

India—Chennai, Bengaluru and Hyderabad. This was followed by the western region, which accounted for about 25 percent of the sample. The central region and the east accounted for about 5 percent of the sample. The regionwise distribution was based on the level of development and economic activity in various regions of the country.

4.5.1 Projects with PE Investment: A Comparative Analysis

Figure 4.1 presents the results of the comparative analysis of residential projects with PE funding as against projects without PE funding. The analysis has been divided into project-level variables, developer-level variables, and macroeconomic-level variables.

An examination of Fig. 4.1 indicates that there are significant differences in residential projects which have PE investments when compared to projects that do not have PE investments. These differences appear more marked at the project level. There are differences in both construction area and land area, which indicates that PE firms invest in projects with larger land area and construction area. The difference in cost of the projects between projects with and without PE investment indicates that PE firms invest in costlier projects. Also, the ratio cost by construction is larger for projects with PE investments than for projects without PE investments.

An examination of developer-level variables such as years of experience and number of projects developed indicates that PE firms respond to experience levels of the developers homogeneously. However, in terms of sqft developed, PE firms prefer developers with larger sqft developed, indicating PE preferences for larger projects and developers who undertake the same. This difference is significant at 10 percent.

When examining macroeconomic characteristics, it is observed that PE firms prefer to invest in regions with high growth in Housing Price Index (HPI) and Consumer Price Index (CPI). The growth of population or the level of corruption/competitiveness of the state does not affect the decisions of PE firms to invest in residential projects in India.

An analysis of the differences between projects with and without PE investments indicates that project-level characteristics are the greatest influencers in the decision of PE firms to invest in residential projects in India. The affinity to choose developers who develop larger projects rather than developers who have more experience in terms of years or projects developed reveals PE firms' predilection toward considerably sized projects. Thus, PE firms seem to emerge principally as capital providers to residential real estate projects. This is further reinstated by the fact that competitive/corruption levels in the state did not significantly alter between PE firms and non-PE firms.

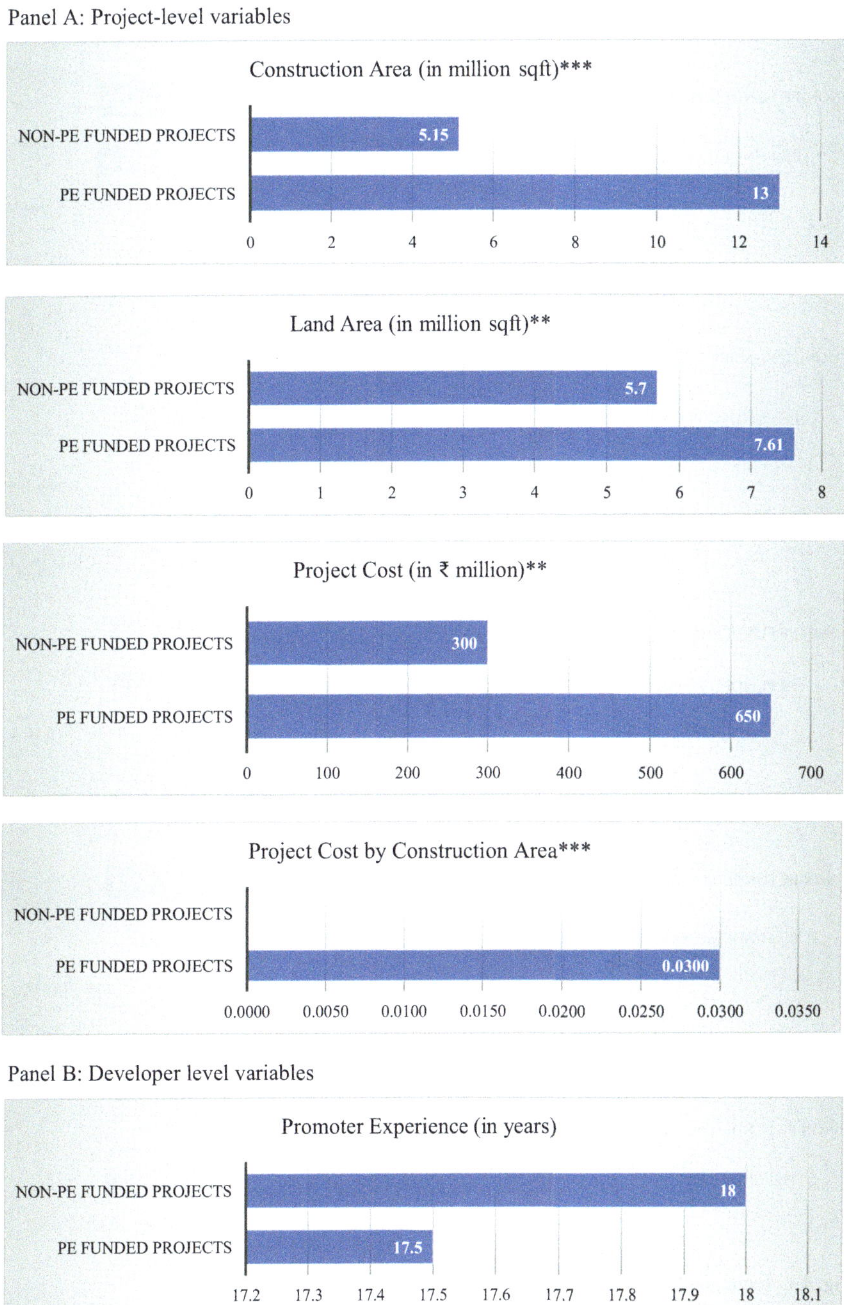

Fig. 4.1 Comparative analysis of residential projects with PE funding versus residential projects without PE funding. *** 99% CI, **95% CI

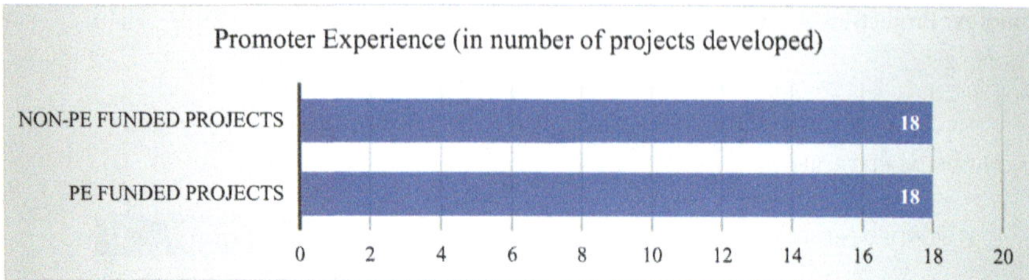

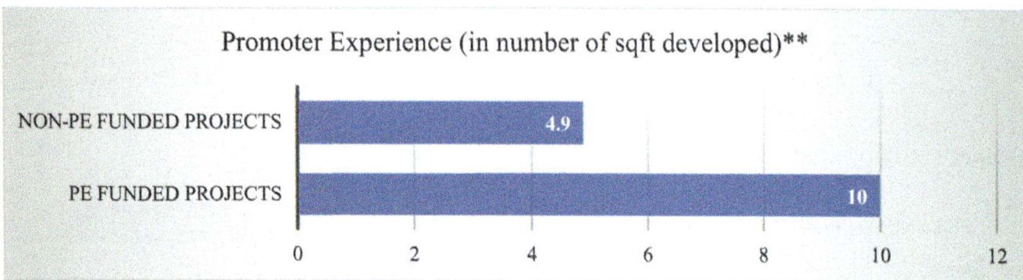

Panel C: Macroeconomic variables

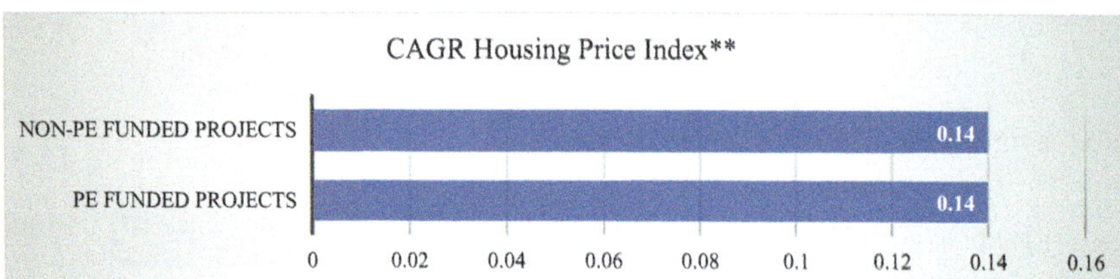

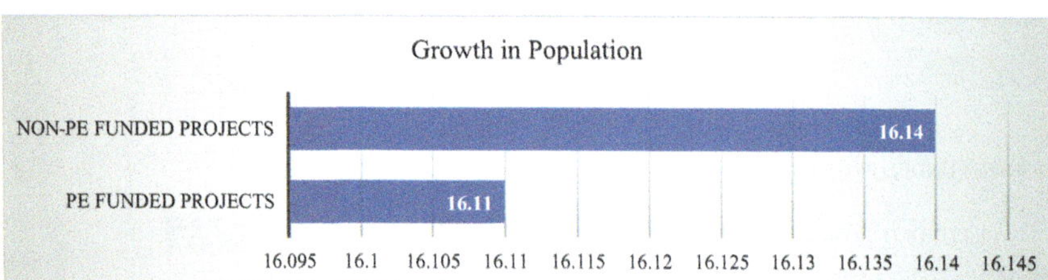

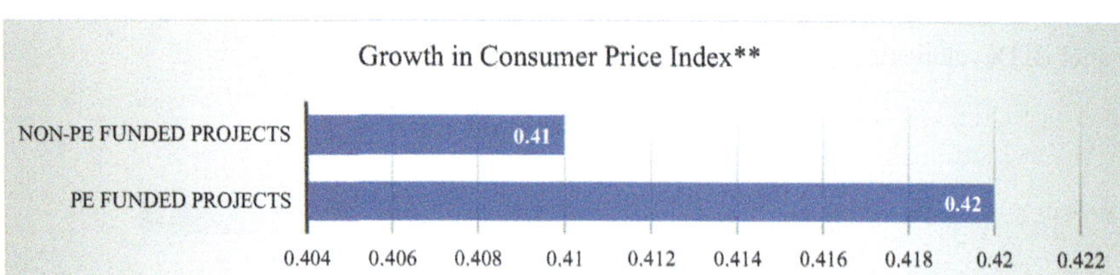

Fig. 4.1 (continued)

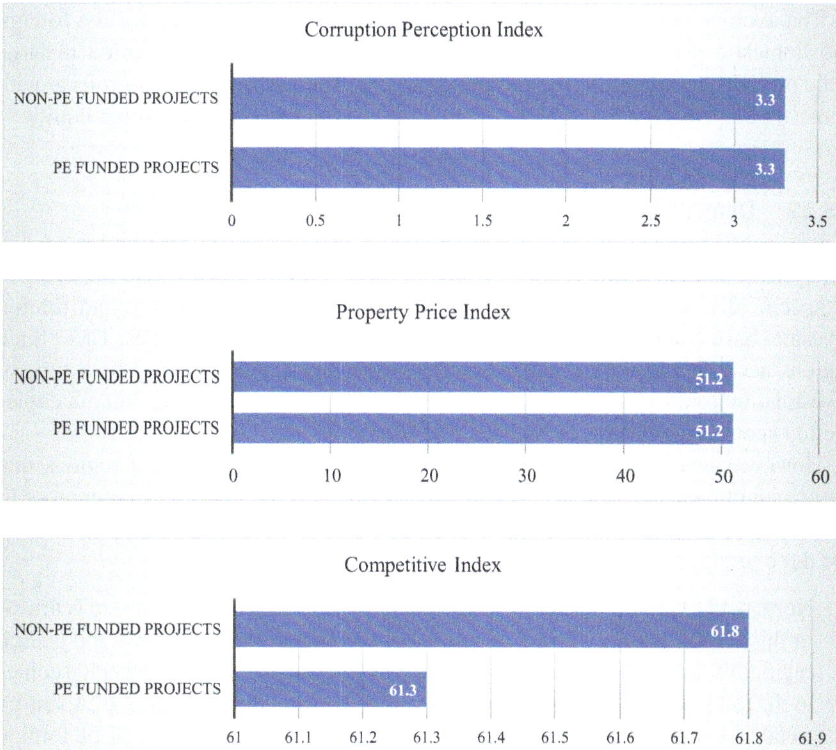

Fig. 4.1 (continued)

4.5.2 *Comparative Analysis of PE Investors*

4.5.2.1 Deal Characteristics

The dataset shows that the total number of deals closed by domestic investors was 52 percent higher compared to the foreign investors.[8] Analysis also reveals that in case of domestic PE investors, four out of every five projects attract investment through project-level investment. However, in case of foreign investors the difference in the two modes of investment is not significant. Fifty-eight percent of the deals which had foreign equity investors were project financed and the rest were investments made at a company level. This comparison clearly highlights that the investment preference of the domestic investors was heavily skewed toward project-level investment mode, whereas the foreign investors do not seem to show a significant preference for any one of the investment modes. It is also seen that the overall deal size was considerably higher for the foreign investors during all periods except 2010.

[8] A domestic PE investor had their registered offices within the boundaries of India, while a foreign investor had their registered offices outside the boundaries of India.

The average developable area of various projects was compared for the foreign and domestic investors. It is seen that domestic investors have invested in large scale projects compared to the foreign investors. The built-up area of projects with domestic PE was 28 percent higher compared to the projects with foreign equity.

4.5.2.2 Demographics

Analysis of domestic and foreign investors based on the geographical preferences or specifically the location of projects reveals that both the domestic and foreign investors have comparable preferences for North, West and South zones. These three regions account for more than 90 percent of the investment made by both type of investors. In terms of total number of deals, the southern part of the country occupies the top spot closely followed by West and North.

However, when the average deal sizes are reviewed for the three regions that attract significant investment, the differences between the investing preferences of the domestic and foreign investors are exemplified. The results are summarized for the three regions for both types of investors.

1. North—In case of domestic investors, at US$40.1 million, the deal size is lowest in this region among all the geographical locations (excluding east and central regions of the country). Moreover, northern region also stands third when it comes to the total number of deals that were finalized during the study period. A similar trend is evident for foreign investors also, but the investment size of foreign investor is 62 percent higher compared to the domestic investors. However, these results are not found to be statistically significant.
2. South—Compared to the other regions, the deal size significantly improves for both domestic and foreign investors when the southern region of the country is considered from an investment perspective. The average deal size increases by 24 percent in case of foreign investor and by 8.5 percent in case of domestic investor when the deal sizes are compared to the northern region. It is also seen that the southern part of the country also occupies the top slots in terms of the total number of deals finalized. In this case, the difference in the investment sizes of foreign and domestic PE investors and domestic is the highest among all regions. The deal size of foreign investors is 84 percent higher compared to domestic investors. The results are statistically significant on a 95 percent confidence interval.
3. West—The western region of the country, which is the hub of industrial and financial activity in the country, occupies the top slot when the average size of the real estate deals is considered. Compared to the southern region, the average deal size increased by 39 percent in case of domestic investors. However, the increase in deal size is only 11 percent for the foreign investors when compared to the southern region. When compared across the type of investors, the foreign investors invest 50 percent more compared to domestic investors on a per deal basis. This result is also highly significant.

Initial results also show that the focus of both the domestic and foreign investors is still largely on metro cities. Non-metro cities have a very small share in terms of the total number of projects that were taken up by developers and those that attracted PE, through either of foreign or domestic investors. When the investment choices of the investors are evaluated based on the metro status of the city, it is seen that foreign investors invested US$4.75 billion across 61 deals. Further analysis shows that 40 percent of the investment was directed toward non-metro cities whereas 60 percent of the investment was made in metro cities. Domestic investors invested US$6.5 billion across 137 deals, making the mean investment size as US$47.5 million. The investment was also directed mainly toward metro cities, which account for 60 percent of the total investment. Among metro cities, the mean investment size of foreign investors is 87 percent higher compared to the domestic investors. The difference is only 32 percent when the investment size is compared for the non-metro cities.

4.5.2.3 Project Segment

Foreign investors invested US$2.92 billion across 39 projects. 25 percent of this investment was in the luxury space, whereas a majority of the investment, 71 percent of the net investment, was in the non-luxury (mid–budget) category. In case of domestic investors, US$4.1 billion was invested across 89 projects. A major part of this investment, 64 percent of the total, was directed toward non-luxury housing projects, whereas 33 percent of the investment was in the luxury space. The low-budget housing concept is still evolving in the Indian real estate market as it accounted for less than 5 percent of the portfolio of both foreign and domestic investors in terms of the total money invested. The average developable area of various projects was also compared for the foreign and domestic investors. It is seen that domestic investors invested in larger scale projects as compared to the foreign investors. The built-up area of projects with domestic PE was 28 percent higher compared to the projects with foreign equity.

Figure 4.2 provides a summary of the analysis between foreign and domestic PE investors in real estate projects with a summary of the results of the nonparametric Mann–Whitney test. Table 4.3 provides a snapshot of the differences between foreign and domestic PE investors in real estate projects based on parameters chosen.

4.5.3 Comparison of Dedicated and Diversified Investors

4.5.3.1 Deal Characteristics

A comparison between the two types of investors on the basis of mode of investment shows that diversified investors on an average invest a larger amount on a per deal basis compared to the dedicated investors. When compared across the project-level mode of investment, the mean investment of diversified investors is found to

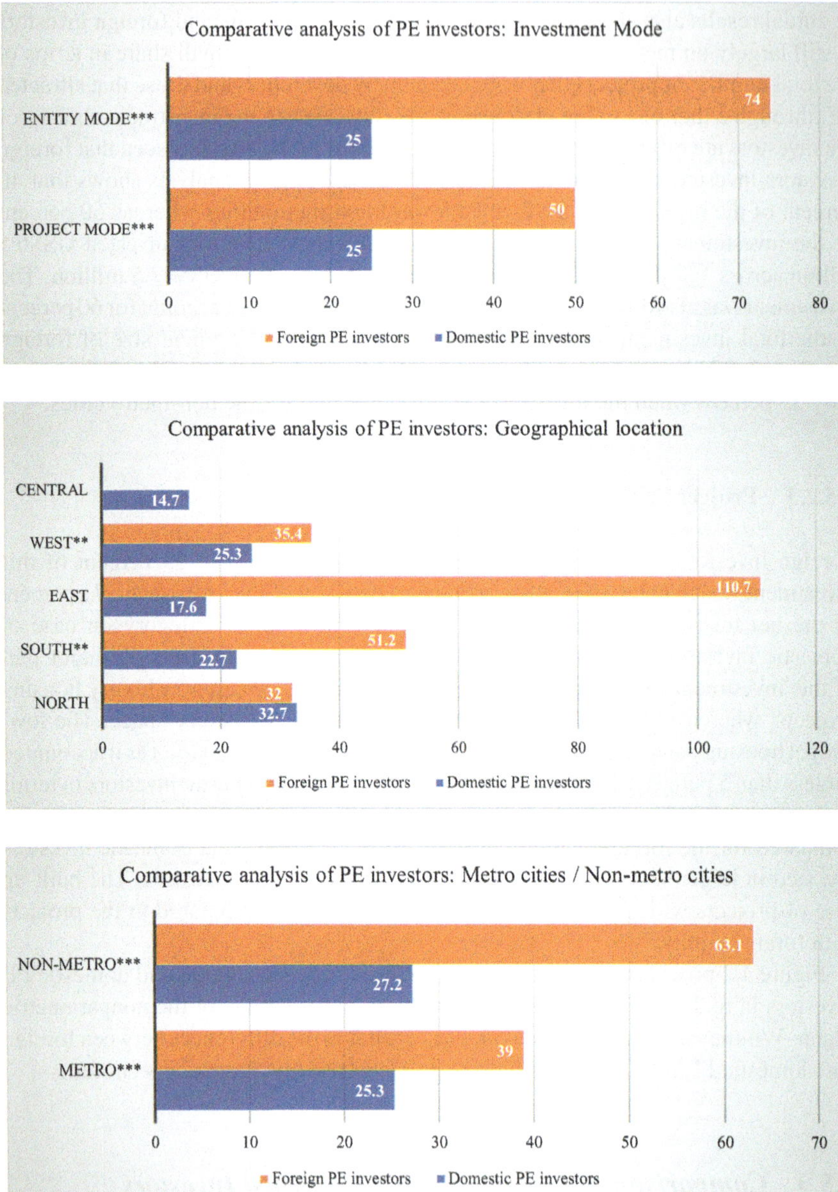

Fig. 4.2 Comparative analysis of PE investors: domestic PE investors versus foreign PE investors. *** significant at 99% CI, ** significant at 95% CI

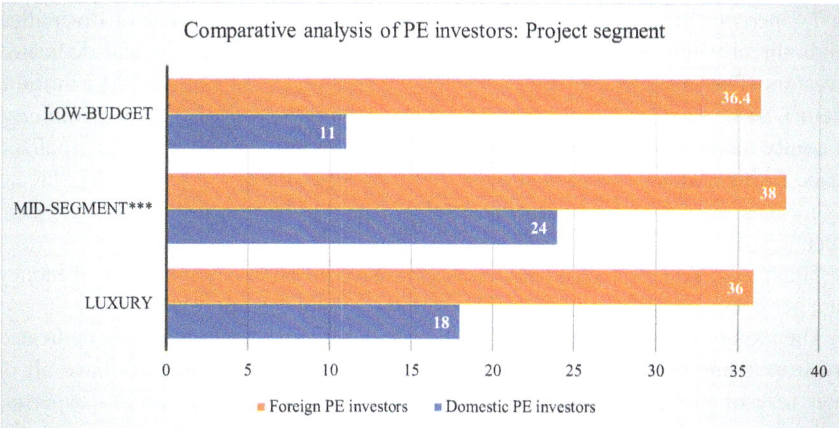

Fig. 4.2 (continued)

Table 4.3 Summary of differences: domestic PE investors versus foreign PE investors

Parameters		Domestic investors	Foreign investors
Deal characteristics	Number of deals	52 percent higher	
	Type of investment	4 out of every 5 projects attract investment through project-level investment	58 percent of deals were project financed, rest were company level
	Deal size	Invested US$6.5 billion US$ across 137 projects making the average deal size US$47.5 million	Significantly higher; US$4.9 billion across 62 projects making the average deal size US$79.3 million
	Average built-up area	28 percent larger	
Demographics	Geographical preferences	Comparable preferences, first for south, second west, third north	Comparable preferences, first for south, second west, third north
	City characteristics	Preference for metro cities	Preference for metro cities, the investment size of foreign investors is 85 percent in major metros
Project segment		64 percent of total investment was directed toward non-luxury housing projects whereas 33 percent of the investment was in the luxury space,	Foreign investors invested US$2.92 billion across 39 projects. 25 percent of this investment was in the luxury space whereas a majority of the investment, 71 percent of the net investment, was in the non-luxury category

be 7.7 percent higher than the dedicated investors. The investment of diversified funds directly into the company is also much higher compared to the dedicated investors. The mean investment size of diversified investors was US$90.7 million, about US$34.3 million higher than the dedicated funds. It is also seen that in case of equity mode, both the type of investors lag behind in terms of the total finalized deals. Although the average deal size involving general purpose funds is 61 percent higher than the dedicated funds, the result is found to be insignificant on statistical level.

The results show that diversified investors have invested larger amount of money on a per deal basis.

The literature on the subject gives evidence on superior performance of dedicated investors compared to the diversified ones. Since dedicated investors have all of their investments in the real estate projects, they gain a higher level of expertise in the investing in apartments, townships, etc. This also allows them to assess the investments more thoroughly compared to general purpose investors. The better insight and knowledge of the industry also allows them to focus on promising new ventures which have to potential for high returns. This is also evident from the high bias shown by dedicated investors toward project mode of investment. 77 percent of the total investment made by dedicated investors was through project mode. This indicated that dedicated investors are more interested in evaluating projects on a merit basis and investing in them rather than investing based on the reputation of the developer. Objective evaluation of the project and ease of exit are the key parameters that these investors consider while investing.

In case of diversified investors, 53 percent of the total money was invested through the project mode showing that this category of investors does not show any special preference for either mode.

4.5.3.2 Demographics

Both the dedicated and diversified investors also have a high preference for North, West and South zones. With regard to geographical investment, the results show that both the dedicated and diversified investors also have a high preference for North, West and South zones. These three regions account for more than 90 percent of the investment made by both type of investors. In terms of total number of deals, the southern part of the country occupies the top spot closely followed by West and North. However, when the average deal sizes are reviewed for the three regions that attract significant investment, the differences between the investing preferences of the dedicated and diversified investors are found to be different.

The results are summarized for the three regions for both types of investors.

1. North—In case of dedicated investors, at US$49.6 million, the deal size is lowest in this region among all the geographical locations (excluding east and central regions of the country). Moreover, northern region also stands second when it comes to the total number of deals that were finalized during the study period.

A similar trend is evident for diversified investors also but their investment size is marginally lower compared to the dedicated investors. However, these results are not found to be statistically significant.

2. South—The average deal size of projects with dedicated investors marginally drops when the southern region is considered. It is observed that the average deal size of diversified investors is 30 percent higher compared to dedicated investor. However, this result is found to be statistically insignificant.
3. West—In case of dedicated investors, the highest average deal size is achieved in the western region. Booming property prices have driven the dedicated investors to invest heavily in the region as it accounts for 50 percent of their total investment in India. Moreover, the average deal size of dedicated investors is 33 percent higher compared to diversified investors.

Both dedicated and general purpose investors have focused their investments in well-developed, urbanized and well-connected cities. In case of dedicated investors, about 95 percent of the total US$6.5 billion was invested in metro cities. A similar trend is observed in case of diversified investors where 97.5 percent of the US$4.8 billion was invested in the top tier cities. There is no significant difference between both investors when types of cities are compared. Diversified investors invested US$5.3 million more on a per deal basis when metro cities are considered, whereas the investment size of dedicated investors was 6 percent higher in case of second-tier cities. These differences were not significant on a statistical level.

Dedicated investors invested a total of US$3.95 billion across 74 deals compared to the US$2.7 billion invested by diversified investors across 52 deals. The average deal size of both the type of investors is found to be comparable, around US$53 million, across metro cities.

In case of non-metro cities, dedicated investors invested US$2.4 billion across 40 deals, marginally more than the US$2.1 billion invested by diversified investors across 31 deals. The deal size of diversified investors was found to be US$4 million more than the dedicated PE investors. However, the results are found to be statistically not significant across both the types of cities.

4.5.3.3 Project Segment

Dedicated investors use project mode of investment with 77 percent of investment made through project mode. Diversified investors on the other hand use project mode of investment with 53 percent of investment made through project mode. Similar to the trend observed earlier, both the dedicated and diversified investors have chosen to focus their investment in the luxury segment. The average deal size of dedicated investors was found to be 55 percent higher compared to diversified investors in the luxury segment, whereas the deal size of diversified investors was found to be 15 percent higher than dedicated investors in case of the non-luxury segment. However, the results were not significant on a statistical level.

Figure 4.3 provides a summary of the analysis between dedicated and diversified PE funds in real estate projects with a summary of the results of the nonparametric Mann–Whitney test. Table 4.4 provides a snapshot of the differences between dedicated and diversified funds in real estate projects based on parameters chosen.

4.5.4 *Factors Influencing Extent of PE Investment in Residential Real Estate Projects*

To conclude this study, a Tobit regression was carried out to determine the factors that affect the extent of PE investment in residential real estate projects in India.

The dependent variable ranges from > 0 to 100 percent indicating the stake of PE investment in the real estate project. Table 4.5 presents the description of the variables used in the regression analysis, while Fig. 4.4 presents the *tobit* regression estimates for the extent of PE investment in residential real estate projects in India.

An examination of Fig. 4.4 indicates that variables LAND and CONSLAND have opposing signs but are not significant. Variable SOUTH is positively significant at 95 percent CI while variables NORTH and WEST are not significant. INVEST is also not significant. Considering developer-level variables, PEXPYRS does not emerge significant. PEXPPD is negatively and strongly significant at 99 percent CI while PEXPSQFT is positively significant at 10 percent level.

The results indicate that project-level variables do not influence the level of PE investment in residential real estate projects. Although project-level variables appear to have significant differences in PE-funded and non-PE-funded projects, these variables do not have a standing in the amount of investment the PE firm wants to infuse into the project. When considering location demographics, the variable SOUTH emerges positively significant indicating that PE firms prefer to take larger stakes in residential projects in South India when compared to North India or West India. The variable INVEST does not appear significant suggesting that the size of the deal did not influence the stake of the PE firm. The strong negative significance of the variable FOREIGN indicates that foreign PE firms take decidedly smaller stakes in projects. The comparative analysis shows that investment sizes of foreign firms are larger than those of domestic firms. More analysis using project size and cost would throw light on the relative sizes of foreign PE firms as compared to domestic PE firms. With regard to developer-level variables, the non-significance of PEXPYRS suggests that experience of the promoter by way of years does not influence the size of PE investment. However, the strong negative significance of PEXPPD and the positive significance of PEXPSQFT suggest that PE firms take into consideration the actual work done by promoters before taking stakes in projects. When considering the number of projects developed, the fewer the number of projects developed by the promoter, the larger the stake of the PE firm in the project. This could be because promoters with lesser number of projects developed are still building their name and reputation in the market. They still look for adequate capital to fund their

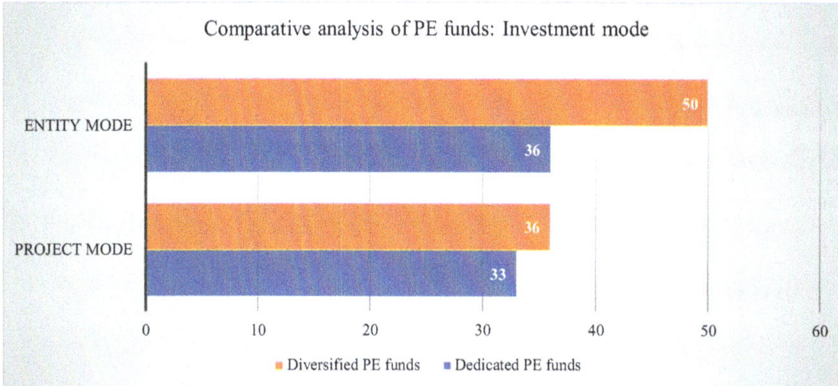

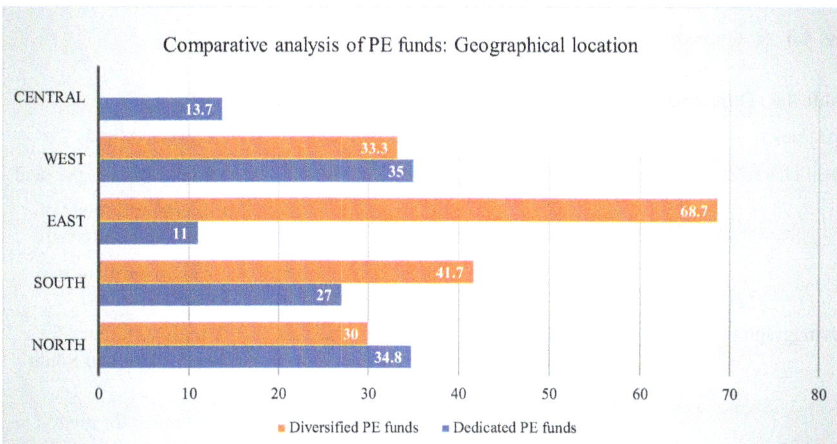

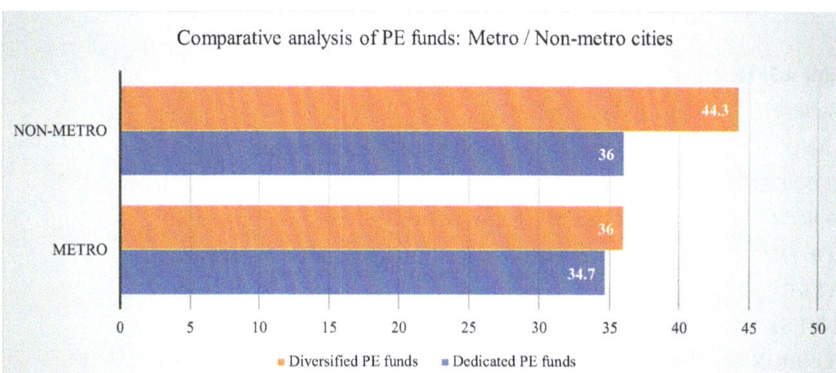

Fig. 4.3 Comparative analysis of PE funds: dedicated PE funds versus diversified PE funds. *** significant at 99% CI, ** significant at 95% CI

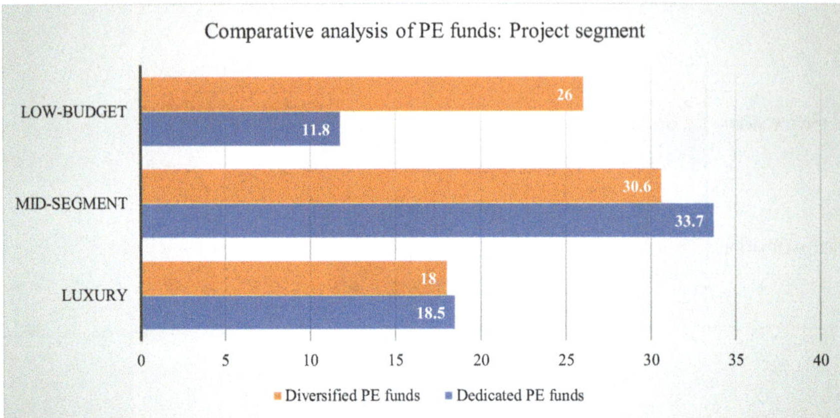

Fig. 4.3 (continued)

Table 4.4 Differences between dedicated PE funds and diversified PE funds

Parameters		Dedicated funds	Diversified funds
Deal characteristics	Number of deals		Larger amounts per deal
	Type of investment		Project-level mode of investment preferred
	Deal size	Mean investment size US$56.4 million	Mean investment size US$90.7 million
Demographics	Geographical preferences	A high preference for North, West and South zones	A high preference for North, West and South zones
	City characteristics	Preference for metro cities	Preference for metro cities
Project segment		Luxury segment	Luxury segment

Table 4.5 Description of the variables used in the Tobit regression

Variable	Description
LAND	Indicates the land area of the project, in acres
CONSLAND	Indicated the construction by land ratio or Floor Space Index
NORTH	Indicates that the project was developed in North India
SOUTH	Indicates that the project was developed in North India
WEST	Indicates that the project was developed in North India
INVEST	Investment size of the PE firm, in US$, Million
FOREIGN	Indicates if the PE firm was a foreign investor
PEXPYRS	Indicates the promoter experience, in years
PEXPPD	Indicates the promoter experience, in number of projects developed
PEXPSQFT	Indicates the promoter experience, in number of sqft developed

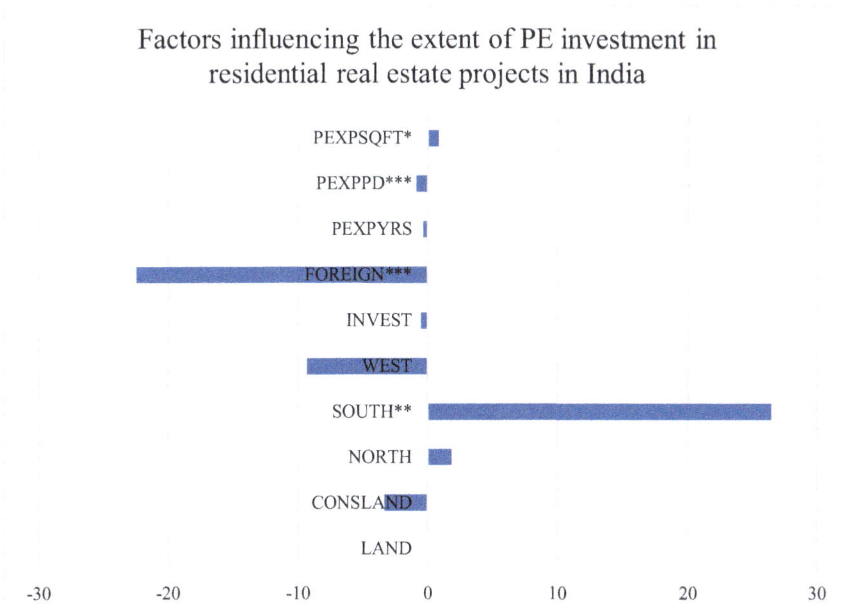

Fig. 4.4 Factors influencing the extent of PE investment in residential real estate projects in India. *** significant at 99% CI, ** significant at 95% CI

projects and thus depend on PE to fund large chunks of their projects. However, while considering promoter experience in terms of square feet developed, results suggest that PE firms choose promoters who have experience in larger projects, i.e., developing projects with significantly larger areas. PE firms take significantly larger stakes with promoters who develop larger projects indicating their affinity to provide capital and support larger-sized projects.

4.6 Discussion

4.6.1 PE Versus Non-PE-Funded Projects

The above analysis provides several interesting insights. First, PE has emerged as an additional source of capital for financing real estate projects in India. So far, developers of real estate had to rely on capital markets and debt financing in the form of bank loans for developing projects. The emergence of PE has expanded the pool of capital that real estate developers can get access.

However, PE firms seem to be investing only in niche areas in the residential real estate sector. This is visible by the comparative analysis of projects with and without PE investments. Majority of the PE investments in the housing sector continue to happen in the luxury sector, which indicates that the focus of PE is on quality projects. Project-level variables indicate that PE firms prefer to invest in projects with larger land and construction areas. Given that such projects are automatically more expensive, PE firms seen to be investing in significantly costlier projects. Further, PE investments are seen in more commonly in Northern and Western India. They also have a significantly higher cost by construction ratio.

Contrary to expectation, the role of developer experience is confounded by other investor and project-level parameters. Developer history and experience in developing projects did not significantly affect decision making of PE investors. Experience levels of real estate developers in terms of years of experience and projects developed influence PE and non-PE investors homogeneously. However, developers who develop significantly larger projects (in terms of sqft) and with larger land banks were able to attract PE funding more easily.

PE firms also seem to be investing in regions with promising growth potential, in terms of real estate. Regions with high growth in Housing Price Index and Consumer Price Index have witnessed larger investments from PE firms. However, corruption levels and competitive index levels affect PE and non-PE investors homogeneously, with no significant differences due to the impact of these factors.

4.6.2 Foreign Versus Domestic Investors

From the analysis foreign versus domestic investors, the sheer number of projects financed by domestic PE investors as compared to foreign investors provides evidence that Indian residential real estate projects are primarily sourcing capital from domestic PE investors. However, in terms of project size, foreign PE investors seem to be able to support larger project sizes. Average deal sizes of foreign investors were US$79.3 million as against US$47.5 million for domestic investors. Thus, it can be constructed that foreign PE firms, from their end, have developed a sense of comfort when investing in housing projects and are thus investing larger amounts in them.

Investment modes can be of two types—project-level investments and entity-level investments. Project-level investments are investments directly into the project, with characteristics such as long life, relatively low cost projects and low risk. Here, the returns to the investor depend only on the profitability levels of the project. Entity-level investments are characterized by investors becoming partners or stakeholders in the company. The capital is invested into the company that develops the real estate projects, and the profitability of the investment depends on the astuteness of the developer in investing the money in the best possible way across real estate ventures. From our analysis, it is evident that project-level investment is the preferred mode of investment for domestic investors. This allows for easier monitoring and tracking of cash flows. However, foreign investors do not show any significant preference for any of the investment modes.

The results show that both the domestic and foreign investors have comparable preferences for North, West and South zones. These three regions account for more than 90 percent of the investment made by both type of investors. In terms of total number of deals, the southern part of the country occupies the top spot closely followed by West and North. When the status of the city is examined, initial results show that the focus of both domestic and foreign investors is still largely on metro cities in terms of the total number of projects that were taken up by developers and those that attracted private equity, through either of foreign or domestic investors. Usually, metro cities are more developed and are characterized by better infrastructure, higher land prices and greater accessibility to economic zones, ports and other amenities. This shows that PE firms are providing capital in urban housing projects without too much focus on rural housing projects where demand and shortages are far greater.

An examination of the segment of the project reveals that foreign PE firms preferred to invest in high-end luxury and mid-segment projects. This classification is done subjectively based on the cost of the property, the income segment that the developer targets, location and other amenities provided to the residents. Cost of the living space, and average prices of the property at the project location were used to classify the projects into these categories.

The non-significance of other city characteristics implies that foreign and domestic investors do not differentiate with respect to competitive scores, corruption levels and other macroeconomic city/state characteristics. Deal characteristics seem to be differentiating factors for these capital providers rather than location, which can be assumed to have been taken care of by the promoter.

4.6.3 Dedicated Versus Diversified Investors

An examination of trends of dedicated and diversified funds shows that diversified funds invest in more number of projects and with larger sizes. However, extant literature provides evidence of superior performance of dedicated investors compared to the diversified ones. Since dedicated investors have all of their investments in the real estate projects, they gain a higher level of expertise in the investing in apartments, townships, etc. This also allows them to assess the investments more thoroughly compared to general purpose investors. The better insight and knowledge of the industry also allows them to focus on promising new ventures which have the potential for high returns. The preference to a project mode of investment also suggests that dedicated funds consider objective evaluation of the project and ease of exit as key parameters while investing.

When demographics are considered, it is noted that both dedicated and diversified funds invest in all regions of demand without confining themselves to particular areas. Although the south has the highest by number of projects, dedicated investors have largest investment sizes in western India suggesting that they harvest largest profits in regions of extremely high demand. Similar to foreign and domestic investors, both dedicated and general purpose investors have focused their investments in well developed, urbanized and well-connected cities. Similar to trends observed earlier, dedicated and diversified funds also show preference for luxury segments.

4.6.4 Factors Influencing Extent of PE Investment in Residential Real Estate Projects

The regression analysis to identify the factors affecting the stake of PE investments in residential real estate projects show that promoter-level characteristics affected the stake holding of PE firms. Deal-level characteristics such as land area, investment size, and demographics do not influence the extent to which PE invests in such projects. The general experience level of the promoter also emerged non-significant. However, experience with number of projects developed and square feet developed negatively and positively, respectively, affect the stake of PE firms' investment in the real estate project. From this analysis, it is seen that PE firms complement promoters experience when it comes to the extent of capital investment in real estate projects. PE firms prefer promoters who have developed larger projects and take larger investment stakes in them. The negative significance of projects developed shows that PE firms take larger stakes with promoters who have fewer number of projects developed.

4.7 Implications and Conclusion

This study presents an analysis of PE investments in residential real estate projects in India. The results of the analysis offer interesting insights which provide significant implications for policy makers and practitioners.

First, PE is an alternate capital source which can be used to finance residential real estate projects in the country. PE is being increasingly used as a viable source of capital to fund non-conventional asset classes such as infrastructure and real estate. In infrastructure, research in the Indian energy projects showed that PE investments led to lower cost per capacity and increased estimated time to commission the project. This led to better efficiency and lower actual delays. Thus, PE firms can provide benefits in addition to the capital they impart to these sectors and can be harnessed successfully in this regard.

Second, the analysis shows that PE firms have invested capital in urban housing projects. They have capitalized on the economic boom in India and have concentrated on investing in luxury / mid-luxury segments primarily located in metro cities. However, India's rural housing demand and shortage far exceeds that of its urban counterparts. Further, low-cost housing in India's rural sector is still largely unorganized and lacking. Encouraging PE firms to invest in the same will bring dual advantages. In addition to providing capital to develop rural housing, harnessing managerial advantages of PE can also provide order to this disintegrated sector.

References

Adair, A., Berry, J., McGreal, S., Syacutekora, L., Ghanbari Parsa, A., & Redding, B. (1999). Globalisation of real estate markets in Central Europe. *European Planning Studies, 7*(3), 295–305.

Cushman & Wakefield. (2012). International investment atlas summary. A Cushman and Wakefield Research Publication.

Ernst & Young. (2013). Global market outlook: trends in real estate private equity.

Georgiev, G., Gupta, B., & Kunkel, T. (2003). Benefits of real estate investment—Some diversification benefit in particular allocations. *The Journal of Portfolio Management, 29*(5):28-+. https://doi.org/10.3905/jpm.2003.319903

Gompers, P., & Lerner, J. (1999). The venture capital cycle. MIT Press.

http://www.ficci.com/sector/59/Project_docs/real-eastate-profile.pdf. Accessed October 11, 2013

Rydin, Y. L., Ellison, E. G., Hayward, R. E. H., Parsa, A. R. G., & Taylor, K. (1990). After 1992: Monetary, political and institutional developments linked to the completion of the single market. Working Paper for the Department of Estate Management, University of East London.

Chapter 5
The Case of Indian Power Sector

> *There is a force more powerful than steam and electricity: the will.*
> *—Fernan Caballero*

5.1 Introduction

International Energy Outlook (2013) had estimated that electricity met an increasing share of the world's total energy demand and was the world's fastest-growing form of delivered energy. Future growth in electricity generation was expected to be led by non-OECD Asian countries, including India and China. By 2040, non-OECD countries were expected to account for 64 percent of world electricity use, up from 51 percent in 2010. To support this growth in consumption, substantial increase in generation capacity was needed in the non-OECD countries. World Energy Outlook (2012) also predicted a similar trend. Worldwide capacity additions from 2012 to 2035 were expected to be about 5890 GW, i.e., more than the total installed capacity in the whole world in 2011. Power sector globally required an investment of US$16.9 trillion during 2012–35. Three-fifth of this investment was for generation capacity, while the rest was for improvement in electricity networks.

A key challenge for developing countries is to mobilize the capital needed to finance the capacity additions. While the power sector has been traditionally the domain for public sector investment in emerging countries, it has been gradually liberalized since the 1990s, to attract private sector investment. In recent years, there

This chapter is based on the journal paper titled "Private equity investment in power generation projects: Evidence from India" which appeared in *Venture Capital: An International Journal of Energy Sector Management* Vol 10, Issue 4, 2016 pp. 617–641. https://doi.org/10.1108/IJESM-12-2014-0008.

J. Gemson and Thillai Rajan A., *Private Equity Financing in Infrastructure and Real Estate*, https://doi.org/10.1007/978-981-16-1634-1_5

has been an emergence of new category of private investors, viz., PE investors in the power sector.

PE investment has been estimated at 10 percent of all infrastructure finance since the global financial crisis (Preqin, 2020).[1] In recent years, the fund raising by PE managers to invest in infrastructure has significantly increased. It has been estimated that PE infrastructure assets under management reached a record US$582 billion in June 2019, significantly higher than the US$216 billion for investment raised by 302 PE infrastructure funds between 2006 and 2013 (Preqin, 2014). In fact, the growth of PE investment in infrastructure has been sustained over the years. For example, about US$19.31 billion of PE capital has been invested in infrastructure from 2005 to 2009, which was a 102 percent increase from 2000 to 2005, which saw an investment of US$9.54 billion (VentureXpert, 2010). During the three-year period (2010–12), the infrastructure funds have on an average invested in about 250–300 deals per year, resulting in aggregate annual investments of about US$100–US$120 billion (Inderst, 2013). Developing countries in places like the Middle East, North Africa and South Asia have been driving this trend when compared to the world's traditional financial centers such as New York, London and Singapore (Orr, 2009; Speechley, 2007).

Energy and power sector accounted for 44 percent of the total deals invested by infrastructure funds during 2008–13 (Preqin, 2014). PE investment in energy and power sector during the period 1990–2009 was more than 64 percent of the total PE investment in the three major infrastructure sectors, viz., energy and power, transport and utilities sectors (Gemson, 2013). The dominant share of power sector in PE investment has been observed in both developed and developing economies. For example, in India, during the period 1998–2013, there were an estimated 569 PE deals involving an aggregate investment of US$22.2 billion. Investment in energy and power projects accounted for about 36 percent of the total deals and investments (Venture Intelligence, 2014).

Studies that have looked at the impact of PE investment using data from sectors other than infrastructure are available (e.g., Brav and Gompers, 1997; Hellman and Puri, 2002; Lerner, 1995). Most of these studies showed that PE investment had a positive effect on firm performance. With respect to the infrastructure sector, the study by Gemson et al. (2012) showed that infrastructure projects that had PE investment had significant differences from those that did not have any PE investment. The authors found that projects with PE investment were larger when compared to projects that did not have PE investment, indicating that that PE investment had helped in successfully financing larger projects. In this chapter, we specifically highlight the impact of PE investment in power projects. We do this by comparing private sector power projects that had PE investment vis-à-vis those that did not have any PE investment.

[1] Preqin, 2020 Preqin Global Infrastructure Report (Feb 2020).

5.2 Research Background

Given the immediate need for large investment capital, governments, especially in developing countries, liberalized the power generation sector to private investment (Chan et al., 2009). Generally, private investment in infrastructure projects such as power generation plants has used the project finance structure (Gatti, 2008). The project finance structure results in the creation of an independent entity called the special purpose vehicle, which helps to bring together all the interested parties in a shareholding structure (Gupta and Sravat, 1998). Power sector has attracted sizable investment from private sector over the years. Between 1990 and 2012, 109 countries have had significant private participation in the electricity sector. In electricity generation, there have been 1,891 private sector projects with a total investment of over US$508 billion (PPIAF, 2013). A key feature of private infrastructure funding is the high percentage of debt, averaging about 80 percent.

Traditionally, the main sponsors of the project contributed the required equity capital. These sponsors, also called sponsor equity investors, had some form of product market relationship with the project company (Finnerty, 2013). Examples of sponsor equity investors could be construction companies, fuel suppliers, power purchasers, operating firms, equipment suppliers and so on. Conventionally, equity investors would have access only to the residual cash flows of the corporation. However, sponsor investors who have a product market relationship with the project company would also have access to intermediate cash flows from the project. For example, a sponsor who is also a vendor for the project receives payments for executing various project development activities, much before the project company starts generating equity returns (Gemson et al., 2012).

In recent years, there has been an increased interest from PE investors to invest in power projects, and such investments have grown from being a niche sector into a separate asset class (Narasimhan, 2009). PE funds form a different category of equity investors, called the non-sponsor equity investors. PE investors invest in the equity of the project company (special purpose vehicle) and stay invested for a specific duration (say up to 5–7 years) before they sell their shareholding in the public market or other investors. The PE funds realize their returns on the investment at the time of exit. PE funds are financial investors, who do not share any product market relationships with the project they have invested (Gemson et al., 2012). Investment from such PE funds differ from sponsor equity investors in terms of the timing of cash flow rights. While sponsors get access to intermediate project cash flows for executing project contracts (Chemmanur and John, 1996), PE funds get access only to the residual cash flows after all operational expenses, vendor payments and debt holders have been paid. Usually, much of the investment returns are realized only at exit rather than from intermediate dividend payments. The valuation of the project at exit therefore becomes an important parameter to realize the projected returns, which in turn depends upon the successful completion and operation of the project. It can be safely said that (well, the usual disclaimers apply, here too) since the returns to PE funds are largely dependent on successful project completion, the PE investors would be motivated to monitor their investments actively and strive to add value by providing managerial inputs at different stages of the project (Engel and Stiebale, 2009). Such monitoring can deny opportunities to sponsors to realize extra normal profits through contracts and other product market linkages.

PE funds have traditionally been an important source of capital in the technology and other high growth sectors and industries. However, PE interest in infrastructure projects can be seen only after 2010. Weber and Alfen (2010) and Smit and Trigeorgis (2009) highlight the motivations for PE funds for investing in the infrastructure sector. PE investors are unique as compared to other external investors as they are known for their value addition capabilities (Kortum and Lerner, 2000; Lerner, 1999, 2002) who take an active role in the development of the investee firm (Suchard, 2009). Unlike project lenders, PE investors also actively monitor their investee projects, which help to reduce the information asymmetries that exist in infrastructure projects (Engel and Stiebale, 2009).

The traditional "business as usual" financing methods are no longer adequate to meet the unprecedented demands for capital to finance infrastructure projects, especially in developing countries Dunkerley (1995). Innovative and new financing sources are needed. PE investment would not only provide the financial resources, but also bring in more financial discipline and strategic management expertise to the sector (Orr, 2009). For many years now, governments have been supporting and assisting private investors to invest in infrastructure projects in an effort to bring more efficiency to project construction and operation (Bond and Carter, 1995; Himburg, 1995). Given some of the inherent advantages of PE style of investment, even Multilateral Development Finance Institutions that used to directly invest in infrastructure projects, are now providing a part of their capital to PE investors for investing in infrastructure (Chowdhury et al., 2009). This chapter highlights how PE investment has impacted the power generation projects.

5.3 Methodology and Data

5.3.1 *Selection of Projects*

Use of project finance technique is a commonly seen in private infrastructure projects. The key features of project financing have been well described by Brealey et al. (1996) and Esty (2003). For this study, the dataset comprises only of those projects that have been funded by the project finance method. Since project-financed projects are ring-fenced projects, whose only assets are the project, the project cost information can be obtained in a transparent fashion, without the complex cross-cash flows seen between various projects in a corporate finance scenario.

5.3.2 Project Cost and Time

Cost and time are two of the most important parameters of large construction projects. Therefore, we analyze the effect of intervention (PE investment) on project costs and time taken to commission the project. Power project costs are significantly determined by the plant capacity. Since the projects have different plant capacities, the costs could not be compared directly, without taking into the different capacities. To make it comparable, we determined "unit capacity costs" (i.e., cost per capacity) which was then used as one of the performance parameters. Unit capacity cost was calculated by dividing the project costs with the capacity of the project (Eq. 5.1).

$$\text{Cost per capacity} = \frac{\text{Cost of the project}}{\text{Project capacity}} \tag{5.1}$$

Project commissioning time has been calculated as the duration between the actual year of project commissioning (or the estimated year of commissioning as determined by the project sponsors if the project was under development at the time of data collection) and the year in which the project achieved financial closure (Eq. 5.2). Project commissioning time was calculated from the time of financial closure because achieving financial closure is a significant milestone in the project development and marked the beginning of a period of significant capital expenditure on the project.

$$\begin{aligned}\text{Project commissioning time} = {} & \text{Year of project commissioning (actual or estimated)} \\ & - \text{Year of financial closure}\end{aligned} \tag{5.2}$$

The performance parameters, unit project cost (cost per capacity) and project commissioning time, were analyzed using means comparison, Ordinary Least Squares (OLS) regression and Three-Stage Least Squares (3-SLS) regression.

5.3.3 Comparison of Means

The projects in the dataset were classified into two categories: those that had PE investment and those that did not. The first level of analysis involved comparing the values of unit capacity costs and commissioning time between the two project samples. This was the first step to find out whether projects with PE investment differed from those that did not. Since the data did not exhibit any particular form of distribution, the non-parametric Wilcoxon rank-sum technique was used for comparing the two samples. Further, the dataset was also unbalanced because of differences in sample size and values of other project characteristics. To ensure that the difference in results was not affected by the unbalanced nature of the dataset, a matching technique was used. Sample comparison was done after matching the projects on variables that were expected to affect costs and time, viz., project capacity, geographic location (captured by the state in which the project is being developed) and the year of financial closure. Coarsened Exact Matching (CEM) technique using Stata software, as suggested by Blackwell et al. (2010), was used for matching. CEM was used to match both exact values and values that were closely related. After the matching, the sample of PE and non-PE projects is using Wilcoxon rank-sum test.

5.3.4 OLS Regression

Since the comparison tests between the two project samples showed significant difference, the next step was to identify whether the main variable of interest (which was the presence of PE investment) affected the dependent variables, after controlling for other effects. We used the OLS regression estimation to achieve this objective. The OLS estimation would also be useful to observe the impact of other explanatory variables on the dependent variables. The quality of the dataset can be considered to be good, if the regression estimations of other explanatory variables on the dependent variables were consistent with the existing literature. Equations (5.3) and (5.4) give the estimation model used for calculating cost per capacity and time taken to commission the project.

$$\begin{aligned}\text{UNIT\_ CAP\_ COST} = {} & \alpha_{C0} + \alpha_{C1}\text{PROJTIME} + \alpha_{C2}D\text{\_INVTYPE} \\ & + \alpha_{C3}\text{YEAR\_FINCLOSURE} + \alpha_{C4}\text{LOG(PROJCAP)} \\ & + \alpha_{C5}\text{PROJCOST} + \alpha_{C6}D\text{\_HYDEL} + \alpha_{C7}D\text{\_SOLAR} \\ & + \alpha_{C8}D\text{\_THERMAL} + \alpha_{C9}D\text{\_WIND} + \alpha_{C10}\text{CAGR} \\ & + \alpha_{C11}\text{PPP} + \alpha_{C12}\text{HDI} + \alpha_{C13}\text{CORR} + \alpha_{C14}\text{PRI} \\ & + \alpha_{C15}D\text{\_NORTH} + \alpha_{C16}D\text{\_SOUTH} \\ & + \alpha_{C17}D\text{\_WEST} + u_c \end{aligned} \tag{5.3}$$

$$\begin{aligned}\text{PROJTIME} = {} & \alpha_{t0} + \alpha_{t1}\text{UNIT\_ CAP\_ COST} + \alpha_{t2}D\text{\_ INVTYPE} \\ & + \alpha_{t3}\text{LOG(PROJCAP)} + \alpha_{t4}D\text{\_HYDEL} \\ & + \alpha_{t5}D\text{\_SOLAR} + \alpha_{t6}D\text{\_THERMAL} \\ & + \alpha_{t7}D\text{\_WIND} + \alpha_{t8}\text{GDP\_CAPITA} \\ & + \alpha_{t9}\text{CAGR} + \alpha_{t10}\text{PPP} + \alpha_{t11}\text{HDI} + \alpha_{t12}\text{CORR} \\ & + \alpha_{t13}\text{PRI} + \alpha_{t14}D\text{\_NORTH} + \alpha_{t15}D\text{\_SOUTH} \\ & + \alpha_{t16}D\text{\_WEST} + u_t \end{aligned} \tag{5.4}$$

In Eqs. (5.3) and (5.4), α_{c0} and α_{t0} are constant terms, α_i's are vectors of estimable parameters, and u_i's are disturbance or error terms that capture unobserved effects. The rationale for the choice of explanatory variables is as follows: In power projects, project cost is largely determined by the capacity and the type of technology. Variables that provided this information were therefore included in the estimation for *UNIT_CAP_COST.* Project cost, and thereby unit capacity cost, is also dependent on project complexity and size. Therefore, two variables to capture complexity and size—project cost and project commissioning time—were included in the estimation. Project cost would increase with complexity, even if there is no change in capacity. Similarly, large projects would take more time for commissioning as compared to smaller projects. Year of financial closure was also included as one of the variables to control any time trends that could impact project performance. In addition to the above, other variables were included to capture the differences in project context. Economic variables such as GDP or GDP growth rates or appropriate index values that can be a proxy for differences in project settings are commonly used in literature. For example, Kenny (2009) uses Transparency International Corruption Perception Index values and Business Disclosure Index values in his analysis. Very similar to the Property Rights Index (PRI) used here, Wallsten (2001) uses the International Country Risk Guide Index values to capture risk of expropriation to private investment. Sen and Jamasb (2010) use a reform index to account for the differences in the implementation of power sector reform in various Indian states. Similarly, the PPP Index is used in our estimation to account for the differences in the policy framework to attract private sector investment in infrastructure.

For conceptual clarity, the explanatory variables were divided into project-specific variables and operating environment variables. Description of these variables is given below.

5.3.5 Dependent variables

i. Unit capacity cost, *UNIT_CAP_COST:* This is the total project cost divided by the capacity of the project and is calculated as indicated in Eq. (5.1).
ii. Time taken for project commissioning, *PROJTIME:* This is the actual or estimated time taken to commission the project and is calculated as indicated in Eq. (5.2).

For projects that were completed, actual values at the time of commissioning have been taken for all the variables. For projects that were under development, the most recent information on the projects has been used.

5.3.6 Project-Specific Variables

These variables pertain to the technical and commercial features of the project. The different variables in this category are as follows:

i. Project capacity, *PROJCAP*: This is the installed capacity of the project. This variable has been used to capture the potential economies of scale effect that is commonly seen in infrastructure projects. An inverse relationship can be predicted between project capacity and unit capacity cost. However, with respect to commissioning time, a direct relationship was expected, as a higher capacity indicates a bigger project and therefore a longer commissioning time.
ii. Project cost, *PROJCOST:* This is the estimated total cost of the project. The sample consisted of power projects that were developed in a twelve-year period, 2001–12. To ensure that project costs are comparable, they were converted to 2012 base year values. The year of financial closure was taken as the year of project development. Both *PROJCAP* and *PROJCOST* were included in the estimations, because project cost depends not only on capacity, but also on the type of power plant, such as thermal, wind. As in the case of *PROJCAP*, project cost was expected to have an inverse relationship with unit capacity cost and a direct relationship with commissioning time.
iii. Type of investment, *D_INVTYPE (dummy)*: This variable captured the type of investment, with PE or without PE. Dummy variable had a value of "1" for projects with PE investment, and "0" otherwise. This was the main variable of interest. Since PE investors closely monitored their investments, we hypothesized that projects with PE investment would have lower unit costs and shorter commissioning time as compared to those projects that did not have PE investment.
iv. Year of financial closure, *YEAR_FINCLOSURE*: This indicates the year in which the project achieved financial closure. This variable was used to capture the "time" trend in project development. Since past project development experience can increase the efficiency of future projects, it was expected that unit capacity costs and commissioning time would show a reducing trend in recent years.
v. Sector, *D_THERMAL, D_WIND, D_SOLAR and D_HYDEL (dummy)*: Our sample consisted of five different types of power projects based on the source of fuel: thermal, wind, solar, hydel and biomass. The dependent variables would be significantly influenced by the type of project. For example, solar and wind power plants would have higher unit capacity costs, but lower commissioning time as compared to that of hydel and thermal power plants. Therefore, dummy variables were used to capture the differences in fuel type. Biomass was considered as the base variable in our analysis, and dummy variables were generated for all the other four sectors. Dummy variable had a value of "1" for projects in the respective sector, and "0" otherwise. For example, thermal power projects had a value of "1" for *D_THERMAL* and a value of "0" for the remaining three sector variables.

5.3.7 Operating Environment Variables

Studies like Himburg (1995) and Gatwick and Eberhard (2008) have indicated that operating environments, especially in developing countries, affected the development of infrastructure projects such as power. The following variables have been used to capture the features of the operating environment of the project.

i. Real GDP per capita in 2011, *GDP_CAPITA*: This variable has been used as an indicator of the income and the level of demand for energy in the state where the power project is being setup. States with a higher per capita state GDP would have a higher level of economic activity and, hence, a stronger demand for electricity. It was also expected that states with higher per capita income have a more robust environment for development of infrastructure projects, which would result in lower time taken to complete the project. However, the effect of this variable on unit capacity cost was not clear.
ii. Cumulative Average Growth Rate 2007–2011, *CAGR*: This variable captured the growth rate of the real GDP per capita of the state from 2007 to 2011. In addition to higher GDP per capita, the private sector would also be keen to invest in states where the growth rate of GDP per capita is higher. The effect of this variable on cost and time was expected to be similar to that of *GDP_CAPITA*.
iii. Public–Private Partnership (PPP) Infra Index, *PPP*: The level of infrastructure development within the state by private sector was captured by this variable. A higher index value indicated a supportive environment for private provision of infrastructure. Availability of good-quality infrastructure such as roads, telecommunication and rail links to the project development site is critical for timely and cost-effective development of projects. On the other hand, better infrastructure availability hikes the land rates, which increases the project cost. High land rates may also prove detrimental to the land acquisition process for the project through expensive and long litigations, thereby increasing the expected time taken to commission the project. Thus, on the whole, the effect of *PPP* on unit capacity costs and plant commissioning time is not clear.
iv. Property Rights Index, *PRI*: This variable is an indication of the legal framework available in the state to safeguard the private property of the individuals. A higher value for *PRI* indicates a higher degree of perceived safety for private sector investment and lower risks of expropriation. It was expected that a higher PRI would reduce unit cost and project commissioning time, because of lower investment risk.
v. Human Development Index, *HDI*: The level of human development within the state was captured by this variable. While the variable *GDP_CAPITA* controls for the effect of income on the dependent variables, the *HDI* variable controls for the human and social development levels on the dependent variables. The relationship between *HDI* and the dependent variables is not very clear.
vi. Corruption Index, *CORR:* The level of corruption within the state was captured by this variable. This variable has been included in our analysis because high incidences of corruption increase transaction costs, which in turn could affect

project cost and time. A higher *CORR* value was expected to increase both cost and time.

vii. Region, *(D_NORTH, D_SOUTH and D_WEST) (dummy)*: Region indicates the location of the project. This variable has been included to control for the regional differences in project cost and time. The location of projects was classified in to four regions, North, South, West and East. The East region was used as a base variable, and dummy variables were used for the other three regions.

5.3.8 Robustness of the estimations

The estimated parameters of an OLS regression equation are unbiased, efficient and consistent provided there is a linear relationship between the dependent and independent variables. We checked for the linearity of the OLS equations by plotting the estimated residuals of Eqs. 5.3 and 5.4 with that of the predicted values of their respective dependent variables. The resulting scatter plot of the residuals did not show any significant relationship pattern or curves, which indicated the presence of a linear relationship between the dependent and independent variables. To check for normality of the equations, we plotted the fractiles of error distribution versus the fractiles of a normal distribution. There was no significant parabolic or S-shaped pattern to indicate the presence of skewness or kurtosis in the dataset. Hence, the distribution of the error term was normal. To check for multicollinearity, a correlation coefficient analysis was done. There was no presence of multicollinearity, and the results were acceptable.

Three-Stage Least Squares (3-SLS) Regression

Given the possibility of simultaneity bias between *UNIT_CAP_COST* and *PROJTIME*, a Durbin-Wu-Hausman (DWH) chi-square test was performed to check for endogeneity using instrumental variables (IV). *YEAR_FINCLOSURE* and *PROJCOST* were used as IV for *UNIT_CAP_COST*, and *GDP_CAPITA* was used as an IV for *PROJTIME*. The test using the IV indicated the endogeneity of *PROJTIME* in the *UNIT_CAP_COST* equation and vice versa. Therefore a 3-SLS estimate was adopted for an unbiased and efficient estimation of the simultaneous equations. Equations (5.5) and (5.6) provide the 3-SLS estimations.

$$\begin{aligned}\text{UNIT\_CAP\_COST} = {} & \beta_{C0} + \beta_{C1}\text{PROJTIME} + \beta_{C2}D\text{\_INVTYPE} \\ & + \beta_{C3}\text{LOG(PROJCAP)} + \beta_{C4}D\text{\_HYDEL} \\ & + \beta_{C5}D\text{\_SOLAR} + \beta_{C6}D\text{\_THERMAL} \\ & + \beta_{C7}D\text{\_WIND} + \beta_{c8}GDP\text{\_CAPITA} \\ & + \beta_{C9}\text{CAGR} + \beta_{C10}\text{PPP} + \beta_{C11}\text{HDI} \\ & + \beta_{C12}\text{CORR} + \beta_{C13}\text{PRI} + \beta_{C14}D\text{\_NORTH} \\ & + \beta_{C15}D\text{\_SOUTH} + \beta_{C16}D\text{\_WEST} + w_c \end{aligned} \tag{5.5}$$

$$\begin{aligned}\text{PROJTIME} = {} & \beta_{t0} + \beta_{t1}\text{UNIT\_ CAP\_ COST} + \beta_{t2}D\text{\_INVTYPE} \\ & + \beta_{t3}\text{YEAR\_ FINCLOSURE} + \beta_{t4}\text{PROJCOST} \\ & + \beta_{t5}\text{LOG(PROJCAP)} + \beta_{t6}D\text{\_HYDEL} \\ & + \beta_{t7}D\text{\_SOLAR} + \beta_{t8}D\text{\_THERMAL} \\ & + \beta_{t9}D\text{\_WIND} + \beta_{t10}\text{CAGR} + \beta_{t11}\text{PPP} \\ & + \beta_{t12}\text{HDI} + \beta_{t13}\text{CORR} + \beta_{t14}\text{PRI} \\ & + \beta_{t15}D\text{\_NORTH} + \beta_{t16}D\text{\_SOUTH} + \beta_{t17}D\text{\_WEST} + w_t \end{aligned} \quad (5.6)$$

In Eqs. (5.5) and (5.6), β_{c0} and β_{t0} are constant terms, β_{ci}'s and β_{ti}'s are vectors of estimable parameters, and w_i's are disturbance or error terms that capture unobserved effects. The equations were uniquely identified by ensuring that the number of exogenous variables excluded from each of the equations was at least equal to the number of endogenous variables included in the right-hand side of the equation. The 3-SLS method of estimation was done in STATA.

5.4 Data Sources and Description

Data on power projects was obtained from the World Bank, Venture Intelligence and DealCurry. World Bank database provided data on private power sector investments in the country. Data on projects with PE investment was obtained from Venture Intelligence and DealCurry. Venture Intelligence (www.ventureintelligence.in) and DealCurry (www.dealcurry.com) were leading sources of information on PE investments in India. Information obtained from the databases was also cross-checked with other sources such as the websites of the individual companies, industry reports and various government agencies. Inconsistencies and gaps in project specific variables were addressed by this process. Projects for which there were significant information gaps were excluded from the dataset. Finally, our dataset consisted of a total of 148 projects, which formed the study sample. Out of these, there were 34 projects with PE investment, and the remaining 114 projects did not have PE investment. Table 5.1 provides the data sources for different variables. Table 5.2 provides the summary data of the projects.

Table 5.3 provides the descriptive statistics for the data. Given the wide variation in project capacity, log scale was used for the analysis. The minimum and maximum values even in log scale indicated the wide range in capacity. In tune with project capacity, project cost values also showed a large variation. Cost per capacity (US$ million/MW) varied from 0.39 to 4.16. The time taken to commission the project varied from about a year to about six years. As expected, power projects based on renewable energy (solar, wind and so on) had lower commissioning time as compared to that of conventional hydro and thermal power projects. Table 5.3 also provides the boundary values for the operating environment variables. Real GDP per capita had values from 0.26 to 0.76, indicating that projects had come up in states with

Table 5.1 Data sources

Variable name	Main data sources	Description
Project-specific variables		
Project capacity	World Bank[1] and Venture Intelligence[2] databases	Project size indicator, represented in MW
Project cost	World Bank[1] database. Data was also obtained from the respective project websites and news reports.	Project cost indicator, represented in US$/Mn. All project costs were converted to 2012 base year values.
Type of investment (*dummy*)	World Bank[1] and Venture Intelligence[2] databases	PE indicator, 1 for with PE investment, 0 for without PE investment
Year of financial closure	World Bank[1], Venture Intelligence[2] and DealCurry[3] databases. In addition, data was also obtained from the respective project websites and news reports.	The year when the financial closure of the project was achieved
Estimated commissioning year	World Bank[1] and Venture Intelligence[2] databases. In addition, data was also obtained from the respective project websites and news reports.	The year when the project is expected to be completed and commissioned for use
Sector (thermal/wind/solar/hydel/biomass) *(dummy)*	World Bank[1] and Venture Intelligence[2] databases	The fuel type that is used for power generation in the project
Operating environment variables		
Real GDP per capita	Reserve Bank of India website, RBI (2013); our calculations	State economic effectiveness indicator, represented in dollars/person
Cumulative average growth rate from 2007 to 2011 (CAGR) percent	RBI (2013), our calculations	State-level real GDP per capita growth rate
Property Rights Index	Debroy et al. (2011), our calculations	Land acquisition effectiveness indicator, state-specific, ranging from 0 to 1, averaged for multistate projects
PPP Infra Index	Gowda et al. (2013)	Infrastructure effectiveness indicator, state-specific, ranging from 0 to 100, higher score indicates better infrastructure facility

(continued)

Table 5.1 (continued)

Variable name	Main data sources	Description
Human Development Index	RBI (2013) website	State-level human development indicator, ranging from 0 to 1, higher score indicates higher human development
Corruption Index	Transparency International India (2005)	State-level corruption indicator, ranging from 1 to 7, higher the score, higher the corruption in that state
Region (North/East/West/South) (*dummy*)	World Bank[1] and Venture Intelligence[2] databases	The region where the project was being developed

[1] World Bank Private Participation in Infrastructure database, available at ppi.worldbank.org
[2] Venture Intelligence database, available at www.ventureintelligence.com
[3] DealCurry database, available at www.dealcurry.com

Table 5.2 Summary details of 148 projects used for the study

Project type	No. of projects		
	With PE investment	Without PE investment	Total
Thermal	20	57	77
Hydel	6	20	26
Other renewable energy sources	8	37	45
Total	34	114	148

varying levels of development. CAGR values ranged from 4.54 to 10.44, indicating the variation in the growth rates of states where private power projects were being set up. The values of different indices (*HDI, PRI, CORR* and *PPP*) also underlined the heterogeneous nature of the operating environments.

Figure 5.1 provides the Wilcoxon rank-sum test of the key variables separately for projects with and without PE investment. It can be seen that the difference between project capacity and cost per capacity was statistically significant between the two groups. However, there was no significance difference in project cost. This was consistent with the findings of Gemson et al. (2012), which indicated that PE investments could support larger infrastructure projects at the same cost. There was no

Table 5.3 Descriptive data

Variable description	Variable name	Sample size	Mean	Median	Std. dev.	Min	Max
Dependent variables							
Cost per capacity (US$ Million/MW)	UNIT_CAP_COST	148	1.68	1.33	0.89	0.39	4.16
Time taken to commission the project (in years)	PROJTIME	113	2.57	3	1.55	1	6
Project-specific variables							
Log project capacity (in MW)	Log (PROJCAP)	148	5.11	5.65	1.99	1.39	8.29
Project cost (in 100's of US$ Million)	PROJCOST	148	7.67	3.59	10.57	0.04	69.67
Debt ratio		43	74.89%	75%	20.94%	0%	100%
Operating environment variables							
Real GDP per capita in 2011 (in 1000's of US$)	GDP_CAPITA	148	0.52	0.53	0.14	0.26	0.76
CAGR %	CAGR		7.42	7.86	1.36	4.54	10.44
Human Development Index	HDI	144	0.49	0.51	0.09	0.358	0.652
Property Rights Index	PRI		0.47	0.52	0.19	0.15	0.90
Corruption Index	CORR	114	3.21	3.30	0.33	2.6	4.2
PPP Infra Index	PPP	128	52.55	50.60	14.80	24.1	76.4

significant difference in debt ratio values, indicating that the inherent risk levels of the project were not different between the two groups. Should there have been any significant difference in project risk levels, we perceive this would have been reflected in the debt ratios. There were also significant differences in some of the operating environment variables. The mean values of *CAGR* and *PRI* were significantly different between the two groups. PE investments happened in states that had a higher *CAGR* and a higher level of property rights for private investors. However, it was also interesting to note that there were no significant differences in mean values for *CORR* and *PPP*. This indicated that the importance attached to these factors by PE investors was no different from the importance attached to these factors by other private investors in power projects. In sum, the descriptive statistics highlighted that there were differences between the power projects that had PE investment and those that do not.

5.5 Results and Discussion

5.5.1 Comparison Tests

Figure 5.2 provides the results of comparison tests for cost per capacity. The unmatched sample indicated that the mean cost per capacity for projects with PE investment was US$1.18 million per MW, whereas for projects that did not have PE investment, it was US$1.82 million per MW. The difference was statistically significant at the 99 percent CI. This indicated that projects with PE investment had lower unit capacity costs. When the means were compared after matching the projects on the type of power generation, the results remained the same. Subsequently, we increased the degree of matching by increasing the number of variables used for matching. The results showed that the difference was significant at all levels of the matched pair sampling. However, as expected, the number of observations gradually reduced with the increase in the number of variables used for matching, because of the lack of suitable projects that matches on all the variables chosen between the two groups. The results show that the two samples, i.e., projects with and without PE investment, are statistically different when compared on unit capacity costs.

Results for comparison on time taken to commission the project are given in Fig 5.3. The unmatched sample indicated that the average commissioning time was higher for projects with PE investment (2.97 years as compared to 2.39 years for projects without PE investment), though the difference was not statistically significant. However, matched pair analysis indicated a difference at the 10 percent level when the projects were matched on sector, project capacity, and the state in which the project was being set up. The trend of projects with PE investment having greater commissioning time persisted even in the matched pair analysis.

The comparison tests indicated that projects with PE investment had lower unit capacity costs. There was also a counteractive effect, though not very strong, in the form of longer commissioning time for projects with PE investment. The opposing effects of PE investment on costs and time were interesting. Though the comparison tests indicated significant differences between the two samples, it cannot be said for certain that this difference can be associated with the treatment effect. We probe this further through regression analysis.

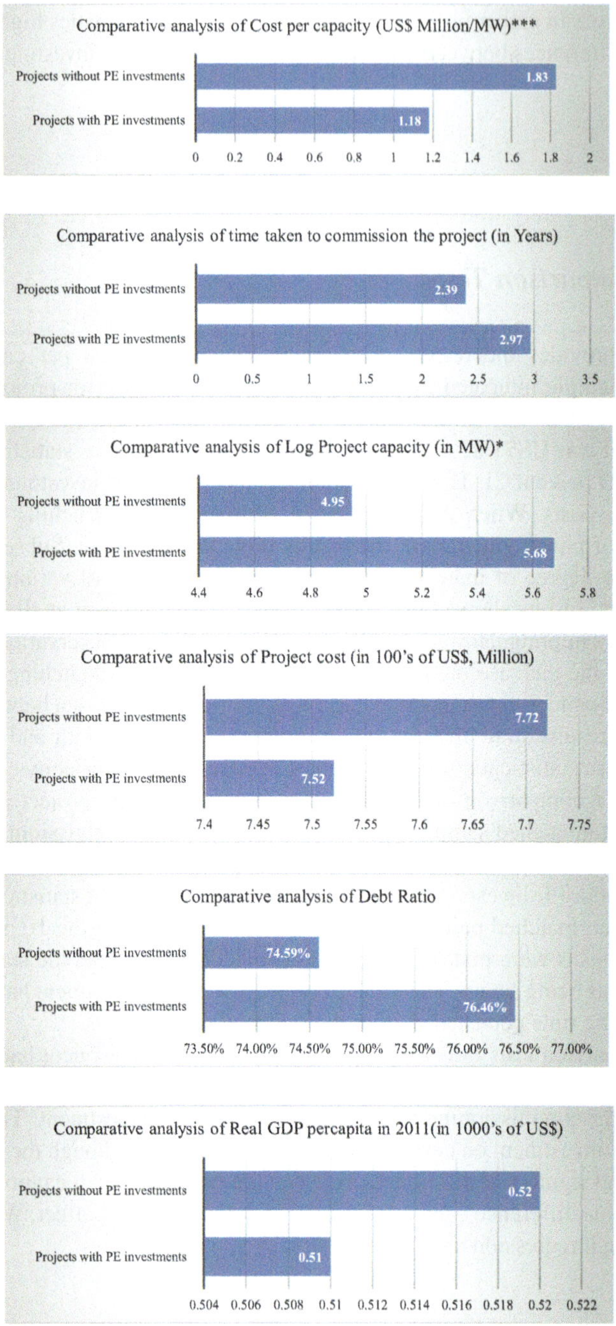

Fig. 5.1 Results of the Wilcoxon rank-sum test of the key variables for projects with and without PE investment
*** significant at 99% CI, ** significant at 95% CI, * significant at 90% CI

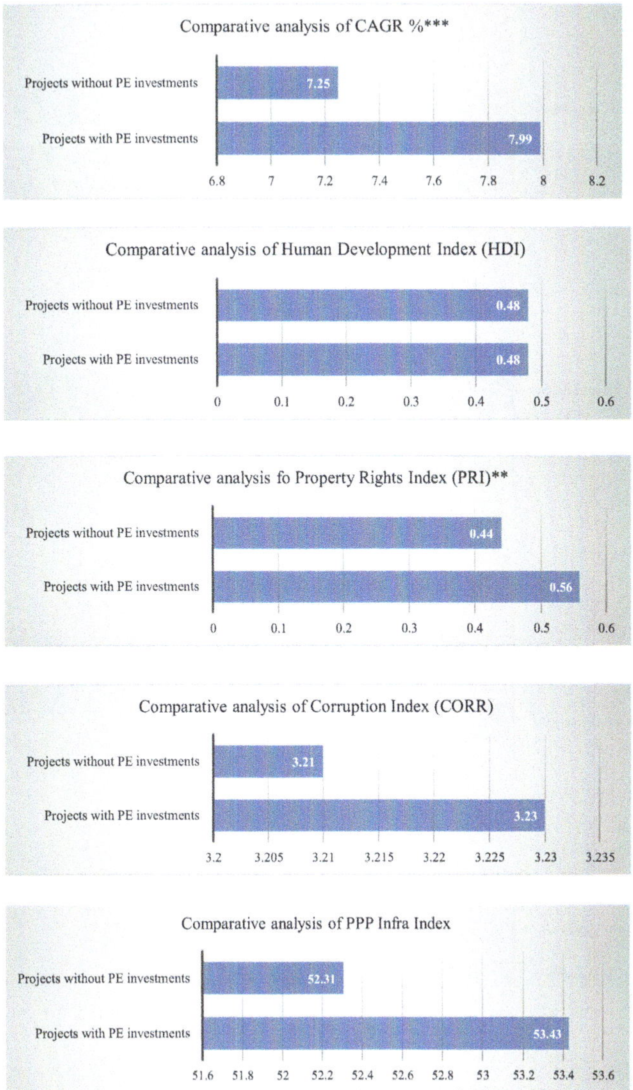

Fig. 5.1 (continued)

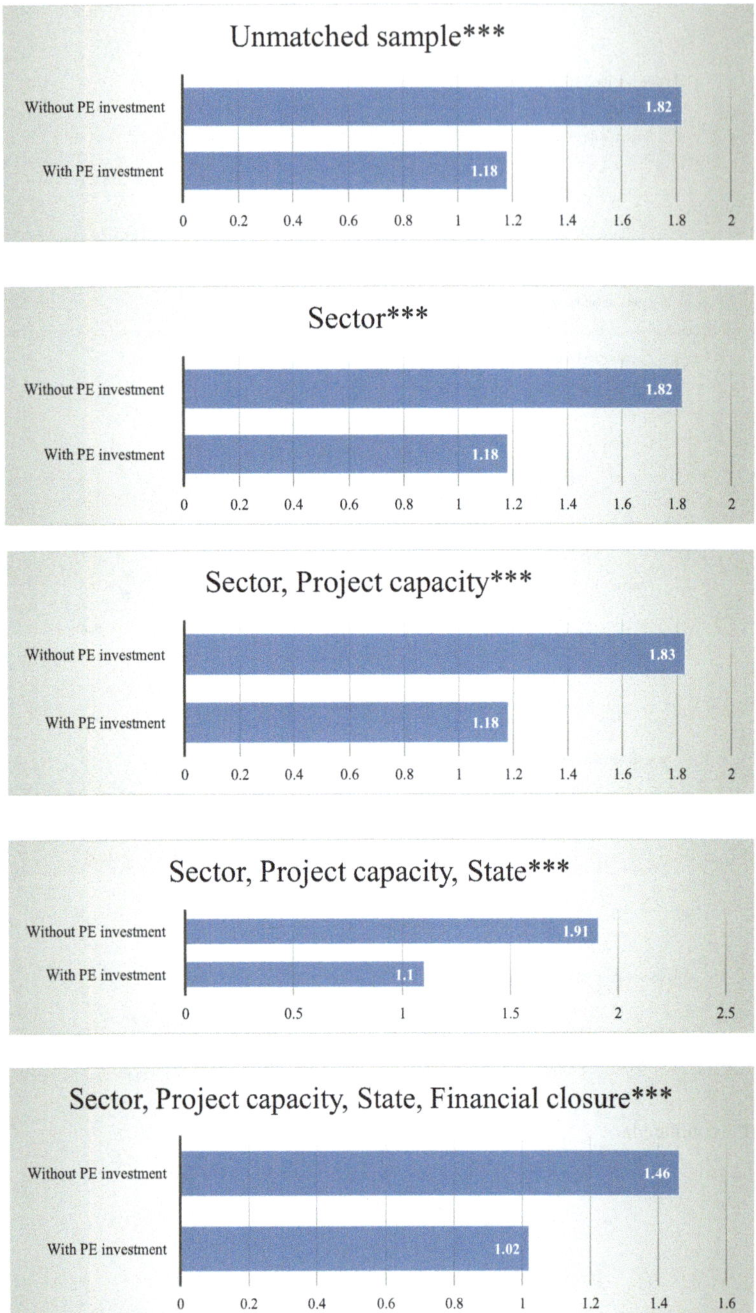

Fig. 5.2 Matched pair sampling results for cost per capacity (MW)
*** significant at 99% CI

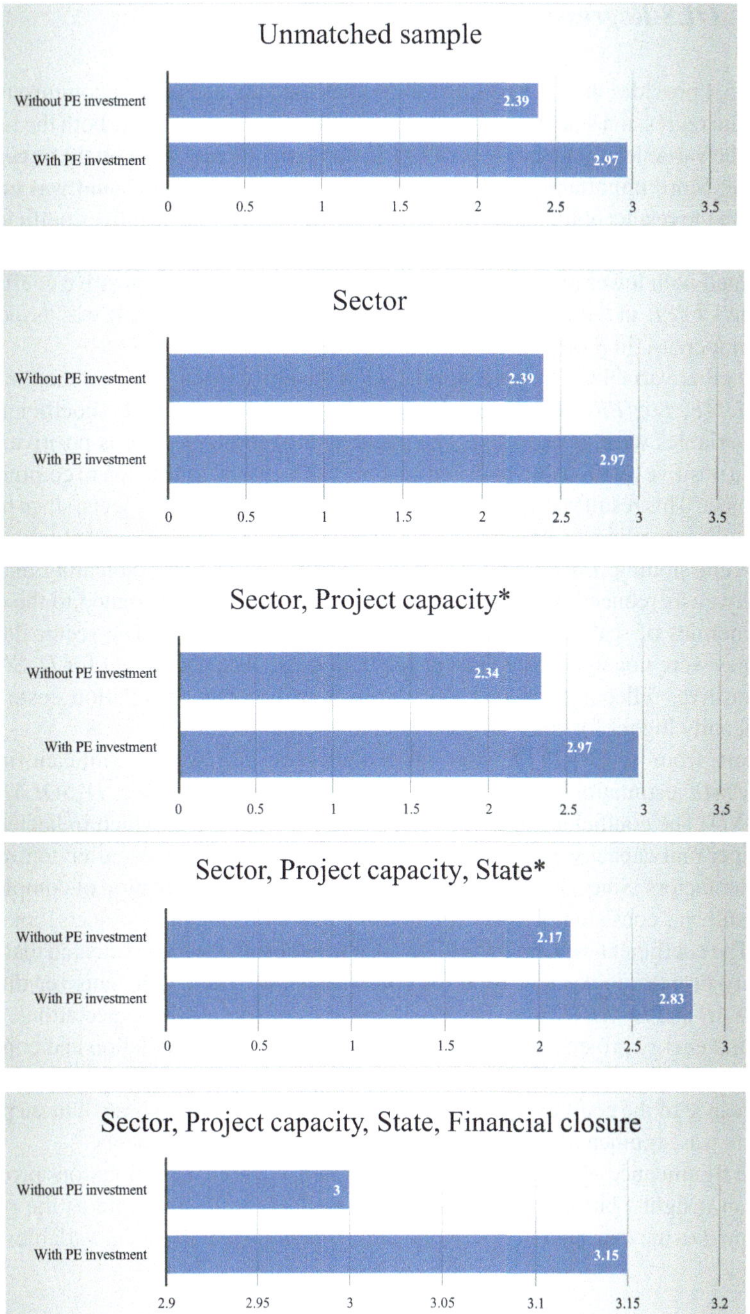

Fig. 5.3 Matched pair sampling results for project commissioning time (years)
* significant at 90% CI

5.5.2 OLS Regression

Figure 5.4 provides the OLS results for cost per capacity and project commissioning time. The regression statistics indicates a good fit of the model. In the both the regressions, the variable of interest, *D_INVTYPE*, had a significant effect on the dependent variable. More importantly, the effect was on opposing directions and was consistent with the results obtained from comparison of means. The negative coefficient of *D_INVTYPE* in the unit capacity cost estimation indicated that PE investment was associated with lower unit capacity costs. On the other hand, the positive coefficient of *D_INVTYPE* in the time estimation indicated that PE investment was associated with an increase in project commissioning time.

The other variables that were significant in the unit capacity cost estimation were *PROJTIME, Log(PROJCAP)* and *D_SOLAR*. The directions of the coefficients of these variables were as expected. The coefficient of *PROJTIME* was positive, indicating a positive relationship between cost per capacity and time taken to commission the project. This result was on expected lines as in infrastructure projects, since higher costs indicated a bigger and possibly a complex project, which needed more time for commissioning. *Log(PROJCAP)* had a negative coefficient, indicating that unit capacity costs reduced with increasing capacity. This can be attributed to the effect of economies of scale commonly seen in infrastructure sector. The sector dummy variables were not significant, except for *D_SOLAR*. The coefficient for *D_SOLAR* was positive, reflecting the fact that the upfront capacity installation costs were significantly higher for solar projects as compared to biomass projects.

Apart from *D_INVTYPE,* the other variables that were significant in the *PROJTIME* estimation were *UNIT_CAP_COST, Log(PROJCAP), D_SOLAR* and *D_WIND*. The coefficient of *UNIT_CAP_COST* was positive, which indicated that as the per unit capacity cost increased, *PROJTIME* also increased, after controlling for other factors. Since unit capacity costs can be seen as an indication of complexity, this result was consistent with the relationship that more complex projects took more time. The coefficient for *Log(PROJCAP)* was also positive, which indicated that large capacity projects took more time for commissioning. The coefficients for dummy *D_SOLAR* and *D_WIND* were negative and were consistent with expectations. Solar and wind energy projects have much shorter development, installation and commissioning time as compared to conventional hydro and thermal power projects. The significance of the coefficients indicated that the commissioning time of these power projects was significantly lower than the conventional power projects.

The significance of the project-specific variables in both the estimations provided no fresh insights, but highlighted the robustness of the data sample as the results confirmed to the expected trends. None of the operating environment variables were

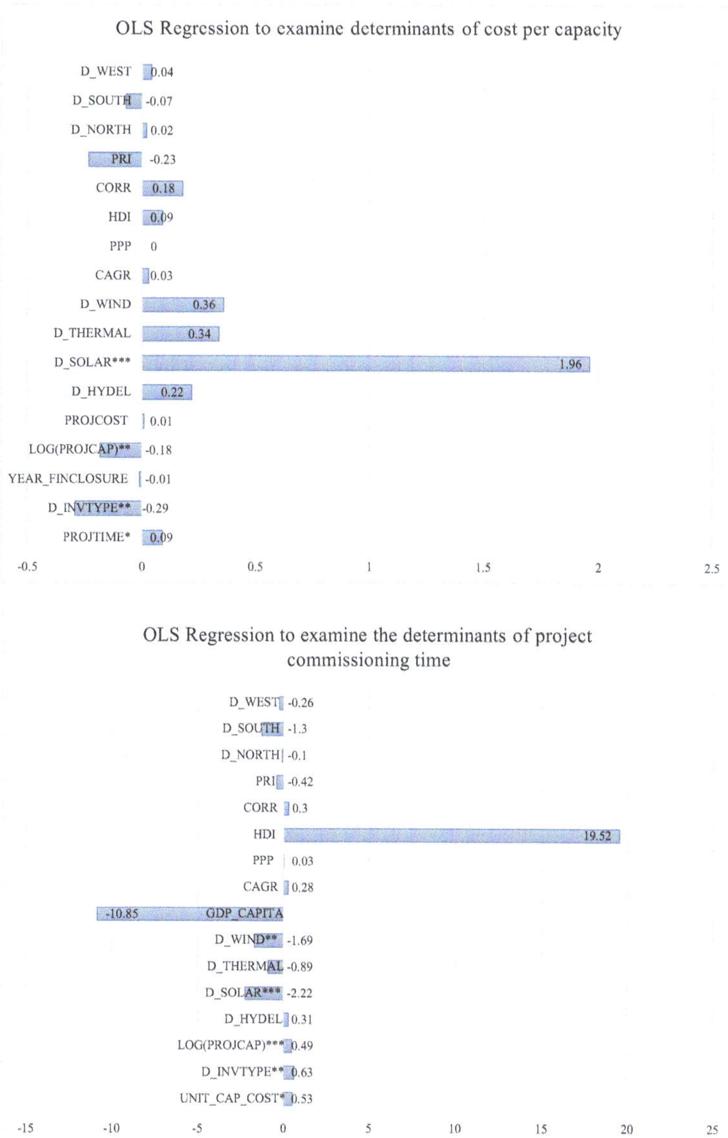

Fig. 5.4 Results for the OLS Regression (N=90): Determinants of cost per capacity & Determinants of project commissioning time

***, **, * indicates significance at 1%, 5% and 10% level, respectively

Table 5.4 DWH test results for endogeneity

Test for the endogeneity unit capacity cost and project commissioning time		
H0 (null hypothesis)	Durbin-Wu-Hausman chi-square test	*P*-value
PROJTIME is exogeneous	3.33, chi-sq(1)	0.0678*
UNIT_CAP_COST is exogeneous	13.62, chi-sq(1)	0.0002***

*, *** Significant at 10% and 1% level of significance, respectively
Instruments for cost per capacity are year of financial closure and project cost
Instruments for estimated time taken to commission the project (years) are real GDP of the state

found to be significant in both the estimations, even though the descriptive data (Table 5.3) shows a wide variation in the operating environment variables. A possible explanation for this is that state-level operating environment variables may not be an appropriate representation of the project operating environment. For example, given the importance of power projects, governments could provide special privileges and concessions that ensure speedy clearances to certain projects to attract investment from private sector. Such project-level concessions might not get fully reflected in the state-level indices that have used in our estimations. No significance was also seen for the regional dummies. A possible reason is that the division of the projects according to regions may not be adequate, since different states are characterized by their own unique socio-political and economic settings. Scope for future work should therefore focus on alternative ways to operationalize and model the operating environment variables.

The OLS results, however, indicate the possibility of simultaneity bias as *PROJTIME* was significant in the *UNIT_CAP_COST* estimation and vice versa. DWH test results (Table 5.4) indicated the endogenous nature of both the variables. Therefore, to increase the robustness of the results, we used a 3-SLS estimation to model the dependent variables.

5.5.3 3-SLS Regression

Figure 5.5 gives the 3-SLS regression results after accounting for the simultaneity of the dependent variables. The coefficient of *D_INVTYPE* was significant for both the equations. The results were consistent with the OLS results and indicated that PE investment had an opposing effect on cost and time. Further, the signs of the coefficients of other project-specific variables in the *UNIT_CAP_COST* equation (Eq. 5.5) remained the same. However, the significance of *PROJTIME* increased from 10 to 5 percent level. Other variables, *Log(PROJCAP)* and *D_SOLAR*, which were significant in OLS regression continued to retain their significance. There was no change in the level of significance of other variables.

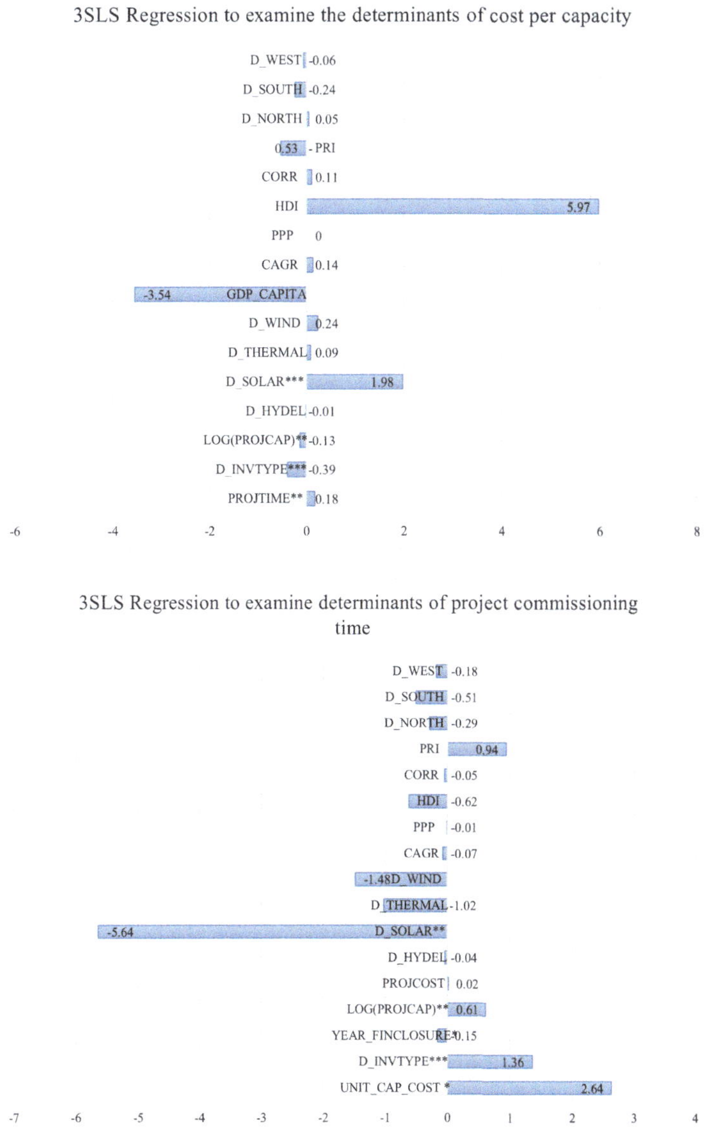

Fig. 5.5 Results for the 3SLS regression (N = 90): Determinants of cost per capacity & Determinants of project commissioning time
***, **, * indicates significance at 1%, 5% and 10% level, respectively

The results of the *PROJTIME* equation (Eq. 5.6) further strengthened the OLS results. The significance of variable *UNIT_CAP_COST* increased from the 10 percent level to 5 percent level, with the coefficient continuing to remain positive. Other variables that were significant in the OLS regression continued to remain significant, except that of *D_WIND*. The 3-SLS estimation indicated that after accounting for simultaneity, PE investment was associated with lower unit capacity costs, but a longer time for project commissioning.

5.6 Summary and Conclusions

This chapter highlights the impact of PE investment in power generation projects. Specifically, the impact was analyzed on two key parameters determining cost (unit capacity cost) and time (project commissioning time). Data from 148 private power generation projects in India that were financed by the project finance method formed the sample for the study. The results showed that PE investment was associated with a significant, but opposite effect on unit capacity costs and project commissioning time.

Unmatched sample analysis indicated that average unit capacity costs for power projects with PE investment was 35 percent lower than that of projects that had no PE investment. The difference in average unit costs was significant even after the projects were matched on different project parameters. Regression estimations showed that PE investment was associated with lower unit capacity costs. The signs of the coefficients of other significant variables in the estimations were as expected, which indicated the robustness of the estimation model.

Comparison tests of project commissioning time indicated that, on an average, projects with PE investment took 24 percent longer time as compared to projects that did not have any PE investment. However, the unmatched sample did not show any statistical significance in the comparison tests. When the samples were compared after matching the projects on sector, project capacity and the state in which the project was being developed, the difference was significant at the 10 percent level. Thus, the strength of the difference between the samples was not as significant for project time as it was for unit capacity costs. However, the regression estimations indicated that PE investment was associated with longer project commissioning time.

Chronic power shortages necessitate the need for large additions in power generation capacity in many developing countries. However, countries which are most in need of cost-effective and affordable power to consumers also find difficulty in mobilizing capital to finance their power projects. Given the large demand for capacity additions, private sources of financing are being used to augment public sector investment. Policy-makers, particularly those in developing countries, are keen to create a facilitating environment that would attract private investment for infrastructure development. An important inference of this study is that the type and source of private capital matters. While private capital in infrastructure has helped to increase efficiencies, the results of this study indicate that new sources of private capital such as PE can help to capture additional benefits that may not be possible with conventional private sector investment.

Attracting PE investment can provide a twofold benefit to the power sector in developing countries: First, it forms an additional source of capital for power sector development. Second, the style of PE investing can contribute to development of projects that have lower capacity costs. PE investors are purely financial investors, and unlike the project sponsors, they do not have any product market linkages (i.e., they are not a supplier of goods and services or a purchaser of outputs) with the projects in which they invest. Therefore, their returns are largely determined by the competitive merits of the projects that they invest in. The results of this study demonstrate the ability of PE investors to select and invest in projects that have lower capital costs. By investing in projects that are more cost competitive, PE investors bring in the discipline of capital markets for infrastructure projects. As the number of projects that have PE investment increases, it would have a favorable impact on the unit capacity costs.

PE investment was also associated with longer commissioning time. Therefore, it might be perceived that PE investment is not desirable from the perspective of achieving faster capacity additions. We however propose that one of the reasons for longer commissioning time can be attributed to the stronger adherence to processes and accountability demanded by the PE investors. Thillairajan and Jain (2013) have indicated that the presence of external investors who demand good governance systems and practices leads to longer project implementation time. While putting in place robust systems and processes that can lead to longer project development time, the benefits of institutionalizing robust systems and processes would extend far beyond the construction phase and contribute to the long-term development of power sector in the country.

The involvement of PE investors benefits the project in two counts. First, at the investment phase, they are able to select better projects using superior screening and selection criteria. PE investors, thus, help to weed out poor and uneconomic projects by disciplining capital availability. Second, in the post-investment phase, active monitoring and managerial contribution to their portfolio of investments ensure project development as planned. We hypothesize that such active monitoring would reduce project over-runs. The jury is still out on the assertion, and hopefully, future studies can provide the evidence to back up the assertion.

References

Blackwell, M., Iacus, S. G., King Porro, G. (2010). CEM: Coarsened exact matching in Stata, Stata corp.

Bond, G., & Carter, L. (1995). Financing energy projects: Experience from the International Finance Corporation. *Energy Policy, 23*(11), 967–975.

Brav, A., & Gompers, P. A. (1997). Myth of reality? The long-run underperformance of initial public offerings: Evidence from venture and non-venture capital backed companies. *Journal of Finance, 52*(5), 1791–1821.

Brealey, R. A., Cooper, I. A., & Habib, M. A. (1996). Using project finance to fund infrastructure investments. *Journal of Applied Corporate Finance, 9*(3), 25–38.

Chan, C., Forwood, D., Roper, H., & Sayers, C. (2009*). Public infrastructure financing: An international perspective.* Productivity Commission Staff Working Paper.

Chemmanur, T. J., & John, K. (1996). Optimal incorporation, structure of debt contracts, and limited-recourse project financing. *Journal of Financial Intermediation, 5*, 372–408.

Chowdhury, A., Orr, R. J., & Settel, D. (2009). Multilaterals and infrastructure funds: A new era. *Journal of Structured Finance, 14*(4), 68–74.

Debroy B., Bhandari, L., & Aiyar, S. S. A. (2011). *Economic Freedom of the States of India 2011*, Academic Foundation, New Delhi. URL: http://www.freetheworld.com/pdf/EconomicFreedom India-2011.pdf. Accessed May 12, 2013.

Dunkerley, J. (1995). Financing the energy sector in developing countries. *Energy Policy, 23*(11), 929–939.

Engel, D., & Stiebale J. (2009). *Private equity, investment and financial constraints—Firm-level evidence for France and the United Kingdom.* Ruhr Economic Papers 0126, Rheinisch-Westfälisches Institut für Wirtschaftsforschung, Ruhr-Universität Bochum, Universität Dortmund, Universität Duisburg-Essen.

Esty, B. C. (2003). *Modern project finance: A casebook.* Wiley.

Finnerty, J. D. (2013). *Project financing: Asset-based financial engineering* (3rd ed). Wiley Finance.

Gatti, S. (2008). *Project finance in theory and practice: Designing, structuring, and financing private and public projects.* Academic Press Advanced Finance Series, Elsevier Inc.

Gatwick, K., & Eberhard, A. (2008). An analysis of independent power projects in Africa: Understanding development and investment outcomes. *Development Policy Review, 26*(3), 309–338.

Gemson, J., Gautami, K. V., & Thillairajan, A. (2012). Impact of private equity investments in infrastructure projects. *Utilities Policy, 21*, 59–65.

Gemson, J. N. (2013). *Syndication and staging as risk management strategies in private equity investments: Evidence from the infrastructure sector.* Unpublished Ph.D. thesis, Indian Institute of Technology Madras.

Gowda, M. V. R., Mukherji, A., Reddy, K. (2013). Most states unprepared for PPP's. *The Hindu Business Line.* January 17. URL:http://www.thehindubusinessline.com/opinion/columns/most-states-unprepared-forppps/article4316517.ece. Accessed May 12, 2013.

Gupta, J. P., & Sravat, A. K. (1998). Development and project financing of private power projects in developing countries: a case study of India. *International Journal of Project Management, 16*(2), 99–105.

Hellman, T., & Puri, M. (2002). Venture capital and the professionalization of start-up firms: Empirical evidence. *Journal of Finance, 57*(1), 169–197.

Himburg, H. (1995). The view from the Overseas Private Investment Corporation (OPIC): Support to power projects in Asia. *Energy Policy, 23*(11), 977–980.

Inderst, G. (2013). *Private infrastructure finance and investment in Europe.* European Investment Bank Working Paper 2013/02.

International Energy Outlook. (2013). *A report published by the US Energy Information Administration.* URL: www.eia.gov/forecasts/ieo/pdf/0484(2013).pdf

Kenny, C. (2009). Is there an anti-corruption agenda in utilities? *Utilieis Policy, 17*, 156–165.

Kortum, S., & Lerner, J. (2000). Assessing the contribution of venture capital to innovation. *RAND Journal of Economics, 31*, 647–692.

Lerner, J. (1995). Venture capitalists and the oversight of private firms. *Journal of Finance, 50*(1), 301–318.

Lerner, J. (1999). The government as a venture capitalist: The long-run effects of the SBIR program. *Journal of Business, 72*, 285–318.

Lerner, J. (2002). Boom and bust in the venture capital industry and the impact on innovation. *Federal Reserve Bank of Atlanta Economic Review*, 25–39.

Narasimhan, T. E. (2009). Power gets a big chunk of private equity pie. *Business Standard*, December 4. URL: http://www.business-standard.com/article/finance/power-gets-a-big-chunk-of-private-equity-pie-109120400017_1.html. Accessed on July 03, 2013

Orr, R. J. (2009). *Pensions and infrastructure: The path to common ground*. Collaboratory for Research on Global Projects, Stanford, California.

PPIAF. (2013). *Public-private infrastructure advisory facility, private participation in infrastructure database*. URL: http://ppi.worldbank.org/explore/ppi_exploreSubSector.aspx?SubSectorID=3

Preqin. (2014). *Preqin global infrastructure report* (p. 13).

RBI. (2013). *Reserve Bank of India website*. URL: http://www.rbi.org.in/scripts/AnnualPublications.aspx?head=Handbook%20of%20Statistics%20on%20Indian%20Economy. Accessed May 10, 2013.

Sen, A., & Jamasb, T. (2010). *The economic effects of electricity deregulation: an empirical analysis of Indian states*. EPRG Working Paper 1001, Cambridge: University of Cambridge.

Smit, H. T. J., & Trigeorgis, L. (2009). Valuing infrastructure investment: An option games approach. *California Management Review, 51*(2), 79–100.

Speechley, T. (2007). *The infrastructure boom and the role of private equity, Private Equity and Hedge Funds by Abraaj Capital*. URL: http://www.abraaj.com/mediacenter/Files/PEandHedgeFunds.pdf

Suchard, J. (2009). The impact of venture capital backing on the corporate governance of Australian initial public offerings. *Journal of Banking and Finance, 33*, 765–774.

Thillairajan, A., & Jain, N. (2013). Project finance and investments in risky environments: evidence from the infrastructure sector. *Journal of Financial Management of Property and Construction, 18*(3), 251–267.

Transparency International India. (2005). *India corruption study 2005*. URL: http://www.transparencyindia.org/resource/survey_study/India%20Corruption%20Study%202005.pdf. Accessed December 10, 2013.

Venture Intelligence. (2014). Available at www.ventureintelligence.com. Accessed March 15, 2014.

VentureXpert. (2010). *Database available from Securities Data Corporation*. Accessed April 15, 2010.

Wallsten, J. S. (2001). An econometric assessment of telecom competition, privatization and regulation in Africa and Latin America. *Journal of Industrial Economics, 49*(1), 1–19.

Weber, B., & Alfen, H. W. (2010). *Infrastructure as an asset class: Investment strategies, project finance and PPP*. Wiley.

World Energy Outlook. (2012). *Factsheet—How will global energy markets evolve till 2035?* URL: http://www.worldenergyoutlook.org/media/weowebsite/2012/factsheets.pdf

Chapter 6
An Overview of Private Equity Financing Strategies

However beautiful the strategy, you should occasionally look at the results.
—Sir Winston Churchill

Traditional sources of financing are available to industries generally through a line of credit such as a loan. Under conventional terms, such processes are mostly standardized and are usually based on the 5 C's of credit—character, capacity, condition, capital, and collateral. This can sometimes make the process tedious, especially for entrepreneurs and non-traditional firms who may not fulfill the regulatory standard and possess the level of information required by lenders. The 2008 financial crisis and its subsequent aftermaths also reduced the ability of traditional lenders to support long-term non-traditional projects.[1] In addition, factors such as uncertainty, asymmetric information, the nature of firm assets, and the conditions in the relevant financial and product markets can also limit access to capital for some potentially profitable firms.[2]

Uncertainty may be a result of unwillingness to forward capital or extend a line of credit, due to the managements' aversion with risk. Asymmetric information is the result of the absence of complete and relevant information. The characteristics of the firm's assets such as intangibility, location and site specificity, purpose or use specificity can affect the type and levels of financing being obtained. Finally, dynamic market conditions, supply chains, and intense competition, and even uncertainty

[1] https://www.itf-oecd.org/sites/default/files/docs/mobilising-private-investment-infrastructure.pdf (accessed 13 April 2022).

[2] Gompers and Lerner (1999).

Some sections of this chapter are based on the journal papers titled "What do PE investors seek From syndication partners? Evidence from the infrastructure sector" which appeared in Public Works and Management Policy, 2015, https://doi.org/10.1177/1087724X15613095, and "A new perspective on private equity stage financing: Evidence from investments in infrastructure" which appeared in *Venture Capital: An International Journal of Entrepreneurial Finance*. 17(4), 299–325, https://doi.org/10.1080/13691066.2015.1052193.

J. Gemson and Thillai Rajan A., *Private Equity Financing in Infrastructure and Real Estate*, https://doi.org/10.1007/978-981-16-1634-1_6

about potential markets may affect the ability of firms to raise capital from traditional sources of financing.

PE has emerged as an important source of capital to sidestep traditional mechanisms and the challenges associated with the same. Although global economic and financial crises often witness a shift toward more conservative funding techniques, there are steep increases and robust activity immediately following them. The period immediately following the subprime crisis (2007 to early 2012) saw almost US$15.25 billion worth of infrastructure funds being raised, and 2021 witnessed historic heights in PE deal making at approximately US$1.2 trillion.[3]

In addition to providing capital, PE brings both competency and efficiency into the sectors they invest in through continuous innovation on several fronts, including technology, design, construction, and operational processes,[4] rightly obtaining the title of value-added capital. Such capital has proven to be very effective and successful. As early as 1980, VC investments offered attractive returns, on an average of 18.9 percent year-on-year, subject to the number of successful investments the investment portfolio contained.[5] In 2013, the total exit value of PEs stood at US$456 billion, 67 percent more than that of the previous year. A study conducted by the American Investment Council in September 2020 concluded the PE funds produced a 14.2 percent median annualized return, net of fees, over the previous ten years. The S&P 500 provided a 13.7 percent return and public pension funds returned 12.8 percent, net of fees, over the same time period.[6] Their immense success coupled with the desire to move away from their traditional forte of investments saw large capital inflows into the infrastructure sector. PE investments in infrastructure saw a 468 percent increase in 2000–2009 with US$202.82 billion worth of infrastructure projects receiving PE investment as compared to US$35.69 billion of the same in 1990–1999.

PE is a popular method to provide capital to infrastructure projects through ready capital and management benefits. While PE is known to sidestep government requirements and bureaucratic delays, such investments could also support larger projects. PE investments seem to play a role in faster, cheaper, and better project delivery, along with lower volatilities, diversification of portfolios and mitigation of inflation. Further, PE investors shared the risk of the project among themselves, thereby reducing the risk faced by the individual sponsors.

While such attractive settings reinstate PE and its outperformance, when large amounts of capital are at stake in a relatively untested sector, it raises questions about the investment strategies of PE firms. The syndication of investment and the staging of investment are strategic and distinctive operational mechanisms used by

---

[3] https://corpgov.law.harvard.edu/2022/02/09/private-equity-2021-year-in-review-and-2022-outlook/.

[4] Thillai Rajan and Menon (2014).

[5] Huntsman and Hoban (1980).

[6] https://www.nytimes.com/2021/12/04/business/is-private-equity-overrated.html#:~:text=As%20of%20September%202020%2C%20private,industry%2C%20using%20the%20latest%20numbers.

PE while infusing capital into investee firms. Syndication of PE investing is the process by which two or more PE firms come together to make common decisions with respect to investing and through this process share in the payoffs. Staging of PE investing is the process by which capital is infused into the investee company in distinct points in time, where the size and timing of cash flows is determined by a prior agreement or a significant development in the company. These two strategies result in or can be a result of the active monitoring and advice that is provided, the screening mechanisms employed, the incentives to exit, informal monitoring, and controls over the compensation of the entrepreneur which include the widespread use of stock grants and stock options.

There is a large body of academic knowledge which has explored syndication of investments and/or the staging of investments, mostly from the venture capital investment point of view, as the mechanisms than venture capitalists use to mitigate agency conflicts among entrepreneurial firms and outside investors. In virtually all such cases, a critical role of venture capitalists is generating information about the firm's prospects to mitigate uncertainty, asymmetric information, the nature of the firm's assets, and the conditions in the relevant financial and product markets.[7]

This section examines the syndication of PE investments and the staging of PE investments as two non-monetary financing strategies[8] employed by PE firms when they invest in the infrastructure sector. While investing in this sector, PE firms are appreciative of infrastructure asset characteristics, large project sizes, project finance structures, and varying risks and risk levels.

6.1 An Overview of Syndication and Staging of PE Investments in Infrastructure

We contend that risk is inherent in the very nature of most investments and hence becomes an important characteristic of infrastructure deals. Sectors and project structures in infrastructures are made known through the extent of risk. The primary risk in investing capital arises from the size of the same, i.e., large sized investments automatically reflect the changing nature of the investors' willingness to bear risks, leading to uncertainty. Next, long gestation periods required for construction of infrastructure assets brings information asymmetry. Then, characteristics of site specificity and asset specificity indicate that such projects must be situated in areas where they are required and constructed as needed. Finally, the nature of the environment housing

[7] Gompers and Lerner (1999).

[8] The use of financial strategies through specialised financial instruments has not proved to be credible. For example: the use of project bonds almost disappeared after the financial crisis of 2008, after the series of downgrades by the Monoline insurers that provided credit insurance to these debt instruments. The demise of the Monoline insurers reduced the potential amount of funds that institutional investors could have committed to various infrastructure investments. Further, Central Banks carried out a series of liquidity injections from 2009 to 2012 which compressed the yields of debt instruments.

the infrastructure asset is of paramount importance. This environment covers demographics as well as legal aspects of the market and the government of the country. Thus, uncertainty, information asymmetry, the nature of the firm's assets, and the financial product markets play crucial roles in in determining financing strategies of PE firms.

We examine 358 worldwide infrastructure deals with PE investments of US$9.74 billion in energy, transport and water and utilities sectors from 1990 to 2009 and analyze the syndication of PE investments and the staging of PE investments.

6.2 The Case of Syndication of PE Investment

This study presents an analysis of PE syndication in infrastructure projects. PE firms are known to form syndicates to mitigate risk through diversification, combat uncertainty and information asymmetry through resource utilization, handle firm specific assets through utilization of capabilities to add and increase value, and lack of information through sharing of information and resources on potential deals, for improved decision making, thus sharing in the payoffs. For a more comprehensive examination, the analysis is divided into three parts. First, infrastructure deals with PE syndication are compared against similar deals without PE syndication. Such an analysis highlights the characteristics of deals with PE syndication. Second, the factors that drive PE syndication are determined. Finally, the extent of PE syndication in infrastructure is examined. The findings indicated that PE syndication was driven largely by the need for local knowledge—which was critical due to the site-specific nature of infrastructure assets, translating into syndication with local partners. As round number increased, diversity of experience took precedence over level of experience, indicating that PE firms formed syndicates with other PE firms to achieve a varied set of skills.

6.3 The Case of Staging of PE Investment

This study examines the staging of PE investments in infrastructure sector. A staged form of capital infusion has often been considered the most potent function,[9] since it makes the much-needed capital, a conditional phenomenon. While PE firms have the option to finance infrastructure project by infusing capital at once, they can choose to disburse the capital in multiple investments, creating the staging function. Such a mechanism has successfully been used in the past to combat risk and uncertainty. This study hypothesizes that the decision to stage investment is a response to the factors that influence infrastructure deals including institutional and financial environments, project structure, and reputation of the PE firm. We find that developing/transition

[9] Sahlman (1990).

economies and markets characterized by high inflation and interest rates increases PE propensity to stage. Further deals with larger investment sizes and younger investee companies pose increased risks, and PE firms seem to use their prior infrastructure experience and bargaining power to stage financing. Our results also confirm that long-term relationships between the PE firm and the investee company are advantageous to both parties. We believe that the positive results acquired through the PE staging strategy will help perpetuate it as one of the best tools available for PE investing in the infrastructure sector.

References

Gompers, P., & Lerner, J. (1999). *The venture capital cycle*. MIT Press.
Huntsman, B., & Hoban, J. (1980). Investment in new enterprises: Some empirical observations on risk, return, and market structure. *Financial Management, 9*, 44–51.
Sahlman, W. (1990). The structure and governance of venture capital organizations. *Journal of Financial Economics, 27*, 473–524.
Thillai Rajan, A., & Menon, S. (2014). Private Equity investment in infrastructure: evidence from India. *The Journal of Private Equity, 17*(4), 40–47.

Chapter 7
The Case of Syndication of PE Investments

One man can be crucial ingredient on a team, but one man cannot make a team.
—Kareem Abdul Jabbar

7.1 Introduction

This chapter examines the syndication of PE investments in the infrastructure sector. Syndication of investments has been recognized as a non-monetary tool used by PE investors to mitigate uncertainty and information asymmetry in difficult environments. The process of syndication has been well researched in academic literature. Most available studies, while acknowledging the international aspects of syndication, base their inquiry in developed countries; few studies synthesize the overall findings of research to support investment decisions at a sector level. Infrastructure projects have long maturities and resource flows into the project only after they become operational, risk characteristics which are different from typical corporate finance projects. With PEs increasing their scale of investing in infrastructure, an examination of syndication would shed insights into strategies used by PE firms when investing in such non-conventional projects, overcoming challenges with respect to asset characteristics and environments that locate these assets. Here we delve into an analysis of the choice for, drivers of, and extent of PE syndication when they invest in infrastructure projects.

This chapter is based on the journal paper titled "What do PE investors seek from syndication partners? Evidence from the infrastructure sector" which appeared in Public Works and Management Policy, 2015, https://doi.org/10.1177/1087724X15613095.

J. Gemson and Thillai Rajan A., *Private Equity Financing in Infrastructure and Real Estate*, https://doi.org/10.1007/978-981-16-1634-1_7

7.2 Introduction to Syndication

The word syndication derives its origins from the word "syndicate". Early written records indicate that the word "syndicate" was used as early as in the 1620s to represent a "council or body of representatives" (French "syndicat" (15c.), from syndic—representative of a corporation). In the latter half of the 1800s, syndicate was used to refer to a combination or association in industry and media, such as a combination of capitalists or companies to carry on some commercial undertaking or an association of publishers for purchasing articles and such for simultaneous publication in a number of newspapers. In the 1900s, syndication was used as a synonym for organized crime, "the Mob".[1]

In simple terms, syndication means teaming up with a partner (Hopp, 2010). In other words, it is a collaboration between legally distinct organizations. Wilson (1968) defined a syndicate as a group of individuals who must make a common decision under uncertainty that will result in a payoff to be shared jointly among them. In this way, the individuals shared the risk that arose due to uncertainty. These individuals were the various stakeholders of the payoff, who were directly affected by the outcome of the same. If these individuals were investors in projects, they were known as an investment syndicate and the company being invested in was referred to as the portfolio company. Therefore, investment syndication was a form of strategic alliance in which two or more investors co-invested in a portfolio company and shared a payoff (Wright & Lockett, 2003).

7.3 Syndication in Financial Markets

Syndication in the financial markets emerged as a result of the need to create strategic alliances and related collaborative relationships that could help improve firm performance. These alliances and relationships could be used to enhance inter organizational networks and relationships and thereby increase value-add; and thus, create competitive advantage for the investor. Syndicates are extremely popular in reality and are very common. Armstrong (2003) suggested that virtually any type of commercial and corporate loan or credit facility can be syndicated.

On the debt side, a syndicate—representing a group of financial institutions—can grant a loan to a single borrower. The lending syndicate includes at least one lead institution, also known as the lead arranger(s). The lead arranger(s) negotiates the terms and conditions of the loan and puts together the syndicate, which finances the borrower. For this, the lead arranger(s) receive(s) an arrangement fee (Gadanecz, 2004). Loan syndication is a popular and important way for commercial borrowers to satisfy their financing needs as well as overcome problems of adverse selection and moral hazard (Jones et al., 2002) and the past few years have witnessed a radical expansion of syndicated loans worldwide.

---

[1] https://www.etymonline.com/word/syndicate.

Syndicated loan commitments totaled US$2 trillion in 2003 (Schure et al., 2005) and syndicated lending represented approximately 51 percent of new corporate financing, generating more underwriting revenue than either the equity or the bond market (Armstrong, 2003; Dennis & Mullineaux, 2000; Jones et al., 2002). In 2021, total corporate lending in the three subsectors of the syndicated loan market in the USA alone was approximately US$2.9 trillion.[2] The shift toward syndicated lending was attributed to the fact that the syndicated loan market combined some of the best features of both commercial banking and investment banking and represent an important source for non-financial firms.

On the equity side, VC/PE syndication is also a common and widely observed phenomenon (Casamatta & Haritchabalet, 2003). Bygrave (1988) suggested that syndication was an important transaction between PE investors. Wright and Lockett (2003) noted that syndication of VC investments in the USA rose sharply in the second half of the 1990s with over three-fifths of all VC investments being syndicated by the end of the decade. Manigart et al. (2002) indicated that over 60 percent of VC investments in the USA were syndicated. Brander et al. (2002) reported from Canadian data that 60 percent of VC investments were syndicated in 1997. Lerner (1994) concluded that syndication was commonplace even in first-round investments. Wright et al. (2005) observed that the internationality of PE in recent years led to foreign PE firms entering overseas markets, thus creating a large wave of cross-border syndication. In Europe, for example, the authors noted that over the period since 1988, the share of inflows of PE from non-domestic sources more than doubled to 45 percent of the market, while the share of total outflows accounted for by international investments rose almost fourfold to 29 percent (EVCA, 2011).

7.4 PE Syndication

PE syndication has been viewed as a relationship between, or a process by which, or a situation where two or more PE firms come together to share in the financing of a particular venture or investment opportunity in the same financing round. This creates a network among the PE firms, where the ties among them are their co-investments (Kogut et al., 2007).

Establishing syndication with desirable and useful partners is arguably the most important aspect of the syndication strategy, as the partners in the syndicate were representative of the quantity of funds (Wang & Wang, 2012) and the quality of expertise available to the investee firm. Both theoretical and empirical research in the USA and Europe were consistent with the hypothesis that proper syndication of investments was a successful non-monetary tool used by PE in response to a difficult environment.

[2] https://iclg.com/practice-areas/lending-and-secured-finance-laws-and-regulations/01-loan-syndications-and-trading-an-overview-of-the-syndicated-loan-market.

7.5 The Structure of PE Syndication Networks

Syndication arose as a direct result created by PE investors' networking relationships. Syndicating through networking relationships can be thought of as an explicit attempt of a PE investor to diversify risk (Chowdhry & Nanda, 1996). Syndication networks were known to improve the quality of deal flow in many ways, and hence, PE firms that were more open to syndication enjoyed more favorable network positions that enabled them to benefit from high-quality relationships (Hopp, 2010).

First, PE firms invited others to coinvest in their promising deals in the expectation of future reciprocity (Bygrave, 1987, 1988; Lerner, 1994). For example, a PE firm entering into a new market could offer a PE existing in that market access to its home market in return for cooperation in the target market. Hochberg et al. (2007) found supportive evidence to that effect. In this way, cross-border deals too were facilitated and syndication between foreign and local partners was stimulated (Tykvova & Schertler, 2011).

Second, by checking each other's willingness to invest in potentially promising deals, PEs pooled correlated signals, thereby selecting better investments. These were done in situations of extreme uncertainty, and the "signals" were used to judge the viability and return potential of investment proposals (Millon & Thakor, 1985; Sah & Stiglitz, 1986; Wilson, 1968). Casamatta and Haritchabalet (2007) viewed these "signals" as a mechanism to screen projects: the preciseness of the signal dependent on the level of experience of the PE investor. With this signal, the PE firm had the opportunity to request a second evaluation, one which would be performed by another PE. While some authors believed that this process improved PE willingness to invest together, Casamatta and Haritchabalet (2007) argued that this was done at the cost of disclosing the existence of the investment opportunity to the other PE thereby making them a potential rival. In that case, in order for the original PE to preserve its monopoly rents, its had no choice but to negotiate with its competitor and share the project's surpluses (circumstantial syndication).

Third, individual PEs tended to have investment expertise and knowledge that was both sector specific and location specific (Hochberg et al., 2007). Industry expertise served as a positive signal and lent legitimacy to lead PE firms (Hopp, 2010). Syndication helped disseminate information across sector boundaries and expanded the spatial radius of exchange, allowing VCs to diversify their portfolios (Sorenson & Stuart, 2001). This was true especially in case of cross-border deals where syndication between foreign partners and local partners seemed to stimulate PE international syndication and expansion of VC financing across borders (Tykvova & Schertler, 2011). This was based on the premise that that the knowledge required for a firm to operate in a foreign environment is different from that accumulated in its home country (Dunning, 1993; Johanson & Vahlne, 1977; Kogut & Zander, 1993; Makela & Maula, 2008).

In addition to improving deal flow, syndication networks also helped add value to their portfolio companies. Syndication networks also facilitated the sharing of information, contracts and resources among PE firms (Bygrave, 1988). Syndication networks helped in expanding the range of target customers or strategic alliance partners for their portfolio companies.

Strong relationships with other PE firms also improved the chances of securing follow-on funding for portfolio companies and indirectly provided access to other PE firms' relationships with service providers such as headhunters and prestigious investment banks (Hochberg et al., 2007).

7.6 The Motivations for PE Syndication

Studies in the past identified and examined many rationales for PE syndication. Some of them are presented below.

(i) **Traditional finance based, risk sharing perspective**

The traditional approach was based on finance theory and viewed syndication as a means of risk sharing via portfolio diversification. In general, PE firms found it more difficult to obtain a fully diversified investment portfolio (Bygrave & Timmons, 1992). This arose partly because of the presence of ex-ante asymmetric information in investment decisions. Further, many contracts that established PE partnerships explicitly prohibited PE firms from investing in other funds (Gompers and Lerner, 1999). The actual risk associated with an investment usually became clear only after the investment was made and the PE firm received access to less biased information (Lockett and Wright, 2001). Ex-ante decision making related to the selection of investments while the ex-post decision making related to the subsequent management of investments. PE investments were also more illiquid (Hand, 2004; Janney & Folta, 2003) as compared to stock investments. As a result, it was more difficult in the short term to adjust a PE firm's portfolio by divesting "lemons" if the risk of an investment turned out to be greater than initially thought. Lockett and Wright (2001) hence stated that PE firms attempted to share the risk associated with a particular investment by involving another PE firm in the financing. The principle of diversification or syndication was based on the idea that by investing in a balanced portfolio of companies, unsystematic risk could be significantly reduced. Lockett and Wright (2001) suggested that when investments were large in comparison to the total size of the VC firm's portfolio, syndication may be appropriate. Brander et al. (2002) concluded that by syndicating, each VC was able to invest in more ventures, given the size of its pool of investment capital, and thus achieve (potentially) greater diversification.

(ii) **Resource-based, risk reduction perspective**

The resource-based risk reduction rationale viewed the exchange of resources between PE firms to be more than purely a financial transaction. The resource-based view of the firm (Penrose, 1959) suggested that firms sought competitive advantage by obtaining control over those factors that increased their competitiveness above that of their closest rivals (Wernefelt, 1984).[3] Better resources allowed VCs to provide better advice and better screening of proposals of entrepreneurs (Brander et al., 2002; Lerner, 1994). "Resources" were factors that could provide competitive advantage and had four distinctive characteristics (Barney, 1991). Firstly, resources were valuable to the firm, either in terms of lower input costs or higher prices of outputs. Secondly, resources were rare or firm-specific. If resources were commonly held, they would not differentiate one firm from another and thus would not provide competitive advantage. Thirdly, resources were imperfectly imitable to sustain the competitive advantage in the long term. Finally, resources were not substitutable. If resources could be replaced using strategically equivalent substitutes, they would not provide competitive advantage. These factors implied that resources could not be instantaneously developed. Rather, they required time to accumulate. Thus, resources were typically assets that had less value when separated from the creating organization (Dierickx and Cool, 1989).

PE firms also tried to reduce the risks associated with investing by sharing information with other PE firms and consequently benefitted from these investments (Bygrave, 1987, 1988; Sahlman, 1988).

(iii) **Uncertainty and information asymmetry**

Literature identified that the most common reason for syndication of PE firms as the need to mitigate and combat uncertainty and information asymmetry (Admati and Pfleiderer, 1994; Hochberg et al., 2007; Lerner, 1994; Lockett and Wright, 2001; Sorenson & Stuart, 2001).

In uncertain environments (with higher asset specificity and correspondingly greater dependence on entrepreneurial effort), PE firms were more likely to encounter unforeseen contingencies and benefitted more from involving partner PEs and their corresponding managerial expertise and financial endowments to either improve selection of funded firms (Lerner, 1994) or diminish individual capital contributions, thereby allowing participating PEs to invest smaller amounts of capital into a larger number of funded firms in an attempt to reduce uncertainty or information asymmetry (Lockett and Wright 1999; Meuleman et al., 2009).

Syndication helped mitigate information asymmetry that arose due to agency problems between the initial PE investor and other potential investors (Admati

---

[3] 2003 Doctoral Thesis of Tuukka Seppa found on the Aalto University https://aaltodoc.aalto.fi/bitstream/handle/123456789/2039/isbn9512264129.pdf?sequence=1&isAllowed=y.

and Pfleiderer, 1994; Fluck et al., 2005). Admati and Pfleiderer (1994) stated that a PE firm who is involved in the firm's daily operations may exploit the information he possessed and overstate the proper price for the securities in the next financing round. They provided a formal model in which PE firms avoided agency conflicts by maintaining a constant share of ownership in a particular venture over time.

Lerner (1994) suggested that syndication may also be a mechanism through which PE firms exploited information asymmetries and colluded to overstate their performance to potential investors. The author argued that since institutional investors examined only end-of-period holdings PE firms could be induced to invest in late rounds of promising firms even if financial returns were low to represent themselves in marketing documents as investors in these firms. This theory was similar to Lakonishok et al.'s (1991) "window dressing" where pension funds adjusted their portfolios at the end of the quarter by buying firms whose shares appreciated and selling "mistakes".

(iv) **Superior selection of investments**

Syndication also led to superior selection of investments by checking each other's willingness to invest in potentially promising deals. Sah and Stiglitz (1986) provided a model of organizational design and pointed out that it was sometimes preferable to have a decision process in which a project must satisfy the evaluation of two separate observers, each of whom had veto power. Another PE firm's willingness to invest in the firm may be an important factor in the lead investor's decision to invest (Pence, 1982).

Though used by Sah and Stiglitz (1986) in a general framework, this model was successfully implemented by Lerner (1994) in his empirical work in biotechnology firms. Basing on Sah and Stiglitz's (1986) paper, Lerner (1994) stated the "selection hypothesis" and concluded that syndication may lead to a superior selection of investments, even in first-round investments.

For firms whose products were far from commercialization, the risks that investors faced were more severe and scrutiny in deal selection through syndication and subsequent managerial advice was an important mechanism to align managerial effort with the goals of the financing PEs (Lerner, 1994). Hence, PEs benefitted from combining their investment expertise when risks are more pronounced.

Brander et al. (2002) modeled the selection hypothesis as a sequential sampling problem where the model suggested that the returns to the syndicated investments should be lower than the returns to stand-alone investments. The primary cost of syndicating was that the PE firm must share in the venture's proceeds. If it were unclear whether the project should be accepted or rejected, a second opinion was valuable, leading the PE firm to pursue syndication.

(v) **The deal flow rationale**

The deal flow rationale required PE firms to be in a position to compete for as many deals as possible so that they could make their investment selections from a wide supply of deals. The deal flow rationale also argued for future reciprocity in PE syndication (Bygrave, 1987, 1988; Lerner, 1994). Hochberg et al. (2007) found supportive evidence for this. This was especially important when the competition for deals was great and the availability of money to invest was high. The deal flow rationale could be thought of arising from the superior selection of investments, where PE firms' decisions to invest in deals was based on mutual sharing of information.

(vi) **Value-add hypothesis**

Another reason for syndication was the value-added hypothesis considered by Brander et al. (2002). Here, PE firms were presumed to add value to ventures rather than simply trying to select the best ventures. Different PE firms had different skills and information. The benefit of seeking syndication was that the value of the project rises if other PE firms got involved.

(vii) **Other motives**

The risk avoidance through risk sharing hypothesis suggested but not tested by Lerner (1994) was also another possible reason for syndication. Gompers and Lerner (1999) suggested that many contracts establishing PE partnerships explicitly prohibited investing in other funds. By syndicating investments with other PE firms, however, the same effect could be achieved. Brander et al. (2002) argued that it might be difficult to test the importance of risk sharing. The relevant risk consideration from the PE firm's point of view was the contribution of a given investment to the overall portfolio risk, and this depended upon the investment's entire covariance structure vis-à-vis other investments in the PE firm's portfolio.

Other motives for syndication suggested by Brander et al. (2002) were the possibility for collusion—by banding together rather than competing, PE firms could try to improve bargaining position with investee firms. The authors suggested another possibility was that syndication had an influence on control rights in the venture, as the question of who controls the venture was an important consideration in VC finance.

Syndication has been examined with varying objectives in corporate finance literature. However, there exists limited knowledge on synthesizing the findings of academic research on the decision to syndicate and the extent of syndication in PE investing to support the investment decisions and strategies at a sector level. This study attempts to explore the conditions which impact the decision of PE investors to syndicate with one another in the same financing round when investing in infrastructure projects. This study analyzed the extent of syndication by studying the characteristics of PE investors in a syndicate. Investor-level characteristics, firm characteristics and deal characteristics were considered against a backdrop of the level of development of an economy.

7.7 Data

For the analysis, we used a sample of 358 infrastructure deals with PE investments. PE firms invested approximately US$9.743 billion over a 20-year period from 1990 to 2009 into infrastructure projects. Out of the 358 deals, 103 deals had PE syndication (28.78 percent of the sample) and 255 deals did not have syndication (71.22 percent of the sample), indicating a larger percentage of deals with stand-alone PE investors. Table 7.1 presents a description of the sample with the number of deals divided into four time periods—1990 to 1994; 1995 to 1999; 2000 to 2004; and 2005 to 2009.

An examination of Table 7.1 revealed a steep increase in the number of deals from 1990 till 2009. Period 1 (1990–1994) saw only 17 deals in infrastructure with PE investments in them. The subsequent period saw a little more than 4 times increase in the number of deals. The number of deals remained steady in the subsequent period but more than doubled in Period 4 (2005–2009).

The total investment also saw an increase throughout the four periods in question. Period 2 (1995–1999) saw a 678 percent increase in the total investment by PE firms in infrastructure deals while in Period 3 (2000–2004), total investment showed a small increase (40 percent). Period 4 (2005–2009) showed a 176 percent increase in

Table 7.1 Description of the sample of infrastructure deals with PE investments, divided into four time periods—1990–1994, 1995–1999, 2000–2004, 2005–2009

Particulars	1990–1994	1995–1999	2000–2004	2005–2009	1990–2009
	Period 1	Period 2	Period 3	Period 4	Overall
Number of deals	17	74	78	189	358
Total investment (in 2009 US$, Million)	248.99	1,936.32	2012.02	5546.63	9743.96
Average investment (in 2009 US$, Million)	14.65	26.17	25.80	29.35	27.22
Median investment (in 2009 US$, Million)	3.82	3.46	9.67	10.48	8.66
Total number of PE investors	26	97	162	282	567
Average number of PE investors	1.529	1.31	2.07	1.49	1.58
Number of investors per US$ Million	1.029	2.060	0.859	0.767	1.379

Source Securities Data Corporation; created and complied by authors total investment compared to the previous one. The total investment in infrastructure also saw a higher rate of growth as compared to the rate of growth of number of deals. While period 4 witnessed a growth rate of 1011 percent in number of deals as compared to period 1, there was a 2127 percent growth rate in the size of the investment between these two periods.

The average investment showed an increase as well, with the highest increase recorded between Period 1 (1990–1994) and Period 2 (1995–2009). However, the median investment decreased between these two time periods. Average investment and median investment recorded a steady increase between Period 3 (2000–2004) and Period 4 (2005–2009).

There was also an increase in the total number of PE investors throughout the periods in question. The average number of PE investors per deal showed no apparent trend between the first two periods; it kept increasing and then decreasing again. The number of PE investors per US$ million showed an increase between Period 1 and Period 2 and thereby a steady decrease between Period 2 and Period 3 and Period 3 and Period 4.

Table 7.2 presents a break-up of the sample into deals in industrial/energy sector, transport sector and water and utilities sector. This information is presented region wise, using 5 regions, namely Africa, Americas, Asia, Europe and the Pacific.

An examination of Table 7.2 revealed the fact that Americas had the highest number of deals in all the three sectors. Energy deals in the USA were the highest in number with 201 investments in infrastructure. The Americas also had the highest investment size—US$6502 million; 265 percent more than the second highest region, Europe, with an investment size of US$1779 million. Asia had a total investment size of about US$1410 million. However, the average investment size in Asia was the highest—about US$52 million. This could be because of the large number of greenfield projects in the developing Asian countries. The Pacific region had the lowest average investment size of US$2 million with a large number of water and utilities deals in the region.

Table 7.2 Break-up of the sample into deals in industrial and energy sector, transport sector and water and utilities sector and presented region-wise

Particulars	Africa	Americas	Asia	Europe	Pacific
Number of deals in industrial and energy sector	0	225	14	44	2
Number of deals in transport sector	1	15	11	7	2
Number of deals in utilities sector	0	15	2	8	12
Total investment size (in 2009 US$, Million)	21.0	6501.9	1409.8	1778.8	32.5
Average investment size (in 2009 US$, Million)	21.0	25.5	52.2	30.1	2.0
Average round number	1	4	1	2.5	3
Total number of PE investors	2	431	35	80	19
Average number of PE investors	2	1.69	1.29	1.35	1.18

Source Securities Data Corporation; created and complied by authors

Americas also had the highest number of PE investors followed by Europe which underscores the fact that PE investors preferred investing in developed regions. The average number of PE investors per deal was between 1 and 2, with the Pacific registering the lowest number of PE investors per deal and Africa having the highest. Americas also had a high average number of PE investors per deal.

7.8 Comparison of the Sample with Other Sectors

Table 7.3 presents the sample of deals in the infrastructure sector in comparison with PE investments in other sectors, namely information technology, medical/health/life science and overall group.

An examination of Table 7.3 showed that infrastructure has by far the least number of deals in the periods in question. Both Information Technology sector and medical, health, and life sciences sector have larger number of deals as well as total investment. However, an examination of the average investment (per deal) and median investment showed that infrastructure sector has larger values thus implying larger sized projects. Thus, it can be constructed that infrastructure deals were larger in size than deals in the information sector or medical, health, and life sciences sector.

A comparison of the number of PE investors among the various sectors revealed that a large number of PEs invested in the Information Technology sector and medical, health, and life sciences sector and the average number of PE investors in a deal was lowest in the infrastructure sector. The number of PE investors investing in deals was almost the same in the other sectors to but vastly different from the infrastructure sector. Further, the number of PE investors per US$ million was also lowest in the infrastructure sector compared to the other sectors. From this, it can be concluded that the nature of PE investing in the infrastructure sector was different from that of PE firms investing in other sectors, notably the Information Technology sector and medical, health, and life sciences sector.

7.9 PE Investors in Infrastructure Projects, Round Wise

Table 7.4 presents a summary snapshot of PE investors in infrastructure projects. The average number of PE firms in a deal was 1.69; however, the sample noted up to 13 PE firms in a syndicate.

Table 7.4 illustrates that round 1 had the maximum number of investments and the largest total amount invested. This is unsurprising because most infrastructure projects are usually designed on a project finance basis and require a large upfront capital infusion. The investment size decreased significantly from round 1 onwards: It fell by about 72 percent to round 2 and then by about 55 percent from round 2 to round 3. This trend continued in our sample, averaging to about a 30 percent drop, through the future rounds.

Table 7.3 Comparison of the sample with other industry sectors—the IT sector, the life-sciences sector and the overall group—and presented in four time periods—1990–1994, 1995–1999 and 2000–2004, 2005–2009

Particulars	1990–1994 Period 1	1995–1999 Period 2	2000–2004 Period 3	2005–2009 Period 4	1990–2009 Overall
Infrastructure					
Number of deals	17	74	78	189	358
Total investment (2009 US$, Billion)	0.25	1.94	2.01	5.55	9.74
Average investment (2009 US$, Million)	14.65	26.17	25.8	29.35	27.22
Median investment (2009 US$, Million)	3.82	3.46	9.67	10.48	8.66
Total number of PE investors	26	97	162	282	567
Average number of PE investors	1.529	1.31	2.07	1.49	1.58
Number of investors per US$ Million	1.029	2.06	0.859	0.767	1.379
Information technology					
Number of deals	1736	4633	8411	4960	19,740
Total investment (2009 US$, Billion)	6.9	51.86	91.72	48.65	199.12
Average investment (2009 US$, Million)	3.98	11.2	10.95	9.81	10.11
Median investment (2009 US$, Million)	1.01	3.7	3.69	2.47	3.02
Total number of PE investors	5472	15,801	30,801	15,468	67,542
Average number of PE investors	3.152	3.411	3.662	3.119	3.422
Number of investors per US$ Million	15.47	4.959	3.861	6.591	7.72
Medical, health, and life sciences					
Number of deals	743	1366	2045	2130	6284
Total investment (2009 US$, Billion)	2.64	11.19	19.19	20.47	53.5
Average investment (2009 US$, Million)	3.56	8.2	9.41	9.61	8.52
Median investment (2009 US$, Million)	1.42	2.71	3.94	2.99	2.95
Total number of PE investors	2268	4461	8381	7903	23,013

(continued)

Table 7.3 (continued)

Particulars	1990–1994	1995–1999	2000–2004	2005–2009	1990–2009
	Period 1	Period 2	Period 3	Period 4	Overall
Average number of PE investors	3.052	3.266	4.098	3.71	3.662
Number of investors per US$ Million	13.662	5.755	4.783	10.297	8.624
Overall group					
Number of deals	3767	8843	13,896	10,005	36,511
Total investment (2009 US$, Billion)	21.61	115.85	174.88	191.16	503.5
Average investment (2009 US$, Million)	5.74	13.11	12.7	19.13	13.85
Median investment (2009 US$, Million)	1.26	3.38	3.66	3	3.07
Total number of PE investors	9983	25,125	45,336	28,426	108,870
Average number of PE investors	2.65	2.841	3.263	2.841	2.982
Number of investors per US$ Million	12.336	5.274	4.19	8.102	7.476

Source Securities Data Corporation; created and complied by authors

Table 7.4 Summary statistics of PE investors in infrastructure projects

Particulars	Rounds of PE Financing			
	1	1–3	4–6	≥7
Number of deals with PE investment	115	224	412	61
Total capital invested (2009 US$, Billion)	5.276	7.45	13.842	1.179
Mean number of PE investors in each deal round	1.39	1.58667	1.93433	1.29
Mean number of new PE investors in each deal round	1.39	1.11	0.69667	0.2
Mean capital invested per PE investor (2009 US$, Million)	36.98	23.0167	12.31	19.08
Mean Age of the PE investors in each round (in years)	17.61	19.6233	24.9033	34.78

Source Securities Data Corporation; created and complied by authors

There was an increase in average number of PE investors (simple average of the number of PE investors per round) as the round number increased along with addition of new PE investors in each round. Although new PE investors were being added to each round, there was no corresponding increase in investment size; in fact, future rounds recorded a decrease in investment size. This implied that new PE investors did not seem to be contributing capital. Approximately, 0.71 new PE investors were added in each round. This showed that there was syndication with new partners as round number increased. However, the mean amount invested per PE investor showed an overall decreasing trend (except in round 4). It fell to half the amount in round 2 and to one-third the amount in the following round 3. However, it increased about a fifth in round 4 but fell back to its decreasing trend from round 5 onwards. Lerner (1994) showed 2.2 new venture investors in round 1 and investment of US$0.5 million per venture investor while round 2 had 1.2 new venture investors and investment of US$0.6 million per venture investor. Round 3 and above had 1.3 new venture investors and investment of US$0.6 million per venture investor. This indicated there was an increase in amount invested per venture investor as round number increased. Thus, it can be construed that the syndication features of PE investing in infrastructure was different from PE investing in other sectors, notably high risk sectors such as the biotechnology sector.

Although there were more PE investors as round number increased, they were not investing as much. This highlighted the fact that the PE investors in round 1 invested the maximum and thus undertook the highest amount of risk. The mean age of PE investors in each round showed a gradual increasing trend. This could also be because of the time duration between rounds. However, most PE investors investing in infrastructure were not recently established PE firms but older ones with average ages of 17.6 years in first-round investments.

7.10 A Comparative Analysis of PE Investments in Infrastructure

Descriptive statistics of infrastructure deals revealed that such deals were larger than most deals in other sectors (refer Table 7.3). Also, previous studies by Hochberg et al. (2007); Sorenson and Stuart (2001); and Lerner (1994) have shown that syndication networks typically enable portfolio diversification and encouraged larger deal flows. Thus, it would be interesting to note if PE syndication could contribute to larger deals, through comparative analysis.

The first set of comparative analysis was between infrastructure deals with PE syndication and those without PE syndication to identify parameters that differed between these two sets of investments. The second set of comparative analysis was performed to examine the extent of PE syndication where deals with fewer members in the syndicate (2–3) have been compared against deals with more number of members in the syndicate (>3). The nonparametric Mann–Whitney U-test was used for significance testing of medians and deals were examined on four parameters—investment size, fund size, investment size as a percentage of fund size and age of the investee company at the time of PE financing.

Figure 7.1 presents the results of the comparative analysis of infrastructure deals with PE investments, where deals with PE syndication have been compared against deals without PE syndication on the following parameters—investment size, fund size, investment size as a percentage of fund size, and age of the investee company at the time of PE financing.

An examination of the results of the comparative analysis (in Fig. 7.1) provides interesting insights on the four parameters analyzed.

First, results indicated that there was no significant difference in investment size between syndicated deals and non-syndicated deals. Median values of deals without PE syndication (US$9.2 million) were slightly higher than median values of deals with PE syndication (US$7.9 million) in our sample, but this difference did not

Fig. 7.1 Comparative analysis of infrastructure deals with PE investments—syndication versus no syndication
*** significant at 99% CI ** significant at 95% CI

emerge statistically significant. This indicated that the size of the project, one of the most compelling characteristics of infrastructure projects, was not a factor that significantly influenced PE investment. It could be hypothesized that PE firms were comfortable with the amount of capital they infused into infrastructure deals and did not find capital requirements a compelling reason to syndicate.

Second, the fund size of syndicated investments (US$823.7 million) was significantly lower than that of non-syndicated investments (US$2022). A larger fund size could indicate a greater reputation for the PE firm, and PE firms with higher reputation did not syndicate as much.

Third, the combination of the first two parameters, the investment size as a percentage of fund size was also significantly different between deals with PE syndication and deals without PE syndication, with the latter reaching lower economies of scale (median value 0.0056 compared to median value 0.012).

Finally, the age of the infrastructure company at the time of PE financing showed no significant difference between syndicated PE investments and non-syndicated PE investments. The age of the investor company has often been used in research to indicate a level of experience. Casamatta and Haritchabalet (2007) found that more experienced VCs did not usually syndicate. However, comparative analysis did not indicate any differences in our sample.

The second set of comparative analysis examined the extent of PE syndication. Descriptive analysis of the sample showed an increasing number of PE firms in the syndicate without any corresponding increase in investment size. In fact, there was a corresponding decrease in investment size as size of the syndicate increased.

Figure 7.2 presents a comparative analysis of infrastructure deals to examine the extent of PE syndication. Syndicated deals with up to three PE investors were compared against syndicated deals with more than three investors to analyze the changes in five parameters due to the extent of syndication.

An examination of the results of the comparative analysis on extent of syndication (in Fig. 7.2) provides interesting insights on the five parameters—investment size, fund size, investment size as a percentage of fund size, investment size per PE partner and age of the investee company.

Investment size was marginally significant at 10 percent level with lower levels of syndication having larger investment size. There was no significant difference between fund size and investment size as a percentage of fund size. The investment size per partner was significant at 1 percent level with PE firms in lower sized syndicates providing larger investment sizes as compared to PE firms in higher sized syndicates. The age of the investee company at the time of PE financing was significantly lower for lower syndication levels as compared to higher syndication levels.

Comparative analysis on the extent of PE syndication further supported the premise that the need for capital was not a reason for syndication. Larger syndicates did not show significant increase in fund size or investment size as a percentage of fund size which implied that an increase in the number of PE firms was not for additional capital requirements. PE firms in lower sized syndicates offered significantly larger investment sizes which implied that PE firms in larger sizes syndicates were possibly included for reasons other than capital requirements.

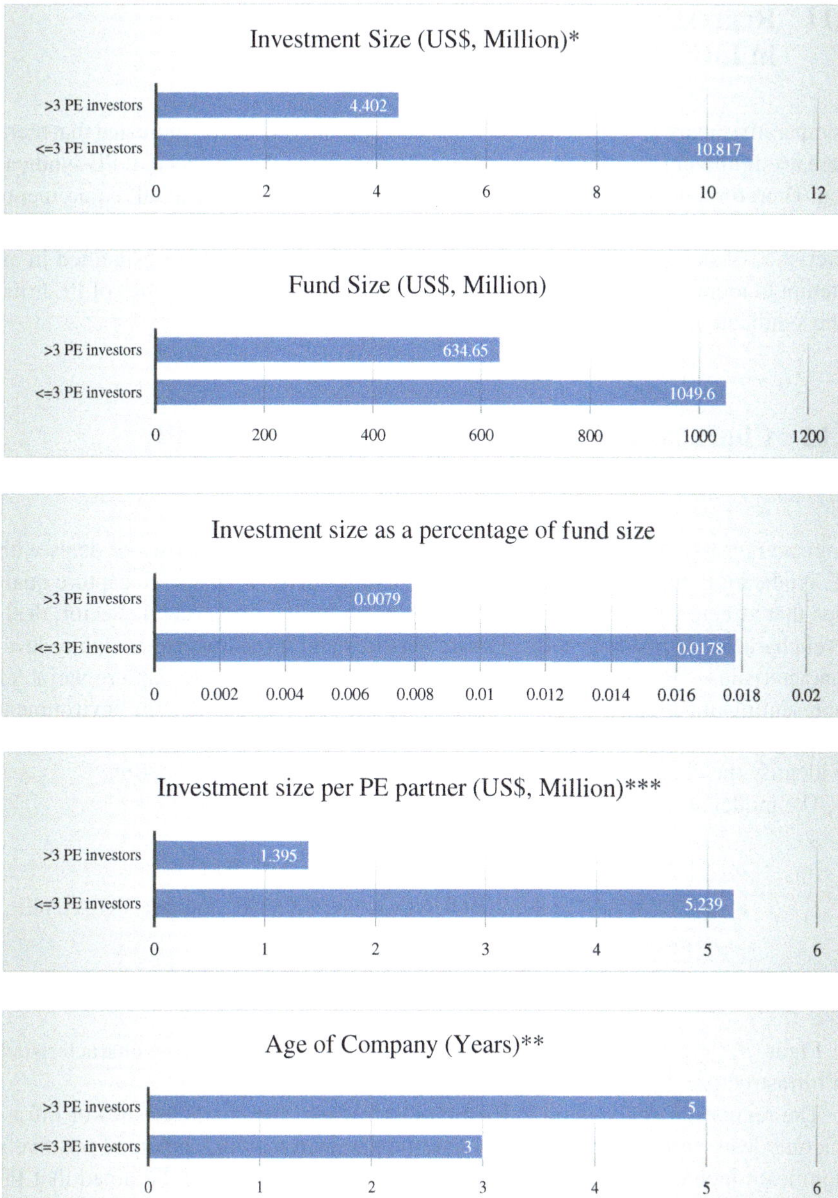

Fig. 7.2 Comparative analysis of infrastructure deals with number of PE investments—extent of syndication
*** significant at 99% CI, ** significant at 95% CI, * significant at 90% CI

7.11 Regression Analysis of PE Investments in Infrastructure

Comparative analysis between deals with and without syndication indicated that there were no significant differences in investment size due to the presence of PE syndication. Therefore, it could be hypothesized that investment size or capital requirements may not be a reason to syndicate in case of infrastructure. In this section, the characteristics of deals that have syndicated investments in them were examined in an attempt to identify the drivers of syndication. Finally, the characteristics of PE firms who syndicate in a deal were also examined.

7.12 Characteristics of Infrastructure Deals with PE Syndication

Logistic regression analysis[4] was used to estimate the characteristics of deals with PE syndication due to the binary nature of the dependent variables. To capture qualities that affected PE firms' decision to syndicate in the infrastructure sector, deal-level characteristics, PE firm-level characteristics and infrastructure company-level characteristics. The rationale for choosing these variables was to capture variables representing uncertainty, information asymmetry, firm's assets, and the environment housing the deal. Table 7.5 presents the variables included in the regression analysis to identify the characteristics of infrastructure deals with PE syndication.

The model to be estimated is given in Eq. 7.1.

$$\begin{aligned} Z_{\mathrm{SYND}_i} = {} & \alpha_{0,i} + \alpha_1(\mathrm{INVEST_i}) + \alpha_2(\mathrm{FUND}_i) + \alpha_3(\mathrm{CAPITAL}_i) \\ & + \alpha_4(\mathrm{COMPAGE}_i) + \alpha_5(\mathrm{ROUND}_i) + \alpha_6(\mathrm{LOCAL}_i) + \alpha_7(\mathrm{GREATAGE}_i) \\ & + \alpha_8(\mathrm{PEINFRA}_i) + \alpha_9(\mathrm{STAGE}_i) + \alpha_{10}(\mathrm{DEV}_i) \\ & + \alpha_{11}(\mathrm{ENER}_i) + \alpha_{12}(\mathrm{TRANS}_i) + \varepsilon_i \end{aligned} \tag{7.1}$$

Figure 7.3 presents the results of the logistic regression exploring characteristics of infrastructure deals with PE syndication.

The regression analysis provided rich insights into the characteristics of infrastructure deals with PE syndication. First, the parameters which emerged positively significant include experience levels of the PE investor(s). It can be noted that PE firm's age positively affected the decision to syndicate. It was seen that the greatest age of the PE firm (GREATAGE) and prior infrastructure experience (PEINFRA) were positively significant at 1 percent and 5 percent significance levels, respectively.

[4] A logistic regression is a specialized regression which is used when the dependant variable takes binary (0 or 1) values. In this regression, a value 1 is assigned to deals that have investments through a PE syndicate, and a value 0 is assigned to deals that have investments when the PE firm is a stand-alone investor.

Table 7.5 Variables included in the regression analysis to identify characteristics of deals with PE syndication

Type	Variable	Description
Dependent variable	SYND	The dependent variable in the logistic regression captures if deals have PE syndication, using a binary notation. A value of 1 indicates that the deal was financed through a PE syndicate, while a value of 0 indicates that the deal was financed through a stand-alone PE investor
Independent variables	INVEST	The log of investment size in the deal, in US$2009 values
	FUND	The log of fund size, in US$2009 values
	CAPITAL	The availability of capital to finance the deal
	COMPAGE	Age of the investee/infrastructure company at the time of PE financing
	ROUND	Round number of the deal
	LOCAL	The presence of a local PE firm financing the deal. This was also captured by a binary variable, 1 indicating if a PE firm financing the deal was situated in the same country as that housing the infrastructure project, 0 indicating if the PE firm financing the deal was an overseas investor. This variable was considered endogeneous to the analysis
	GREATAGE	Age of the PE investor with the greatest age, age being defined as the difference between the year when PE was founded and deal year
	PEINFRA	Infrastructure investing experience of the PE firm(s) captured by a dummy variable, 1 representing if the PE firm(s) has prior infrastructure investing experience, and 0 otherwise
Control variables	STAGE	The stage of current financing round represented by a dummy, 1 indicating acquisition, expansion, and later stage financing, and 0 indicating buyouts and later stage and other financing
	DEV	Level of development represented by a dummy, 1 indicating developed country, 0 otherwise
	ENER	Energy sector being represented by a dummy, 1 indicating energy sector, 0 otherwise
	TRANS	Transport sector being represented by a dummy, 1 indicating transport sector, 0 otherwise

It could be concluded the older PE investors and PE investors with prior infrastructure experience had greater probability for syndication. This showed that older PE firms seemed to be the main drivers of syndication. This indicated that firms with prior infrastructure experience were sought after by other firms for their specific capabilities and knowledge of this sector. Although a large percentage of PE firms

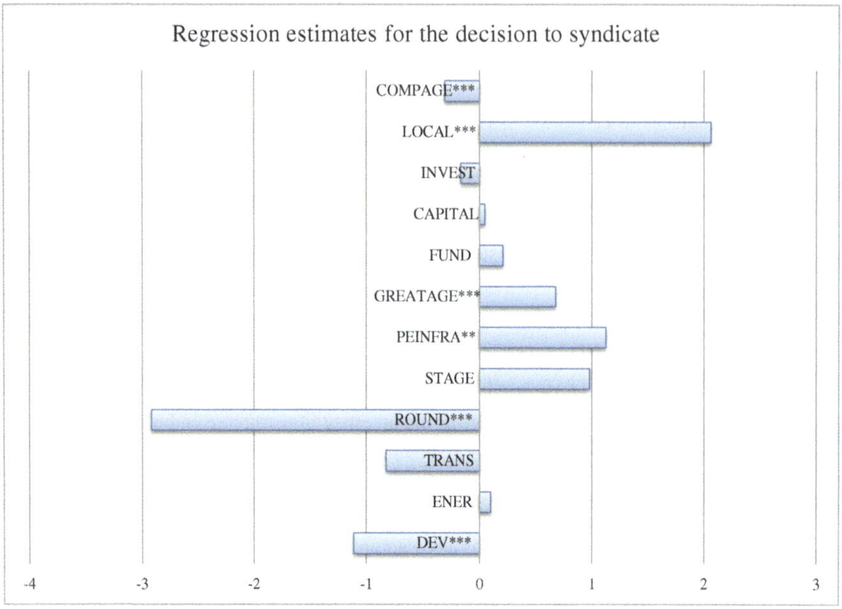

Fig. 7.3 Regression estimates for the decision to syndicate
*** significant at 99% CI, ** significant at 95% CI, * significant at 90% CI

did not syndicate when investing in infrastructure, firms that did preferred to do so with PE firms that had prior investing experience. Lerner (1994) found results on similar lines where he concluded that more established PE firms—which he defined as older and more experienced—drove syndication strategies. However, Casamatta and Haritchabalet (2007) argued that more experienced VC investors did not usually syndicate investments, unless it was with similarly placed investors.

The presence of a local partner (LOCAL) was positively significant. This endogenous variable[5] suggested that when PE investors syndicate they preferred to do so with a local partner. These results were consistent with the findings of Hochberg et al. (2007) and Dai et al. (2009). Manigart et al. (2002) pointed out that there was a wide range of economic, legal, institutional and cultural differences influencing the environments in which PE firms operated. Hochberg et al. (2007) opined that [foreign] PEs recognized their lack of knowledge in local business environments; and partnered with local PEs and were potentially able to alleviate the information asymmetry problem. Tykvova and Schertler (2011) argued that local PE firms potentially had information advantages over foreign PEs. They were able to process "soft" information about local firms and had better knowledge of market conditions, practices, rules, technology and patterns of behavior. Dai et al. (2009) referred to this as the local or proximity hypothesis. This premise also supported the resource-based rationale for syndication.

[5] The variable LOCAL was controlled for endogeneity using the Hausman 2-stage model.

Second, parameters which emerged negatively significant include COMPAGE, ROUND and DEV. Infrastructure company age (COMPAGE) was negatively significant only at 5 percent significance level. The age of the investee company was usually taken as a proxy for information asymmetry or riskiness of the venture (Hopp, 2010). As the company got older, more information was known publicly and encouraged newer PE investors to invest.

The variable round number (ROUND) was negatively significant which implied that more staging resulted in less syndication. Round number was taken to be indicative of the degree of staging in an infrastructure deal. As round number increased, the propensity to stage also increased, thereby reducing the propensity to syndicate. In other studies, round number was taken as a proxy for risk and uncertainty (Dai et al., 2009). Lerner (1994) suggested that with the certification of first-round investors later rounds were relatively less risky.

It was observed that developed country variable (DEV) also emerged negatively significant. This indicated that PE syndication was not popular in developed countries and as investors seemingly had adequate skills and knowledge to be stand-alone investors.

Finally, the variables fund size (FUND), capital availability (CAPITAL) and investment size (INV) did not assume too much importance in this analysis. None of these variables emerged significant. This was contrary to the results of Hopp (2010) who found amount provided significant at 1 percent level. This showed that capital requirements or motives may not the reason for syndication of PE investors in infrastructure.

7.13 Characteristics of PE Firms Who Syndicate

This final section examined the process of syndication and identified the characteristics of PE investors who syndicate with each other. To analyze this further, an index was created which was used to represent the characteristics of the syndicate. Three characteristics were taken to be representative of a PE syndicate included the number of PE investors, their experience and the diversity of experience.

The number of PE investors represented the numerical value of the size of the syndicate. The larger the number of PE firms in the syndicate, the higher the numerical value. The average age of the PE syndicate was the simple average of the age of PE firm(s) at the time of financing the deal. It was used as a proxy to represent the level of experience of the PE firms in the syndicate. The greater the average age, the more the level of experience of the PE syndicate. The standard deviation of age of PE firms in the syndicate was used as a proxy to represent the diversity of experience of the syndicate. The greater the standard deviation, the larger was the diversity of experience of the PE firms in the syndicate.

The index created was calculated using Eq. 7.2

$$\mathrm{INDEX}_i = (\mathrm{NOPE}_i * \mathrm{AVGAGE}_i * \mathrm{SDAGE}_i) \tag{7.2}$$

where

INDEX	represented the index value of *i*th deal
NOPE	represented the number of PE investors in the syndicate in the *i*th deal.
AVGAGE	represented the average age of the PE investors in the *i*th deal.
SDAGE	represented the standard deviation of the age of PE investors in the *i*th deal.

96 deals that had PE investors who syndicated with each other were considered for the analysis. The index ranged from a minimum value of 2.828 (2 relatively young partners) to a maximum value of 5074.101 (5 partners with varied ages). A semi-logarithmic regression was used with dependent variable—Log(Index)—to find out which of the qualities in the syndicate affected the index the most—the size of the syndicate (NOPE), the experience of the partners (AVGAGE) or the diversity of experience (SDAGE) (Fig. 7.4).

From the estimates, it was seen that the number of partners affected the index the most followed by standard deviation of age and then average age. Adding one more partner in the syndicate increased the index by 10.6 percent. Adding 1 more year difference increased the index by 4.7 percent. Adding an additional year increased the index by 2.2 percent. Thus, the size of the syndicate affected the index the most, followed by the diversity of the partners and then by the overall experience of the partners in the syndicate. This theory was consistent with Guo and Jiang (2013) who suggest that at different stages, there were different criteria for addition of investment; the number of additional resources and value-added services were both different.

Next, an independent t-test was performed to compare the difference in index values between earlier rounds (1 and 2) and later rounds (3 and above). 1 and 2 were chosen as earlier rounds because the median value of round number is 2. Lerner (1994) found significant differences in syndication characteristics of PE firms in earlier rounds as compared to later rounds. The independent *t*-test facilitates an evaluation of the same—significant differences in index values between earlier rounds and later

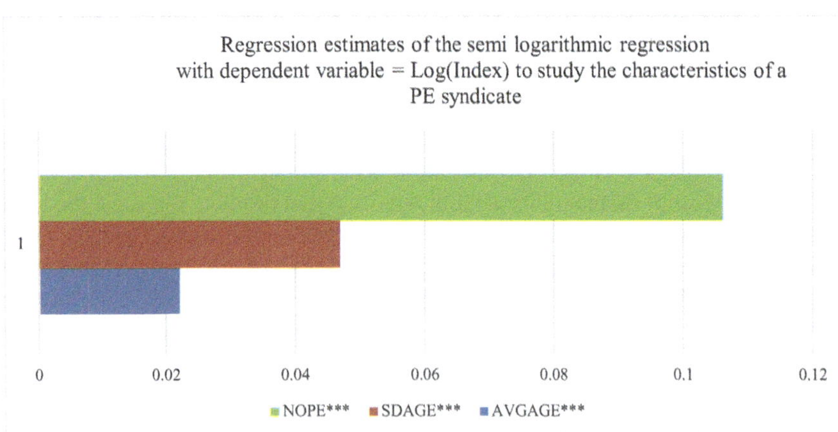

Fig. 7.4 Presents the regression estimates of the semi-logarithmic regression
*** significant at 99% CI

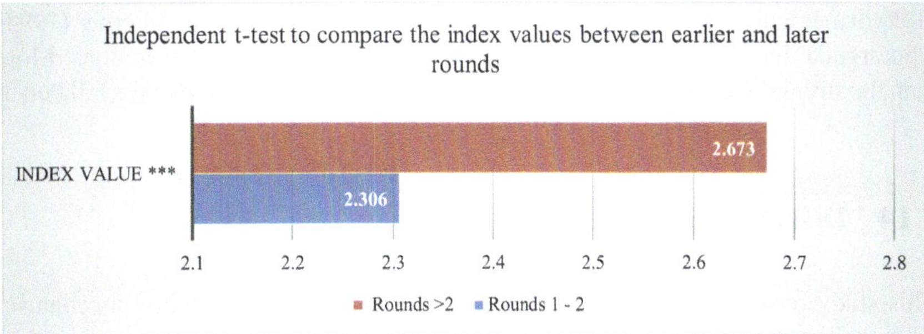

Fig. 7.5 Independent t-test to compare the index values between earlier and later rounds
*** significant at 99% CI

rounds will enhance understanding of the characteristics of PE syndicates as round number increases.

Figure 7.5 presents the results of the independent *t*-test. It was noticed that there was a significant difference between index values in earlier rounds and later rounds. This was significant at 1 percent level and showed that later rounds had significantly higher index values. This supported past studies and confirmed to the premise that characteristics of PE syndicates varied as round number increased.

Finally, to confirm these results and test for the direction of significance, a multivariate regression was run with dependent variable representing the log of the index value. The results are depicted in Fig. 7.6.

An examination of the results in Fig. 7.6 indicated that round number was positively significant at 5 percent level. It can thus be inferred that an increasing round number corresponded to an increasing index value. The index value highlighted a precedence of diversity of experience over just years of experience. This diversity of experience will be beneficial to the syndicate as well, because investors with dissimilar backgrounds and experience may profit by learning from each other

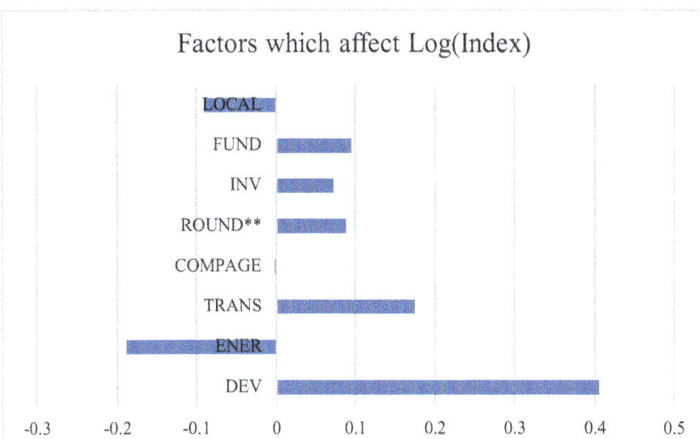

Fig. 7.6 Factors that affect the Log(Index)
** significant at 95% CI

(Tykvova & Schertler, 2011). This result complemented and added to Lerner (1994) who argued that later rounds involved less established venture organizations. More than the strength of establishment, diversity in experience seemed to fit the bill better.

7.14 Discussion

This study provided insights into syndication as a capability building mechanism when infrastructure projects required a varied set of skills other than which could be provided by a single PE investor. It also contrasted ways in which PE investments in infrastructure were different from PE investments in non-infrastructure sectors.

Earlier studies by experts such as Wright and Lockett (2001), Manigart et al. (2002), Brander et al. (2002) and Lerner (2004) found syndication to be extremely common among VC investors. An examination of the trends of syndication in this study revealed, however, that a large number of PE investors did not syndicate when investing in infrastructure. Approximately, 71 percent of the deals in the sample consisted of single PE investors who invested in various sectors in infrastructure with various investment sizes. In spite of such a large percentage of infrastructure deals having only a single PE investor, PE syndication was present even in the first round of investments. There was also an increasing number of PE investors in the syndicate as round number increased, without any corresponding increase in average investment size. Further, smaller sized syndicates had larger investment sizes per deal when compared to larger sized syndicates. This led to the proposition that capital motives might not be a reason to syndicate.

Regression analysis to determine the reasons for PE syndication in infrastructure suggested that syndication was not dominated by a capital motivated phenomenon but arose from a need for resources more than capital. It seemed to be a quest to develop and build on knowledge-based resources, especially with local PE firms, who were assumed to have "soft" skills and knowledge of local laws, workings, governance and the like, which is extremely important while developing infrastructure assets. PE firms found getting local management more of a priority in order to deal with the environmental, regulatory, political and regulatory risks in creating infrastructure assets. Thillai Rajan et al. (2011) stated that the presence of domestic [local] investors seemed to provide a lot of comfort to foreign investors investing in infrastructure projects. The dominance of the resource-based motive was not supported by Lockett and Wright (2001) and Bent et al. (2004), who suggested that the finance-based motive or the need for risk sharing through portfolio diversification was the primary rationale in most PE firms' agenda when they syndicated. These authors, however, found that the risk-based motive took prominence when the PE firms were divided into investing stages (early stage investments/later stage investments) or when there was a need for specific skills to manage investment. These results could be applied to infrastructure asset investing which is usually confined to middle stage/later stage investing and requiring specific skills due to the many unique characteristics of these assets. The findings of this study were in line with Hopp (2010) who analyzed syndication based on the characteristics of the venture and stressed on the importance of the resource-based view of syndication.

Variables such as greatest age of the PE investor, presence of local partner and syndication in the previous round significantly and positively affected the syndication process. Casamatta and Haritchabalet (2007) found that VC firms who did not syndicate were significantly older. This study, however, found that older firms seemed to drive the syndication process and when syndicating preferred a local partner. Therefore, once PE firms decided to syndicate, they looked for partners who could bring in resources other than just capital. The preference for a local PE partner arose from the benefits of having a local partner in the deal. Knowledge of rules for starting businesses, requirements for concession agreements, local environment and language, government rules in developing infrastructure assets, and facilities available for the same varies from region to region. Local companies have superior knowledge of these aspects and practices of business as compared to foreign firms (Tykvova & Schertler, 2011). Also, in developing countries, there is little experience of private capital investments in strategic sectors (Gatti, 2008). Local companies (especially in developing countries) are known also have the ability to influence the local environments in favor of the project (Thillai Rajan et al., 2011). This aspect could make them extremely valuable in the bidding for infrastructure projects which are usually done through floatation of tenders and expression of interests. Local companies could also have closer relationships with local debt markets thus facilitating ease of receiving debt capital for infrastructure asset financing.

Syndication in the previous round increased the probability of future PE syndication in infrastructure. These results were consistent with Hopp (2010).

Regression analysis also indicated a significant negative relationship between round number and PE syndication. Round number in this study was taken as a measure to indicate the level of staging happening in the infrastructure company. This negative relationship suggested that as round number increased, the propensity for PE firms to stage their investments also increased, thereby causing a reduction in PE syndication. From this result, it can be concluded that when there was an opportunity to stage investment, PE firms will prefer to stage and thus reduce syndication.

The extent of syndication was also examined to analyze the characteristics of PE firms in a syndicate. Analysis of the index which depicted the qualities of the syndicate revealed that the diversity of experience of PE firms took precedence over their level of experience. A significantly positive index value as round number increased showed that PE firms provided the infrastructure company with a variety of skills and experience by adding more number of PE firms to the syndicate which seemingly possessed the required know-how. Thus, with increasing round number, infrastructure firms demanded skills more than what was normally possessed by a single PE investor, and PE firms provided the solution by becoming a means of capability provider by syndicating with desirable and useful partners.

7.15 Summary

This study examined the process of syndication by PE firms when they invested in infrastructure projects. A comparative analysis of deals with and without syndication revealed that syndicated deals had lower fund sizes and smaller investment size as a percentage of fund sizes. The non-significance of investment size is one of the most compelling of results of this study. It indicated no inclination by PE toward lowering capital infusion into infrastructure deals.

The regression analysis indicated that previous infrastructure investing experience positively affected the choice of a syndication partner. The infrastructure sector is relatively new in the field to source PE capital, and PE firms with prior experience are perceived as potential partners. Regression analysis indicated that older PEs drove the syndication process. A Hausman 2-stage logit model showed that when PE firms chose to syndicate they preferred to syndicate with local firms. From this, it can be concluded that the resource-based motive of syndication was supported and seemed to take precedence in PE syndication in infrastructure. Further, investment size was not significant, while fund size was marginally significant at 10 percent level. This indicated that the process of syndication was not due to capital constraints but rather a knowledge-motivated phenomenon. PE firms syndicated to have better knowledge of market conditions, practices, rules, technology, and patterns of behavior and to capitalize on the advantages of having a local PE firm in the deal. Older PE firms, who brought with them increased managerial expertise, sought expertise of a different kind by showing an increased propensity to syndicate with local PE firms. The benefits of syndication of this kind [cross-border syndication] seemed to outweigh disadvantages, if any, when PE firms syndicated to gain a better knowledge of market conditions, practices, rules, technology and patterns of behavior and to capitalize on the advantages of having a local PE firm in the deal. Syndication is also seen in developing/transition economies and in younger investee companies where lack of publicly available information seemingly causes increased information asymmetry leading to risky project investments.

Examining the extent of syndication revealed that although the decision to syndicate rested on [the success] of the early rounds, in later rounds, a significant increase in index value implied that there was more syndication in later rounds and PE investors preferred more diversity in experience rather than just more experience. The host of skills required by infrastructure companies in later rounds caused PE firms to syndicate to include PE firms with age diversity.

The resource-based view was found dominant in the process of syndication of PE firms, which seemed to take precedence in PE syndication in infrastructure. Further, it indicated that the process of syndication was not due to capital constraints but was rather a knowledge-motivated phenomenon.

This study highlighted the importance of local knowledge of the environment and its relevance in the choice of an appropriate partner. The resource-based view encompasses both the need for managerial expertise in handling a project and knowledge of the working environment housing the project, both of which help decide what sort of a partner to syndicate with. Capital requirements did not influence syndication strategies which indicated that the traditional finance-based view did not appear to be a cause for syndication in infrastructure projects.

A few limitations were noted in this study which could also offer more scope for future research. While information on PE investments is difficult to gather due to the private nature of their transactions, the data and variables used here were limited to the data available and sourced from the database. Although this database is used frequently for VC/PE research, it lacks details of deals in developing/transition economies as compared to the information available in developed countries. Future studies could access more than one database, assess the completeness of data, perhaps increase the sample size and achieve more insightful results. The time-frame used in this study ends just prior to the global financial crisis. We believe that the infrastructure sector will remain a preferred sector for PE investors in the future; the global financial crisis, the Covid pandemic, and the aftermaths did little to dampen the enthusiasm of PE investments in global infrastructure.

References

Admati, A. R., & Pfleiderer, P. (1994). Robust financial contracting and the role of venture capitalists. *Journal of Finance, 49*, 371–402.

Armstrong, J. (2003). The syndicated loan market: Developments in the North American context. Discussion Paper 2003-15, Bank of Canada.

Barney, J. (1991). Firm resources and sustained competitive advantage. *Journal of Management, 17*(1), 99–120.

Bent, N., Williams, K., & Gilbert, E. (2004). The syndication of private equity investments in South Africa. *South African Journal of Business Management, 35*(4)

Brander, J. A., Amit, R., & Antweiler, W. (2002). Venture-capital syndication: Improved venture selection vs. the value-added hypothesis. *Journal of Economics & Management Strategy, 11*, 423–452.

Bygrave, W. D. (1987). Syndicated investments by venture capital firms: A networking perspective. *Journal of Business Venturing, 2*, 139–154.

Bygrave, W. D. (1988). The structure of the investment networks of venture capital firms. *Journal of Business Venturing, 3*, 137–157.

Bygrave, W.D., & Timmons, J.A. (1992). Venture capital at the crossroads. Harvard Business Press.

Casamatta, C., & Haritchabalet, C. (2003). Learning and syndication in venture capital investments. Discussion Paper 3867, CEPR.

Casamatta, C., & Haritchabalet, C. (2007). Experience, screening and syndication in venture capital investments. *Journal of Financial Intermediation, 16*(3), 368–398.

Chowdhry, B., & Nanda, V. (1996). Stabilization, syndication, and pricing of IPOs. *Journal of Financial and Quantitative Analysis, 31*(1), 25–42.

Dai, N., H. Jo, & Kassicieh, S. (2009). Venture capital ownership type, investment criteria, and venture performance, SCU Leavey School of Business Research Paper No. 09-02, electronic copy available at: http://ssrn.com/abstract=1512012

Dennis, S.A., & Mullineaux, D.J. (2000). Syndicated loans. Discussion paper, California State University at Fullerton, University of Kentucky.

Dierickx, I., & Cool, K. (1989). Asset stock accumulation and sustainability of competitive advantage. *Management Science, 35*(12), 1504–1511.

Dunning, J. H. (1993). *Multinational enterprises and the global economy*. Addison Wesley, New York.
European Venture Capital and Private Equity. (2011). European Private Equity and Venture Capital Association. http://evca.eu/what-are-private-equity-venture-capital/. Accessed 11 November 2012.
Fluck, Z., Garrison, K., & Myers, S. (2005). Venture capital: An experiment in computational corporate finance. American Finance Association Annual Meeting.
Gadanecz, B. (2004). The syndicated loan market: structure, development and implications. BIS Quarterly Review, pp. 75–89.
Gatti, S. (2008). *Project finance in theory and practice: Designing, structuring, and financing private and public projects*. Academic Press Advanced Finance Series, Elsevier Inc.
Gompers, P., and Lerner, J. (1999). *The venture capital cycle*. MIT Press.
Guo, D., & Jiang, K. (2013). Venture capital investment and performance of entrepreneurial firms: Evidence from China. *Journal of Corporate Finance, 22*, 375–395. https://doi.org/10.1016/j.jcorpfin.2013.07.001
Hand, J. (2004). Determinants of the round-to-round returns top Pre-IPO venture investments in US biotechnology companies. University of North Carolina, Working Paper.
Hochberg, Y., Ljungqvist, A., & Lu, Y. (2007). Whom you know matters: Venture capital networks and investment performance. *Journal of Finance, 62*, 251–301.
Hopp, C. (2010). When do venture capitalists collaborate? Evidence on the driving forces of venture capital syndication. *Small Business Economics, 35*, 417–431.
Janney, J. J., & Folta, T. B. (2003). Signaling through private equity placements and its impact on the valuation of biotechnology firms. *Journal of Business Venturing, 18*, 361–380.
Johanson, J. & Vahlne, J. E. (1977). The internationalization process of the firm: A model of knowledge development and increasing foreign market commitments. *Journal of International Business Studies, 8*, 23–32. 10.1057/palgrave.jibs.8490676
Jones, J., Lang, W.W., & Nigro, P. (2002). Recent trends in bank loan syndications: Evidence for 1995 to 1999. Discussion paper, OTS, Economic Analysis Division.
Kogut, B., & Zander, U. (1993). Knowledge of the firm and the evolutionary theory of the multinational corporation. *Journal of International Business Studies, 24*, 625–646. http://dx.doi.org/10.1057/palgrave.jibs.8490248
Kogut, B., Urso, P., & Walker, G. (2007). Emergent properties of a new financial market: American venture capital syndication, 1960–2005. *Management Science, 53*(7), 1181–1198.
Lakonishok, J., Shleifer, A., Thaler, R., & Vishny, R. (1991). Window dressing by pension fund managers. *American Economic Review, 81*(2), 227–231.
Lerner, J. (1994). The syndication of venture capital investments. *Financial Management Association, 23*(3), 293–316.
Lockett, A., & Wright M. (1999). The syndication of private equity: Evidence from the UK. *Venture Capital, 1*(4), 303–324.
Lockett, A., & Wright M. (2001). The syndication of venture capital investments. *Omega. The International Journal of Management Science, 29*, 375–390.
Makela, M. M., & Maula, M. V. J. (2008). Attracting cross-border venture capital: The role of a local investor. *Entrepreneurship and Regional Development, 20*, 237–257.
Manigart, S., Lockett, A., Meuleman, M., Wright, M., Landstrom, H., Bruining, H., Desbrieres, P., & Hommel, U. (2002). Why do European venture capital companies syndicate? Vlerick Leuven Gent Management School Working Paper Series 2002-20, Vlerick Leuven Gent Management School.
Meuleman, M., Wright, M., Manigart, S., & Lockett, A. (2009). Private equity syndication: Agency costs, reputation, and collaboration. *Journal of Business Finance & Accounting, 36*(5–6), 616–644. https://doi.org/10.1111/j.1468-5957.2009.02124.x
Millon, M. H., & Thakor, A. V. (1985). Moral hazard and information sharing: A model of financial information gathering agencies. *Journal of Finance, 40*(5), 1403–1422.
Pence, C. C. (1982). *How venture capitalists make investment decisions*. UMI Research Press.
Penrose, E. (1959). *The theory of the growth of the firm*. Sharpe.

Sah, R. K., & Stiglitz, J. E. (1986). The architecture of economic systems: Hierarchies and polyarchies. *American Economic Review, 76*(4), 716–727.

Sahlman, W. (1988). Aspects of financial contracting in venture capital. *Journal of Applied Corporate Finance, 1*, 23–36.

Sahlman, W. (1990). The structure and governance of venture capital organizations. *Journal of Financial Economics, 27*, 473–524.

Schure, P., Scoones, D., & Gu, Q. (2005). A theory of loan syndication. *Finance Research Letters, 2*, 165–172.

Sorenson, O., & Stuart, T. E. (2001). Syndication networks and the spatial distribution of venture capital investments. *American Journal of Sociology, 106*(6), 1546–1588.

Thillai Rajan, A., Doshi, M., & Gemson, J. (2011). Fueling growth and economic development: An analysis of private equity investments in real estate and infrastructure. India venture capital and private equity report, Indian Institute of Technology, Madras.

Tykvova, T., & Schertler, A. (2011). Cross-border venture capital flows and local ties: Evidence from developed countries. *The Quarterly Review of Economics and Finance, 51*, 36–48.

Wang, L., & Wang, S. (2012). Endogenous networks in investment syndication. *Journal of Corporate Finance, 18*, 640–663.

Wernefelt, B. (1984). A resource based view of the firm. *Strategic Management Journal, 5*, 171–180.

Wilson, R. (1968). The theory of syndicates. *Econometrica, 36*(1), 119–132.

Wright, M., & Lockett, A. (2003). The structure and management of alliances: Syndication in the venture capital industry. *Journal of Management Studies, 40*(8), 2073–2102.

Wright, M., Filatotchev, I., Hoskinsson, R. E., & Peng, M. W. (2005). Strategy research in conventional economies: Challenging the conventional wisdom. *Jornal of Management Studies*, https://doi.org/10.1111/j.1467-6486.2005.00487.x

Chapter 8
The Case of Staging of PE Investments

Those who plan do better than those who do not plan, even though they rarely stick to the plan.
—Sir Winston Churchill

8.1 Introduction

This chapter analyzes the staging of PE investments in the infrastructure sector. Staging refers to the process by which PE firms infuse capital into the investee company at specific points in time. Just like PE syndication, staging is a strategic and distinctive operational management used by PE investors. In this chapter, we examine two operational aspects of the staging function—first, when staging is a strategic management function employed by PE firms to monitor and evaluate the prospects of the firm, in an infrastructure setting, and second, staging as a real options decision to combat risk and information asymmetry, in infrastructure projects. Infrastructure projects, commonly designed on a project finance structure, are different from conventional corporate finance projects. They require large upfront investments and capital outlays; with capital outflows used to repay costs only after the project becomes operational. This capital is usually provided by sponsors who are connected with the project development or operations in some way or the other. However, in recent times, PE, as purely financial investors, have been actively investing in this sector. Present for financial motives alone, PE has the option to finance the project by infusing capital at once, or staging infusions through multiple investments. In

This chapter is based on the journal paper titled "A new perspective on private equity stage financing: Evidence from investments in infrastructure" which appeared in *Venture Capital: An International Journal of Entrepreneurial Finance*. 17(4), 299–325, https://doi.org/10.1080/13691066.2015.1052193. Parts of this chapter are also sourced from the paper titled "Staging of investment as a strategic management function employed by private equity firms: Evidence from the infrastructure sector", presented at the Innovation in Public Finance Conference, June 17–19, 2013, Milano, Italy, editors: Marco Giorgino, Guillermo Aranda-Mena, and Barbara Monda.

J. Gemson and Thillai Rajan A., *Private Equity Financing in Infrastructure and Real Estate*, https://doi.org/10.1007/978-981-16-1634-1_8

case the PE firm decides to disburse the capital in multiple investments, it creates the staging function, a mechanism successfully used by VC firms to combat risk and uncertainty. We empirically analyze the choice for, the motives behind, and the determinants of PE staging in the infrastructure sector.

8.2 An Introduction to Staging

The process of staging in finance has always been in reference to investment and refers to the process of investing in specific points in time. The staging process usually involves a choice between investing in a lumpsum or a whole and precludes the same, and investing in parts to execute a planned strategy. For example, the staging process will smooth the ride to minimize any effects of uncertainty in market downturns for an investor who may be show aversion to investing large sums of money into the market at one instance. It could be referred to as a tool employed to cushion a short-term being or state. In entrepreneurial financing, VC investors use the staging process to combat asymmetric information, to protect the investor from risk, especially if the entrepreneur has superior knowledge and a favorable exit option. Thus, such a strategy is usually one that aims at minimizing risk to the investor.

The process of staging is especially popular in the USA (Wang & Zhou, 2004) and has almost found universal use (Neher, 1999). Hopp (2008) presumed that the use of staged financial structure can be as important as the provision of capital.

8.3 Staging of PE Investments

In PE investing, the stock purchase agreement entered into by the PE investor and the investee company fixed the amount and timing of the investment (Sahlman, 1990). Each successive stage is either predetermined or conditional on performance. If the successive stage is predetermined, staging is akin to round financing and no explicit commitment for an additional round of financing is made. If the successive stage is conditional on performance, it is known as milestone financing where the financing firm receives a new capital injection contingent upon certain criteria being met. It is generally tied to a significant development in the company, such as satisfying targets such as completion of design, pilot production, first profitability, introduction of a second product, or an Initial Public Offering (Kozmetsky et al., 1985; Krohmer et al., 2009; Plummer, 1987). In round financing, each new capital infusion was negotiated separately, whereas in milestone financing, the decision on whether to inject new capital was made contingent on the portfolio company meeting predefined targets in terms of product development or financial figures, making it less efficient as compared to milestone financing. The choice between round financing and milestone financing could perhaps be attributed to role and bargaining power of the VC as compared the entrepreneur (Talmor & Cuny, 2005).

According to Sahlman (1990), PE firms generally invested more than once during the life of each company, and the amount invested often increased with each successive round. The capital invested at each point was expected to be sufficient to take the investee company to the next stage of development but the company required additional capital to make further progress.

From the investors' point of view, the funding requirements of the project were spread out over time and the capital infusions took place in smaller increments, rather than in a large upfront payment (Sahlman, 1990). From the investee company's point of view, staging suggested that the capital required for the project was not available at the outset but became available later at specific points of time.

Sahlman (1990) considered staged capital infusions the most potent control mechanism a VC firm could employ. This was because staging made capital, which was a scarce and expensive resource for the investee company, a conditional phenomenon, just short of denying capital to them altogether. The investee companies accepted the staged capital process because they usually had no other means for obtaining capital but had the confidence in their ability to meet the targets. It also provided incentives to the investee company's management team to continuously work toward attaining targets set by the PE investor. For the PE investor, staging protected capital from bad projects as it created an option to abandon the project and not invest further in it. Whether to invest by injecting capital was often dependent on the outcome of the evaluation of previous investment operations (Guo et al., 2008). PE firms monitored a firm's progress and discontinued funding the project if they learnt negative information about future prospects (Gompers, 1995). Thus, it reduced the risk of investing further in projects which had no favorable prospects.

The decision to stage is determined by the inherent uncertainty and the degree of asymmetric information present in the project. Krohmer et al. (2009) suggested that the staging decision was essentially a signal of the investor's preference for the level of control he wished to exercise, as well as the amount of resources he chose to allocate—resources which might be in the form of capital, managerial support, knowledge transfer, time and support. This stemmed from the "monitoring hypothesis" of staging, which argued that the staging of capital infusions was a substitute for intensive monitoring by the PE investor. Effective monitoring of investee firms can be costly for PE firms (Bottazzi et al., 2008; Gompers, 1995; Kaplan & Stromberg, 2003, 2004; Sahlman, 1990) because in addition to financing, PE firms also spent considerable time visiting the investee firm and working closely with the management to increase the efficiency of the investee firm (Chemmanur et al., 2009; Tian, 2011). On the other hand, the mechanism of staging was also costly as it involved negotiation and contracting costs (Kaplan & Stromberg, 2003), time and resources. Further, staging encouraged short-term success rather than long-term value creation (Tian, 2011). Also, lags in the implementation of the project due to non-availability of funding increased costs for the investee firm necessitating economies of scale, longer development cycles and delays in market entry (Tian, 2011). Wang and Zhou (2004) suggested that staging also led to underinvestment problems and could be inferior to upfront financing because PE firms might tend not to invest in a project's early stages when the viability of the project did not look too promising ex-ante.

Thus, the monitoring hypothesis suggested that the PE firm will try to balance the costs of intensive monitoring with the costs of staging, to achieve a balance.

8.4 Staging as a Strategic Management Function

As a strategic management function, staging can be thought of as a mechanism employed by the PE firm to combat the PE–entrepreneur relationship, i.e., agency relationship, that is characterized by behavioral uncertainty—attributable to self-interest and opportunism and keep the project under control (Wang & Zhou, 2004).

Regular monitoring is usually costly and cannot not be performed continuously, and therefore, the PE firm monitored the activities of the investee firm at periodic intervals of time, making duration and the intensity of monitoring negatively related to expected agency costs. Gompers (1995) who argued this hypothesis found that agency costs increased as tangibility of the assets declined, and the duration of financing was related to the nature of the firm's assets. Higher industry ratios of tangible assets to total assets, lower market-to-book ratios, and lower R&D intensities were associated with longer funding duration. Firms that went public received significantly more financing and a greater number of rounds than firms that were acquired or liquidated.

Bergemann and Hege (1998) proposed a mathematical model to analyze the optimal financing of venture projects when learning and moral hazard interacted. They presupposed a wealth constrained entrepreneur who offered an investment opportunity to a VC where the project could either succeed or fail. The successful completion of the project required funds for its development. The rate of investment controlled the probability of success and a higher investment accelerated the process of discovery. The authors concluded that short-term financing could never be optimal. Short-term financing is distinct from staged financing and is a financial policy where the entrepreneur attracts funds on a competitive basis in each period. Toward the end of the efficient investment horizon, the expected return was insufficient to cover the necessary outlays for both partners. The efficient solution could only be achieved by a long-term contract which allowed for intertemporal risk sharing. This view was in line with that of Megginson and Weiss (1991), Anand and Galetovic (1997) and Cumming and MacIntosh (2001) who reported that venture financing was frequently supported by long-term relationships and that a longer duration (relationship) of VC investments reduced information asymmetry. Megginson and Weiss (1991) also suggested that the longer the relationship between the VC investor and the investee, the greater the certification effect.

Wang and Zhou (2004) offered a formal model for staged financing in controlling risks and moral hazard in VC. They obtained a closed-form solution by which analysis of the complementary roles of staged financing and contracting could be made. They showed that in addition to contracting, staged financing was an effective mechanism for VCs to reduce agency costs and control risks. They suggested that with the flexibility of staged financing, many projects, which might otherwise be abandoned under upfront financing, became profitable. They also showed that the efficiency of staged financing was best for highly promising firms.

The advantages of this process were twofold. There were reduced losses from potentially bad decisions, and PE firms desisted from throwing money into bad projects (Wang & Zhou, 2004). Hellman (1998) argued that VCs provide staged financing in order to avoid risks. Gompers (1995) likened the role of staged capital infusions to that of debt in highly leveraged transactions keeping the owner/manager on a "tight leash". Capital was not easily available and hence could not be wastefully spent. Also, the capital available needed to be utilized wisely to show progress in the firm. If there was no progress, the firm's prospects may not look very favorable during the next round of evaluation and capital could then get reduced or stopped altogether. Thus, staging was a tool used to alleviate information asymmetry and agency problems, creating a monitoring relationship between the investor and the investee, a premise also supported by Dai (2011).

8.5 Staging as a Real Options Decision

As a real options decision, staging enabled the PE investor by providing a choice, as information became available. The staging function allowed the PE investor to invest as a lumpsum or at regular intervals (Gemson and Rajan, 2015); to wait before investing; or abandon the venture (investment) whenever the forward looking net present value (NPV) of the project was negative (Cornelli and Yosha, 2003); or to abandon the entrepreneur's project if it failed to meet stage targets (Admati & Pfleiderer, 1994; Gompers, 1995; Kaplan & Stromberg, 2003, 2004).

Cornelli and Yosha (2003) examined staging as a real options decision by modeling the interim performance of the VC—or the performance of the VC between two rounds of financing, referring to it as a "signal". The "signal" was observed by the VC and the entrepreneur as the short-term performance which enabled both parties to update their expectations about the project's quality. After observing it, the VC decided to refinance the project or get out. Thus, the VC was given the option to abandon the investment if in the medium term they received bad news. By abandoning the venture, the PE investor will not invest further in the project, causing a conflict of interest between the PE investor, who provided the funds and the infrastructure company, who needed to continue with the project.

Li (2008) also took a real options perspective of VC staging and viewed staging as a choice between holding the current option to invest and investing presently and obtaining the option to invest subsequently. The author proposed that the staging decision depended on the factors that influenced the value of the two options, including various sources of uncertainty and competition. The study focused on two forms of endogenous uncertainty in VC—project-specific uncertainty concerning the costs of completing the project and behavioral uncertainty, which was the relationship between the VC and the entrepreneur. To examine the real options view on staging, the study analyzed the funding duration of VC investments in the USA from 1975 to 2005. Using 3737 VC firms and 15,786 portfolio companies, the author presented empirical analysis and provided evidence consistent with the real options view—market uncertainty encouraged the VC firm to delay; while competition, project-specific uncertainty, and agency concerns prompted the VC firm to invest sooner. Empirical results indicated that it was important to consider the broader decision context beyond agency concerns in examining VC staging.

Tian (2011) studied the causes and consequences of VC stage financing at an entrepreneurial firm level and built on the agency model by suggesting three hypotheses. First, the author proposed the "monitoring hypothesis" stating that staging of capital infusions and monitoring were substitutes for each other since they were both costly to incur. The author argued that the VC investor should balance the cost of monitoring and engage in stage financing of entrepreneurial firm only if effective monitoring was too costly. Second, the "hold-up hypothesis" argued that once the VC investor invested in an entrepreneurial firm, the entrepreneur had the ability to leave the firm for a better career. Staging here mitigated such a hold-up problem as it reduced the amount of VC investment tied up to the firm. Finally, the author proposed the "learning hypothesis" whereby a real option was available for the VC investor to abandon financing the project after each financing round based on what the VC learned between the financing rounds. To test the implications of these hypotheses, the author used geographical location information about the entrepreneurial firm and the distance between the VC investor and the firm. The author analyzed 27,461 US firms that received first round financing from VC firms between 1980 and 2006. On the causes of VC staging, the author concluded that VC investors located farther away from the entrepreneurial firm tended to finance the firm with larger number of financing rounds, shorter duration between successive rounds and a smaller amount in each round. The VC's propensity to stage was independent of whether or not the firm was located in a close-knit entrepreneurial community. On the consequences of VC stage financing, the author concluded that the number of VC financing rounds positively affected the entrepreneurial firm's propensity to exit through an IPO, and that it was positively related to the entrepreneurial firm's operating performance in the IPO year. It also affected the entrepreneurial firm's post-IPO survival rate, provided the firm was located far away from the VC investor in all three cases. The author's evidence was consistent with the monitoring hypothesis but did not support the hold-up hypothesis and the learning hypothesis.

This chapter examines staging as a PE investment function used by PE firms to alleviate risk and information asymmetry problems and attempts to synthesize the strategic management control function and the real options decision of PE staging at an industry level (infrastructure sector). It explores the differences between deals where PE firms staged their investments against deals where PE firms did not stage their investments. It examines the characteristics that encouraged PE firms to stage their investments, staging being a monitoring process. It shed light on the duration of PE investments in infrastructure deals.

8.6 Data

For the analysis, we used a sample of 358 infrastructure deals with PE investments. PE firms invested approximately US$9.743 billion over a 20-year period from 1990 to 2009 into infrastructure projects.

Table 8.1 provides a time-series snapshot of the 358 deals in the sample divided into four time periods—period 1 (1990–1994), period 2 (1995–1999), period 3 (2000–2004) and period 4 (2005–2009). It provides summary information on the years and amounts of PE financing for the sample. It also provides details of the number of deals, total amount invested (US$, million), and the number of new firms in each year in the sample. Details of the largest round which was funded in that year as well as the lowest round which was funded in each year along with the average age of the infrastructure company receiving PE funding (in years) are also presented. The number of deals represented the number of transactions where PE firms invested in infrastructure deals in that year. The PE investment size represented in 2009 US$, million was the amount of capital infused by the PE firms. The number of new firms receiving PE funding represented the new infrastructure portfolio companies receiving PE funding. The largest round represented the numerical value of the largest financing round while the smallest round represented the numerical value of the smallest financing round. The average age of the infrastructure company receiving PE funding was the simple average of the ages of the infrastructure companies that received PE financing in that year.

171 firms received 358 individual rounds of PE financing, i.e., about US$9.74 billion over the period. An examination of Table 8.1 revealed that the early 1990s (period 1) saw a modest number of deals as well as smaller investment amounts into infrastructure. The latter half of the 90s saw a gradual increase in the number of deals and investment sizes. Between 1995 and 1997, there was a fivefold increase in the number of infrastructure deals receiving PE investment. The amount of PE investment showed a remarkable 1177 percent increase in 1997 as compared to 1995. The early 2000s (period 3) saw a plateauing of PE activity in infrastructure, while the

Table 8.1 Time series summary of the sample of infrastructure deals from 1990 to 2009 that have PE investments in them

Financing year	No. of deals	PE investment size (US$, Million)	Number of new firms receiving PE funding	Largest round	Lowest round	Average age of infrastructure company receiving PE funding (years)
1990–1994	17	248.99	9	12	1	12.28
1995–1999	74	1936.32	38	11	1	8.78
2000–2004	78	2012.02	41	9	1	7.98
2005–2009	189	5546.628	83	17	1	6.3

Source Securities Data Corporation, complied by authors, Josephine Gemson unpublished thesis mid-2000s saw a spurt in the number of new firms receiving PE funding as well as an increase in the PE investment amount into infrastructure. Altogether, the increase in the size of investment into infrastructure deals was far greater than the increase in number of deals being financed by PE.

The 2000s also witnessed an increase in the number of new firms receiving PE financing. This was reaffirmed by the fact that the lowest round of funding was 1 throughout most of the sample period. PE financing was seen in up to 17 rounds. However, only around ten companies had more than ten rounds of PE financing. The average age of the infrastructure company that received PE financing in the sample had a lower limit of 3.5 years and went up to a high of 12 years. This showed that infrastructure companies did not receive PE financing at seed/start-up stage but were financed by PE toward mid/late stages.

Of the 358 infrastructure deals with PE financing in them, 111 deals had one round of financing while 247 deals had multiple rounds of financing or staging in them. Table 8.2 provides a summary of the 247 infrastructure deals that had staging in them.

Details of round 1–6 were provided along with summated details of round 7 and above. The average round duration between two successive rounds was 243.5 days or 0.66 of a year. The time duration was highest between round 1 and round 2 with

Table 8.2 Summary statistics for the sample of deals with PE staging

Particulars	Rounds of external financing						
	1	2	3	4	5	6	≥7
Number of observations	44	46	31	27	21	18	60
Average duration from previous round (days)		311.88	283.73	226.33	241.00	248.80	184.61
Age of the company at the time of PE financing (years)	3.72	5.00	3.84	3.96	3.91	5.06	6.33
Minimum age of company at the time of PE financing (years)	0	0	1	1	1	1	2
Maximum age of the company at the time of PE financing (years)	21	28	16	29	29	18	21
Median age of the company at the time of PE financing (years)	1	2	2	3	3	3	5
Total amount invested (2009 US$, Million)	1306.43	673.63	343.72	373.19	232.15	212.89	1178.59
Average amount invested (2009 US$, Million)	29.69	14.64	11.09	13.82	11.06	11.83	19.64
Mean number of PE investors in each round	1.25	1.43	1.81	2.15	1.86	1.61	1.33
Mean age of the PE investors in each round (years)	20.02	19.81	23.09	25.61	24.10	26.00	35.21

Source Securities Data Corporation, complied by authors, Josephine Gemson unpublished thesis an average of 311.878 days. This could be because of the large upfront payments required by infrastructure projects. The round duration seemed to show a decrease as round number increased with a 20 percent decrease in duration between round 1 and round 6.

Infrastructure companies were financed by PE firms at the time of inception (minimum age of PE financing is 0 years). However, the average age of the infrastructure company at the time of PE financing at round 1 was 3.7 years. It increased to 5 years at round 2 due to the addition of new deals in the sample.[1] It then fell back to its trend of 3.8 years in round 3 after which it followed a gradual upward trend with increasing time to finance the project. The maximum age of the infrastructure company receiving PE financing in the sample was between 16 and 29 years. Even though the maximum age of infrastructure company at PE financing was high, the median age remained comparatively low. This indicated a wide variation in the age of the infrastructure companies receiving PE financing.

The total amount invested per round was highest in round 1 with US$1306.432 million. This was consistent with the characteristic of large initial capital requirements of infrastructure projects. The total amount invested in round 2 showed an almost 50 percent decrease from that invested in round 1. The amount invested in the subsequent rounds also showed a decrease, except between rounds 3 and 4, which recorded a 9 percent increase to US$373.196 million. The average amount invested per round was also highest in the first round with US$29.692 million; thereafter, there was a sharp decrease in amount invested to US$14.644 million, showing a 51 percent decrease. Average amount invested between rounds 2 and 3 showed a 24 percent decrease after which a 25 percent increase was recorded between rounds 3 and 4. Average investment size then remained between US$11–12 million in rounds 5 and 6.

The mean number of PE investors in each round showed a gradual increase till round 4, which recorded a 72 percent increase in number between round 1 and round 4. However, from round 4, there was a gradual decrease in the number of PE investors financing each round.

8.7 Comparative Analysis of Staged PE Investments in Infrastructure

Descriptive statistics of staged PE investments in infrastructure revealed that staging was a rather popular investment strategy.

In this section, we conduct a comparative analysis to draw insights from the staging mechanism. Two sets of comparative analyses were conducted. The first

[1] The average age of the PE firm at the time of PE financing in round 2 increased to 5 years and then fell back to 3.84 years in round 3. This is because round 2 saw an increase in number of new deals in addition to the infrastructure deals that were present in round 1, which increased the average age to 5 years.

section compared infrastructure deals where PE investments were staged with deals where PE investments were not staged. 31 percent of the deals in the sample were not staged and had only a single round of PE financing in them. This brought out disparities in deals due to PE staging. The second section compared deals that had PE staging or multiple rounds of PE financing in them. Here, the level or percentage of reinvestment by a PE firm was compared to examine if the nature of the transaction was affected by reinvestment characteristics which represented length of associations between PE investors and investee firms. First, staged deals with the exact same PE firm(s) investing in them were compared against staged deals where at least one new PE firm(s) was present in financing the successive round. Next, staged deals with at least one PE reinvestor were compared against staged deals where there are all new PE investors in the subsequent financing round. The non-parametric Mann–Whitney U-test was used for the analysis in order to identify differences in medians of select parameters of the deals.

8.8 Analysis of Investments with PE Staging Versus Investments Without PE Staging

Figure 8.1 provides the summary of differences in infrastructure deals with one round of PE financing versus many rounds of PE financing. Out of the 358 deals in the sample, infrastructure deals with first round of financing between 2007 and 2009, which did not have a follow-up investment within the sample period in question, were excluded from the analysis. This was done to ensure that no staged PE financing was considered as non-staged PE financing. Out of the 111 deals which were single round deals, 17 deals were excluded amounting to a total of 94 deals which had no staged PE investments, while 247 deals have PE staging in them. Comparative analysis was done across four parameters—the investment size per deal, the fund size, the investment size as a percentage of fund size and the age of the investee company at the time of PE financing.

Infrastructure projects which are commonly financed on project finance basis usually have capital commitments spread out in stages. Further, Dai (2011) found that the round size (investment size) in staged financing was significantly smaller on an average than in the average single round sample.

An examination of Fig. 8.1 revealed that investment size per deal was significantly larger when PE investors invested in just one round as compared to when they invested in multiple rounds in infrastructure companies. PE investors seemed to be investing almost 1.8 times with US$17.1 million when they invested in a single round as compared to US$6.8 million a deal when they invested in more than one round. This value was significant at the 99 percent CI. This result was consistent with Dai's (2011). Fund sizes when PE investors invested in only one round were significantly smaller when compared to when PE investors invested in many rounds. This value was also significant at the 99 percent CI. PE investors with smaller funds seemed to

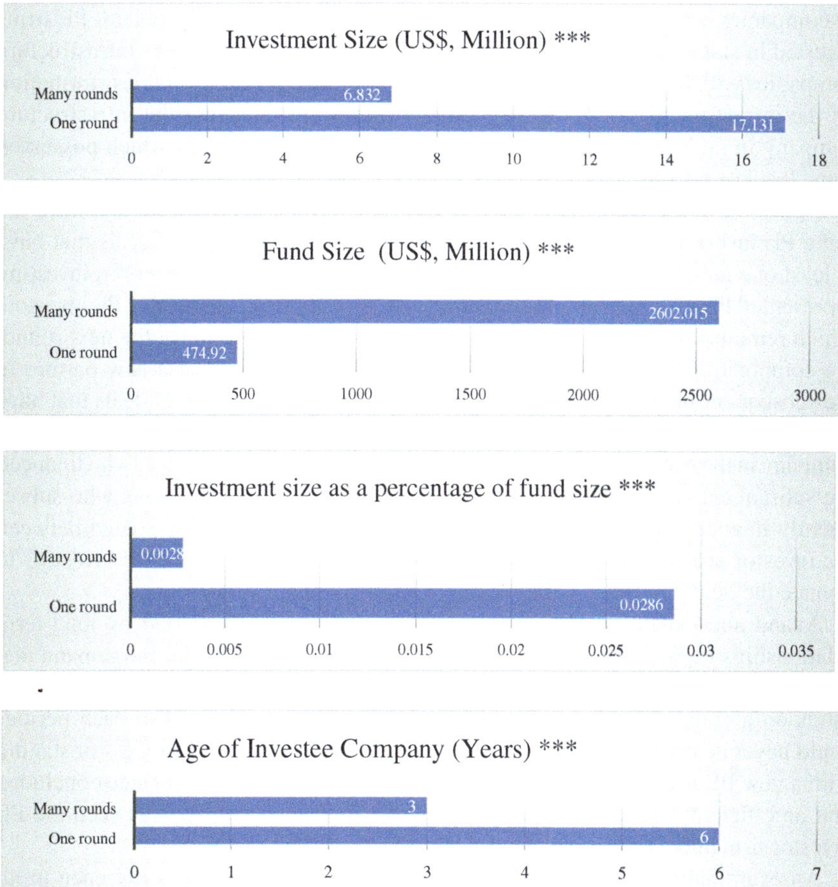

Fig. 8.1 Comparative analysis of infrastructure deals with PE investments—one round versus many rounds
*** significant at 99% CI

be investing larger investment sizes in one single round as compared to PE investors with larger funds. This implied that PE investors with larger fund sizes had more bargaining power and thus invested with lower amounts per deal and in many rounds as compared to PE investors with smaller fund sizes. In case of round one PE investors, the investment size as a percentage of fund size was 2.8 percent, while in the case of many rounds, it was ten times lower with 0.28 percent of fund size. This value was also significant at 99 percent CI.

The age of the investee company at the time of PE financing was significantly larger when there was only one round of PE financing as compared to when there are multiple rounds of PE financing. Gompers (1995) argued that early stage companies had short or no histories and were difficult to evaluate. Therefore, when investing in companies where information asymmetry was likely to be a problem, PE firms invested in stages. This implied that PE firms would prefer to finance infrastructure companies with one larger round when there was more publicly available information on the infrastructure company. However, if they were financing the infrastructure company in multiple rounds, they invested in younger companies which possessed some level of information asymmetry.

Figure 8.2 presents a comparative analysis of infrastructure deals that have the same PE investor(s) reinvesting in the subsequent round as against deals that have at least one new PE investor in the next round. The same PE investor(s) reinvesting represented PE which comprised one single PE investor or a syndicate of PE investors which remained constant. In case of at least one new PE investor in the next round, the composition of the PE syndicate varied with the addition of a new partner in the subsequent financing round. Figure 4.3 presents a comparison of deals that have at least one of the PE investors in the syndicate who reinvested in the infrastructure company in the subsequent round versus deals with all new PE investors who financed the subsequent stage. The presence of at least one of the PE investors who subsequently financed the next round denoted a past association which existed between the investor and the investee company, against an entire new set of PE investors to finance the deal.

Anand and Galetovic (1997) viewed staging as being supported by long-term relationships between the PE investor and the investee firm, while Bergemann and Hege (1998) stated that short-term financing (where the investee company attracts funds on a competitive basis [from different PE firms] at the end of each period) could never be optimal. Short-term financing here refereed to the process of staging with a new PE investor(s) in each financing round. Bergemann and Hege concluded that an efficient solution can be achieved by a long-term contract between the PE investor firm and the investee company.

An examination of Fig. 8.2 showed that there was significant difference in all the four parameters chosen for the analysis—the investment size, the fund size, the investment size as a percentage of fund size, and the age of the investee company at the time of PE financing. The same PE investor(s) who continued to reinvest in the investee company in subsequent rounds had significantly larger investment sizes with averages of US$17 million as compared to investment size of new PE investors in subsequent rounds with averages of US$14.7 million. This was significant at the 99 percent CI. Their fund sizes were also significantly larger than fund sizes of syndicates with at least one new PE investor(s) investing in the next round with averages fund sizes of the former being almost five times larger. This too was significant at the 99 percent CI. Investment size as a percentage of fund size of same PE investor(s) who reinvested was significantly smaller with only 1 percent of the fund size per deal while at least one new PE investors in the subsequent round invested almost 15 percent of their fund sizes per deal.

When the age of the investee company at the time of PE financing was examined, the same PE investor(s) who reinvested in deals did so in significantly younger companies as compared to at least one new PE investor(s) investing in the next round. PE investors who invested in younger companies did so by investing their

Fig. 8.2 Comparative analysis of staged PE investments: same PE investor reinvesting in next round versus at least one new PE investor in the next round
*** significant at 99% CI

capital in staged financing while new PE investors in each round preferred older companies that had more publicly available information.

An examination of Fig. 8.3 revealed no significant difference in investment size with respect to deals that had at least one old PE investor reinvesting in the subsequent round or deals that had all new PE firms investing in the subsequent round. The fund size of PE firms that reinvested was however significantly larger than one-time PE investors in staged deals by almost 3.5 times. Mean fund sizes of syndicates with at least one PE firm that reinvested in the subsequent round stood at US$4409 million while single time PE investors had fund sizes of US$1307 million. The investment size as a percentage of fund size was significantly larger for deals with all new PE investors who invested an average of 31 percent of the funds in the infrastructure deal.

The age of the infrastructure company at the time of PE financing where at least one PE firm reinvested was significantly lower than when all new PE firms came in for a one-time investment. This showed that PE firms that reinvested, tackled information asymmetry problems by staging their capital but where one-time PE investors were concerned, they still needed sufficient publicly available information

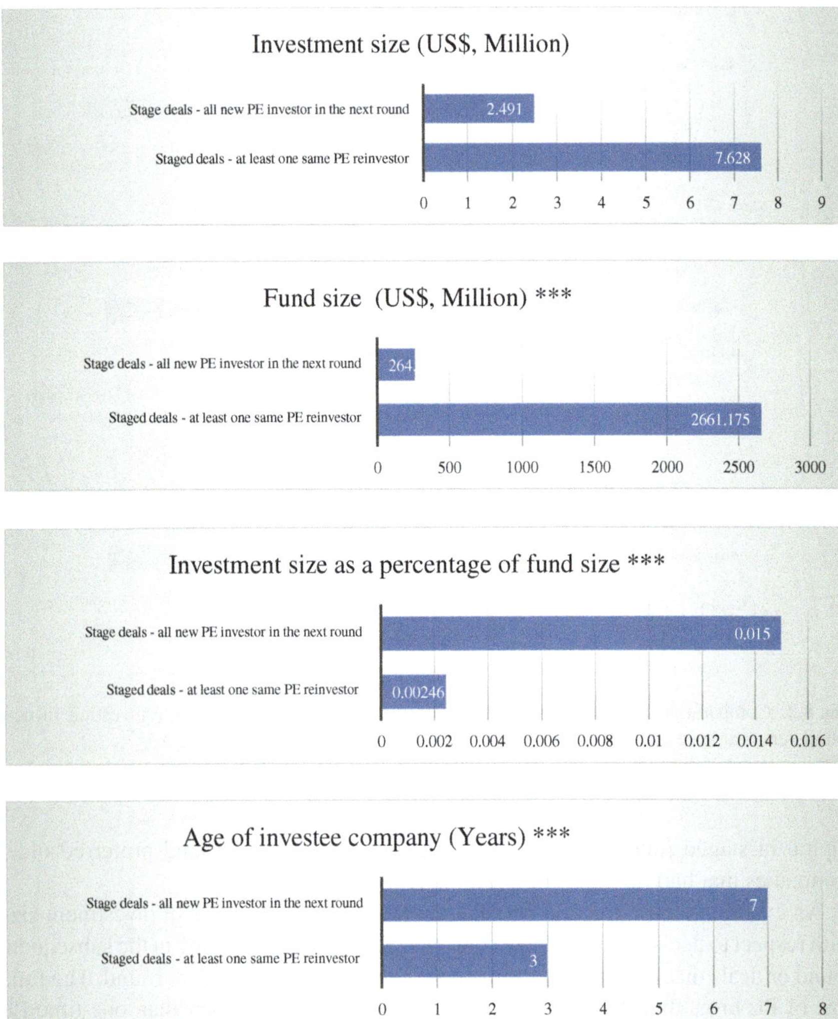

Fig. 8.3 Comparative analysis of staged PE investments: Same PE investor reinvesting in next round versus at least one new PE investor in the next round
*** significant at 99% CI

to make an informed investment. Figure 8.4 presents a graph summarizing the fund size, investment size as a percentage of fund size and age of the investee company at the time of PE financing parameters considered in the analysis across the nature of PE investors investing in subsequent rounds.

Staged capital infusions by PE investors to the infrastructure company differed due to the source of capital. PE investors who continued to invest in subsequent rounds were able to provide larger investment sizes per infrastructure deal than PE investors who did not invest in subsequent rounds. Further, these investors invested in significantly younger companies as well. Thus, it was advantageous for investee companies to have PE investors who continued to invest in subsequent rounds and have long-term relationships with them. From the PE investors' point of view, although the PE investors who continued to reinvest in subsequent rounds provided larger investment sizes per deal, they were not being taxed as much because they possessed significantly larger fund sizes. Further, investment sizes as a percentage of fund size were also significantly smaller for these PE investors. With empirical evidence, this supported the premise of Anand and Galetovic (1997) and Bergemann and Hege (1998) who stated that long-term relationships between the PE investors and investee firms resulted in optimal financing solutions.

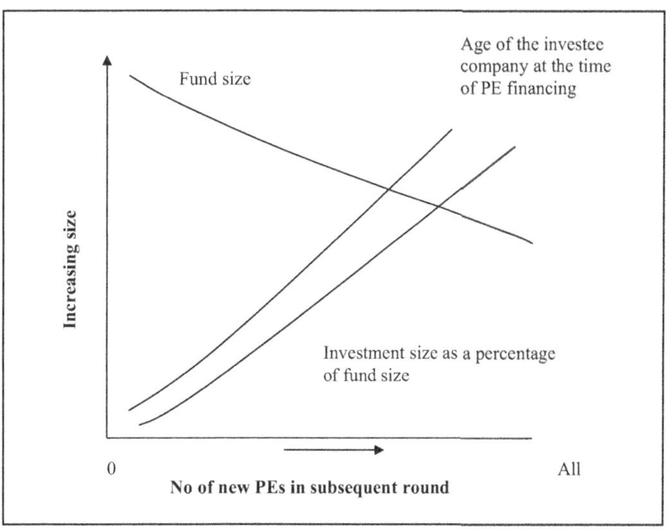

Fig. 8.4 Graph summarizing the parameters—fund size, investment size as a percentage of fund size and age of the infrastructure company at the time of PE financing—across the nature of PE investors investing in subsequent rounds in infrastructure firms

8.9 Regression Analysis of Staged PE Investments in Infrastructure

Comparative analysis in the preceding section indicated that there were significant differences in investment size per deal, fund sizes per deal, and age of the infrastructure company at the time of PE financing when PE firms staged their investment. Thus, it could be hypothesized that there exist certain characteristics that encourage PE firms to stage their investments when investing in the infrastructure sector. In this section, regression analysis will be used to determine the factors that drive PE firms to stage their investments in infrastructure projects.

8.10 Drivers of PE Staging in Infrastructure Projects

We conduct regression analysis to examine deal qualities that encouraged PE firms to stage their investments. Staging in this context was defined as a follow-up investment in the infrastructure project within two years from the previous investment. The follow-up investment was made after careful monitoring of the infrastructure firm and evaluating its prospects (Sahlman, 1990). Any follow-up investment into the infrastructure company within a span of two years (0–2 years) was taken to be staging as a result of monitoring. Such deals were assigned the value of 1.[2] Investments that happened after a two-year period (2–5 years) were taken as deals where staging was not a result of monitoring. Such deals were assigned a value of 0. Any follow-up investment after five years was assumed to be a fresh investment in the infrastructure firm due to the changing market conditions. The sample did not contain any deals with follow-up investment of greater than five years.

To ensure that deals satisfy the condition, deals which had their last financing in 2007 or later without a follow-up investment till 2009 have been excluded from the analysis. This was done to ensure that all deals pertained to the definition of staging as a monitoring function as put forth earlier in this section. Further, deals with round numbers greater than 1 which received PE financing between 1990 and 1992 have been excluded from the analysis. 252 deals in the sample satisfied the above conditions and have been included in the analysis (Table 8.3).

The model to be estimated is found in Eq. 8.1 (Fig. 8.5).

[2] A logistic regression, used to examine the drivers of PE staging in infrastructure projects, is a specialized regression which is used when the dependant variable takes binary (0/1) values. In this regression, a value 1 is assigned to deals that have a follow-up investment into the infrastructure company within a span of two years (0–2 years), and a value 0 is assigned to deals that has a follow-up investment after a two-year period (2–5 years).

Table 8.3 Presents the variables included in the regression analysis to identify the characteristics of infrastructure deals with PE syndication

Type	Variable	Description
Dependant variable	STAGEFUN	The follow-up investment was made after careful monitoring of the infrastructure firm and evaluating its prospects. A follow-up investment made between 0 and 2 years was assigned the value of 1, while a follow-up investment made between 2 and 5 years was assigned a value of 0
Independent variables	INTEREST	Real interest rate of the country in the year PE financed the infrastructure project
	STOCK	The stocks traded (as a percentage of GDP) in the country in the year PE financed the infrastructure project
	GROWGDP	The growth rate of GDP (as a percentage) from the previous year, in the country in the year PE financed the infrastructure project
	FDI	The FDI inflow into the country in the year PE financed the infrastructure project
	CPI	The Consumer Price Index of the country in the year PE financed the infrastructure project
	MARKCAP	The market capitalization (as a percentage of GDP) in the country in the year PE financed the infrastructure project
	SPGLOBAL	The S&P Global Equity Index value (annual percentage change) of the country in the year PE financed the infrastructure project
	COMPAGE	The age of the infrastructure project (in years) at the time of PE financing
	INVEST	The total value (in US$ million, 2009 values) of PE investment into the infrastructure project
	STAGE	The stage of the infrastructure project, at the current financing round. Represented by a dummy variable, 1 representing acquisition, expansion and later stage financing, and 0 represents buyouts and later stage and other financing
	FUND	The total size (in US$ million, 2009 values) of the fund used by the PE firm to finance the infrastructure deal. This variable has been adjusted for endogeneity before being used in the analysis, to control for PE firm age and PE fund age using the Hausman two-stage model
	PEAGE	The age of the PE firm (in years) at the time of PE financing
	PEINFRA	Dummy representing prior experience of the PE firm in the infrastructure sector, 1 representing a previous investment in infrastructure, 0 otherwise

(continued)

Table 8.3 (continued)

Type	Variable	Description
	LOCAL	Dummy variable, 1 representing if the PE firm is located in the same country as the infrastructure project, 0 otherwise
	SYNDICATE	The presence of a syndicate in the deal when the PE firm invested into the project. Represented by a dummy variable, 1 representing the presence of a syndicate, 0 otherwise
Control variables	ROUND	Numerical value of the round that was currently being financed by the PE firm, also representing the earliest round the PE firm financed the infrastructure company
	ENER/TRANS	Sector variables represented one of the three sectors of the infrastructure deal—the industrial/energy sector, the transport sector and the water and utilities sector. It was taken as a proxy to represent the riskiness of each sector. In this study, two dummy variables were used—ENER—where the energy sector was represented by a dummy and TRANS—where the transport sector was represented by a dummy

$$
\begin{aligned}
Z_{STA_i} = {} & \alpha_{0,i} + \alpha_1(\mathrm{INTEREST}_i) + \alpha_2(\mathrm{STOCK}_i) + \alpha_3(\mathrm{GROWGDP}_i) \\
& + \alpha_4(\mathrm{FDI}_i) + \alpha_5(\mathrm{CPI}_i) + \alpha_6(\mathrm{MARKCAP}_i) + \alpha_7(\mathrm{SPGLOBAL}_i) \\
& + \alpha_8(\mathrm{COMPAGE}_i) + \alpha_8(\mathrm{INVEST}_i) + \alpha_8(\mathrm{SYNDICATE}_i) \\
& + \alpha_9(\mathrm{STAGE}_i) + \alpha_{10}(\mathrm{FUND}_i) + \alpha_{11}(\mathrm{PEAGE}_i) \\
& + \alpha_{12}(\mathrm{PEINFRA}_i) + \alpha_{13}(\mathrm{LOCAL}_i) + \alpha_{14}(\mathrm{ENER}_i) \\
& + \alpha_{15}(\mathrm{TRANS}_i) + \alpha_{16}(\mathrm{ROUND}_i) + \varepsilon_i
\end{aligned} \tag{8.1}
$$

The regression analysis provided rich insights into the characteristics of infrastructure deals with PE staging. First, the parameters that emerged positively significant include the variables INTEREST (99 percent CI), INVEST (95 percent CI), FUND (90 percent CI) and GROWGDP (90 percent CI). The positive significance of the INTEREST variable indicates that regions with high interest rates (developing and transition economies) warrant staging on investments. The positive significance of the INVEST variable indicates that larger investment sizes encourage the use of staging by PE firms. The larger the investment size, the more was the risk involved, and the more was the propensity to stage. This result was consistent with Neher (1999) who found that PE firms tried to minimize the amount of capital committed to the investee firm by investing in stages.

The positive significance of the FUND variable indicates that a larger fund size amounts to increased bargaining power. PE firms will utilize their position to stage

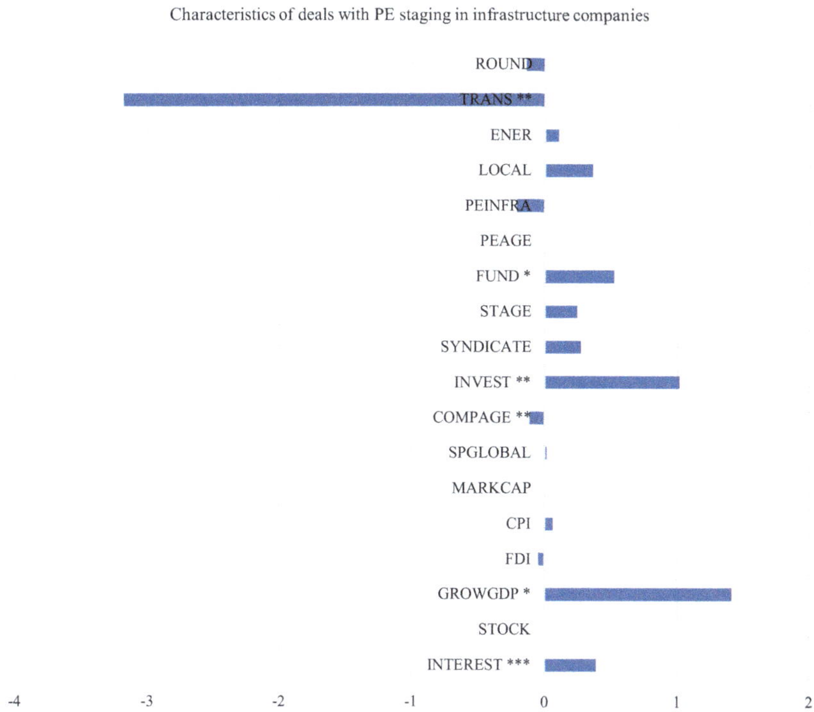

Fig. 8.5 Provides the characteristics of deals with PE staging in infrastructure companies. *** significant at 99% CI, ** significant at 95% CI

capital investment. Finally, the positive significance of the variable GROWGDP indicates that countries witnessing growing markets with high values of stocks traded (as a percentage of GDP) and higher growth rates of GDP, i.e., developing and transition economies house most Greenfield infrastructure projects, indicating favorable investment opportunities. Thus, PE firms can capitalize on these investment opportunities by staging their investment, a mechanism that allows for lowering risk positions in uncertain environments.

Next, the parameters that emerged negatively significant are COMPAGE (95 percent CI) and TRANS (95 percent CI). The age of the investee company at the time of PE financing (COMPAGE) was a negative driver to staging. This was significant at the 1 percent level. The age of the infrastructure company was analogous to the information asymmetry that prevailed about the company or the riskiness of the venture (Hopp, 2010). Gompers (1995) argued that in early stages, the lack of publicly available information was bound to be a problem and PE firms tackled this by investing in stages. Thus, when the company was younger or when there was lesser amount of publicly available information about it, PE firms preferred to invest in the company in stages.

The transport sector (TRANS) saw less of staged PE investment compared to the other two sectors in question—the energy sector and the water and utilities sector. This was significant at the 5 percent level. This implied that PE firms found investing in the transport sector less risky as compared to investing in other sectors. This could perhaps be due to the nature of financing projects in the transport sector. The transport sector is more homogeneous than other sectors (Singh, 2009); therefore, experience with one project could account for the lower risk levels while investing in other projects.

PE firm characteristics—the age of the PE firm at the time of financing (PEAGE) and the presence of local PE firm (LOCINV) were also not significantly related to staging. This indicated that experience of a PE firm or the possession of local knowledge did not render the PE firm at an advantage when the PE firm decided if capital was to be staged when investing in an infrastructure deal. PE firms were taken to be homogeneous when they decided whether to stage investments or not into infrastructure deals.

8.11 Analysis of the Time Duration Between Two Successive Rounds of Financing

This final section analyzed the factors affecting the time duration of two successive rounds of PE investments in infrastructure.[3] Funding duration is the time elapsed between two adjacent rounds of financing (Li, 2008). A shorter duration implied that the infrastructure company received its next round of financing sooner than if there is a longer funding duration.

Table 8.4 presents the variables included in the duration analysis and Figure 8.6 presents the estimation results of the duration analysis.

An examination of the variables in the analysis indicated that country development variable which differentiated developed economies from developing/transition economies (DEV) and the transport sector (TRANS) positively affected funding duration. These results were significant at 5 percent level and implied that deals in developed economies or the transport sector have longer funding durations and therefore less staging. This could be because developed economies/transport sector were perceived to be less risky which warranted less monitoring and consequently less staging.

The age of the investee at the time of PE financing (COMPAGE) positively affected the duration of funding. This was significant at the 1 percent level. This result was

[3] In this study, a "failure-time process" or a "survival-time process" is used to evaluate duration data. The data referred to the points in time when the "units" (investee company) received funding. At any point in time, the units (investee company) were "at risk" of being funded or had the propensity to receive a subsequent funding round. The "event" referred to the funding process or the capital infusion into the investee company.

Table 8.4 Variables included in the duration analysis

Type	Variable	Description
Dependant variable	DURATION	Duration of financing round, represented by Log (days)
Independent variables	DEV	Level of development represented by a dummy, 1 indicating developed country, 0 otherwise
	ENER	Energy sector being represented by a dummy, 1 indicating energy sector, 0 otherwise
	TRANS	Transport sector being represented by a dummy, 1 indicating transport sector, 0 otherwise
	COMPAGE	Age of the investee company at the time of PE financing
	ROUND	Round Number, used to represent level of staging
	LOCPAT	Local PE partner represented by a dummy, 1 indicating the presence of a local firm in the syndicate, 0 otherwise
	PREVSYN	Presence of syndication in the previous round represented by a dummy, 1 indicating the presence of syndication in the immediate previous round, 0 otherwise
	PEREINV	Percentage of PE investors who are reinvesting in the deal, from the previous round

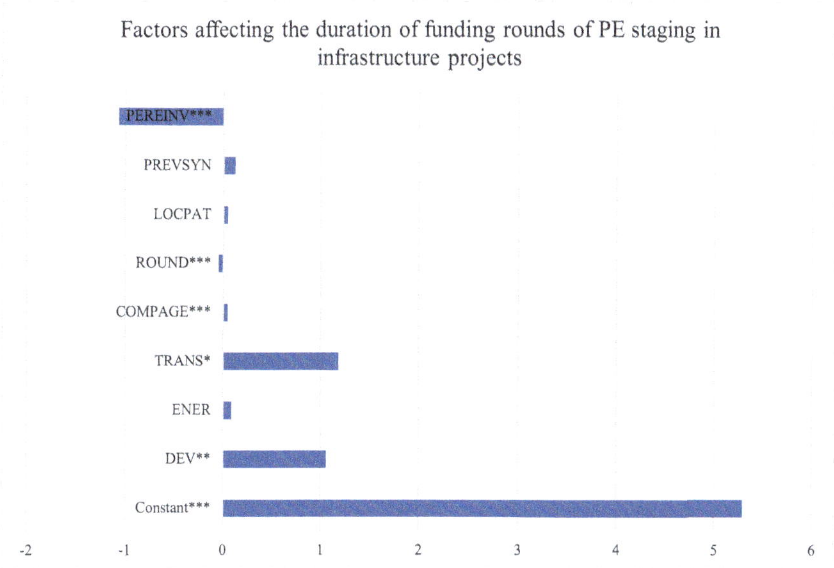

Fig. 8.6 Regression estimates for duration of financing round, ***significant at 99% CI. **significant at 95% CI, *significant at 90% CI

consistent with Gompers (1995) and Li's (2008) who found a positively significant effect of funding duration on low-technology firms. Tian (2011) concluded that younger investee companies had a higher degree of staging. Gompers (1995) concluded that firm age may be vital in measuring potential asymmetric information for low-technology firms—in this case infrastructure companies.

Round number (ROUND) was negatively significant at 1 percent level. Round number in this study represented the level of staging; therefore, an increase in round number implied more staging. In other studies, round number was considered a proxy for uncertainty (Dai et al., 2009). Lerner (1994) suggested that with the certification of first round investors, later rounds were relatively less risky and thus funding occurred easily and more frequently.

PE firm-level characteristics such as the presence of local partner/local knowledge (LOCPAT) and syndication in the previous round (PREVSYN) did not affect the duration of funding. Therefore, it can be concluded that staging was not a function of the characteristics of the PE investor, but a function of the risk and uncertainty associated with the infrastructure company.

Percentage of PE investors investing in the next round (PEREINV) was negatively significant at 1 percent level. This entailed that PE firms which reinvested into the infrastructure company do so at shorter durations that when new PE firms invest in the subsequent round. This was consistent with the results in the previous section.

8.12 Discussion

This study examined 358 infrastructure deals to analyze the staging strategy of PE firms when they invested in infrastructure firms. The analysis gave insights into staging as a strategic management function to combat information asymmetry and uncertainty when PE firms invested in infrastructure, a sector recently ventured into.

An examination of the trends of staging in the sample of infrastructure deals revealed that 247 deals or 69 percent of the sample had PE staging. This was consistent with past studies such as Wang and Zhou (2004), Hopp (2008), and Neher (1999) who acknowledged the wide use of staging by PE firms. Thus, staging was a popular strategy used by PE firms when investing in infrastructure projects. The reasons for the popularity were highlighted in the study. When deals with staged PE investments were compared against deals without staged PE investments, PE firms with larger fund sizes were found to invest with smaller investment sizes and smaller investment sizes as a percentage of fund size, despite the fact that infrastructure projects generally had significantly larger investment sizes. This put PE firms at an advantage over the infrastructure firm. This was perhaps because PE firms with larger fund sizes had more bargaining power, and could influence investment decisions, thus working these decisions to their benefit.

Long-term relationships between PE investors and investee firms where PE firms continued to reinvest in investee companies resulted in advantages for both parties. In the case of long-term relationships that are characterized by staged infusion of capital from the PE firm to the investor, the syndicate which remained constant throughout the investor–investee relationship was able to invest significantly larger amounts of capital at significantly lower investment size as a percentage of fund size than if the syndicate added new PE firms in subsequent rounds. These firms could support larger infrastructure projects with lower economies of scale. This long-term relationship between the PE investor and the investee company created an advantageous situation by learning by monitoring. These PE investors invested in significantly younger companies as compared to new PE investors that invested in a following round and depended on publicly available information.

An analysis of the drivers of syndication indicated that when PE firms invested in stages, firm-level characteristics such as age of the PE firm (used to represent experience level of the PE) and local partner (used to represent local knowledge) did not seem to influence their decisions. The variables—investee company age and investment size—were the only ones which emerged significant indicating that PE investors protected their investments through staging. Staging was primarily targeted at reducing information asymmetry and uncertainty by allowing PE firms take decisions about investing capital as situations unfolded. In developing infrastructure assets, risk levels in the precompletion phase are very different from the post-completion phase. Until the asset becomes operational and starts producing cash flows, it is worth very little. Further, the physical asset specificity characteristic of the asset makes it useful for little else. Thus, PE firms prefer to monitor the progress of the infrastructure firm and invest as the prospects of the firm are positive. The hypothesis of staging being used as a monitoring mechanism was established in this study. PE firms when investing in infrastructure used staging as a means to monitor and evaluate the prospects of the infrastructure company. Results of the analysis indicated that if PE firms decided to infuse more capital into the company, they did so within a span of two years from the previous investment. The descriptive statistics also supported this premise and the maximum average duration between two successive rounds of funding was 311 days or less than a year. The sample used for the study also did not feature any infrastructure project which received subsequent funding after five years. This implied that PE firms were careful in choosing the right kind of infrastructure projects to invest in.

Duration analysis of the time between investments indicated characteristics of deals such as deals in developed countries and transport deals that were perceived to reduce the risk of PE investors. Investee company age positively affected the duration of PE funding. This implied that older companies were perceived to be significantly less risky. The construction stage of the infrastructure asset was considered most risky, which warranted continuous monitoring leading to staged investment. Older infrastructure companies were usually in the operations/maintenance phase where the risk was considerably low leading to less monitoring and subsequently less staging.

Round number negatively influenced the duration of PE funding. Round number, in this study, was used to represent the level of staging in the deal. A higher round number represented greater staging and therefore lower time duration between two successive rounds. The percentage of PE investors investing from the previous round also negatively influenced the duration of PE funding. An increasing percentage of PE investors reinvesting in the subsequent round implied that these investors preferred to monitor their investments more and therefore stage more, leading to lower time gaps between financing rounds.

8.13 Summary

This study examined the staging of capital infusions when PE firms invested in infrastructure projects. A comparative analysis of deals with and without PE staging indicated that investment size per deal was significantly smaller in staged deals as compared to deals that were not staged even though PE firms who did so had significantly larger fund sizes compared to PE firms who invested in one-off deals. PE firms who staged investments also invested in younger infrastructure companies. Comparative analysis of staged PE investments in infrastructure indicated that PE firms who continued to reinvest in subsequent rounds invested with larger investment sizes per deal and had larger fund sizes but had significantly smaller investment sizes as a percentage of fund size per deal. They also invested in significantly younger infrastructure companies.

Regression analysis into the drivers of syndication indicated that uncertainty and information asymmetry surrounding the infrastructure firm was the most prominent reason that led to staging of PE capital. PE firm characteristics or country risks characteristics did not seem to matter, highlighting the fact that PE firms were homogeneous when it came to the decision to stage investments into infrastructure.

Analysis into the time duration between two successive rounds indicated that company age positively affected the round duration while the percentage of PE investors reinvesting in a subsequent round, and round number negatively affected round duration. Country development variable and sector variable (transport sector) positively affected round duration which implies that PE firms found developed countries and transport sector less risky and hence has longer durations of financing (and consequently less staging). PE firm-level characteristics did not affect the duration between subsequent financing rounds which indicated that staging or the frequency of staging did not depend on the qualities of the PE firm as much as the risk and uncertainty surrounding the infrastructure deal did.

References

Admati, A. R., & Pfleiderer, P. (1994). Robust financial contracting and the role of venture capitalists. *Journal of Finance, 49*, 371–402.

Anand, B., & Galetovic, A. (1997). Small but powerful: the economics of venture capital. Working Paper, Yale School of Management.

Bergemann, D., & Hege, U. (1998). Venture capital financing, moral hazard, and learning. *Journal of Banking and Finance, 22*, 703–735.

Bottazzi, L., Da Rin, M., & Hellmann, T. (2008). Who are the active investors? Evidence from venture capital. *Journal of Financial Economics, 89*, 488–512.

Chemmanur, T., Krishnan, K., & Nandy, D. (2009). How does venture capital financing improve efficiency in private firms? A look beneath the surface. Unpublished working paper, Boston College.

Cornelli, F., & Yosha, O. (2003). Stage financing and the role of convertible securities. *Review of Economic Studies, 70*, 1–32.

Cumming, D. J., & MacIntosh, J. G. (2001). Venture capital investment duration in Canada and the United States. *Journal of Multinational Financial Management, 11*, 445–463.

Dai, N. (2011). Monitoring via staging: Evidence from private investments in public equity. *Journal of Banking and Finance, 35*, 3417–3431.

Dai, N., H. Jo, & Kassicieh, S. (2009). Venture capital ownership type, investment criteria, and venture performance, SCU Leavey School of Business Research Paper No. 09-02, electronic copy available at: http://ssrn.com/abstract=1512012

Gompers, P. (1995). Optimal investments, monitoring, and the staging of venture capital. *Journal of Finance, 50*, 1461–1489.

Guo, J., Yan, W., & Zhang, G. (2008). Stage investment cost and adding investment triggers in venture capital. Systems Engineering—Theory and Practice, 28(8), 38–43.

Hopp, C. (2008). Nothing ventured—nothing gained? Empirical evidence on venture capital financing in Switzerland. Research paper series 23, Thurgau Institute of Economics.

Hopp, C. (2010). When do venture capitalists collaborate? Evidence on the driving forces of venture capital syndication. *Small Business Economics, 35*, 417–431.

Kaplan, S., & Stromberg, P. (2003). Financial contracting theory meets the real word: An empirical analysis of venture capital contracts. *Review of Economic Studies, 70*, 281–315.

Kaplan, S., & Stromberg, P. (2004). Characteristics, contracts, and actions: Evidence from venture capitalist analyses. *Journal of Finance, 59*, 2177–2210.

Kozmetsky, G., Gill, M. D., & Smilor, R. W. (1985). *Financing and managing fast-growth companies: The venture capital process*. Lexington Books.

Krohmer, P., Lauterbach, R., & Calanog, V. (2009). The bright and dark side of staging: Investment performance and the varying motives of private equity firms. *Journal of Banking & Finance, 33*, 1597–1609.

Lerner, J. (1994). The syndication of venture capital investments. *Financial Management Association, 23*(3), 293–316.

Li, Y. (2008). Duration analysis of venture capital staging: A real options perspective. *Journal of Business Venturing, 23*, 497–512.

Megginson, W. L., & Weiss, K. A. (1991). Venture capitalist certification in initial public offerings. *Journal of Finance, XLVI, 3*, 879–903.

Neher, D. (1999). Staging: An agency perspective. *Review of Economic Studies, 66*, 255–274.

Plummer, J. L. (1987). *QED report on venture capital financial analysis*. QED Research Inc.

Sahlman, W. (1990). The structure and governance of venture capital organizations. *Journal of Financial Economics, 27*, 473–524.

Singh, R. (2009). Delays and Cost Overruns in Infrastructure Projects: An enquiry into extents, causes and remedies. *Centre for Development Economics, Delhi School of Economics*, Working Paper No. 181.

Talmor, E., & Cuny, C.J. (2005). The staging of venture capital financing: Milestone vs. rounds. EFA 2005 Moscow Meeting Paper.

Tian, X. (2011). The causes and consequences of venture capital stage financing. *Journal of Financial Economics, 101*, 132–159.

Wang, S., & Zhou, H. (2004). Staged financing in venture capital: Moral hazard and risks. *Journal of Corporate Finance, 10*, 131–155.

Chapter 9
Value Addition by Private Equity Investors: Infrastructure

Start by doing what's necessary, then do what's possible; and suddenly you are doing the impossible.
—Saint Francis of Assisi

9.1 Overview

Despite the growing policy focus on infrastructure, the sector continues to face many challenges characterized by implementation and financing risks. First, infrastructure as a business requires sufficient land for developing the project. However, regulatory frameworks around land acquisition, environmental clearances and tax regulations continue to be unclear, especially in many emerging economies where the need for infrastructure capacity creation is even more dire. In the words of a project developer engaged in developing toll roads in India,

> Majority of infrastructure developers end up with unviable projects because of regulatory delays around acquiring land and providing environmental clearances. Most of these problems were not expected at the time of bidding for projects and the developers thought that the government would enable the necessary provisions in good faith for smooth development of the project.

Another developer who has developed multiple infrastructure projects also echoed a similar viewpoint.

> There has been a systemic failure at different levels, which has left the developers all by themselves to handle the problems in the sector.

Second the sector is characterized by bureaucracy, corruption and poorly structured or open ended provisions in good faith contracts, which are dampeners for private investors, and even more so in the case of global investors. A global infrastructure focused investor opines,

J. Gemson and Thillai Rajan A., *Private Equity Financing in Infrastructure and Real Estate*, https://doi.org/10.1007/978-981-16-1634-1_9

Inability to enforce contracts is a big issue for foreign investors since they are unlikely to have the same degree of familiarity with people, systems and processes as a domestic investor and are more likely to rely on contracts for their business operations.

While most countries might have a strong legal regime and autonomous judiciary, recourse to the legal process can be very time consuming and expensive in many. India is one example.

Third, just as any other industry, infrastructure is also plagued by revenue risks, market risks, operational risks and construction risks. While the assets have long lives and the demand for infrastructure products or services may not have the fluctuation seen in a fad economy, it is nevertheless exposed to the various shocks to the system. For example, road traffic is a function of economic growth. Any fluctuation in economic growth can therefore impact toll collections, and this is a risk that the developers have to bear. Another example of risk is the COVID-induced freeze on air travel in 2019 and 2020. As a response to the COVID pandemic, most countries shut down their air traffic significantly during the period 2019–2021, which dramatically reduced the air traffic and affected the revenues of airport operators. Airports Authority of India, the public sector agency operating many Indian airports, was expected to post a loss for FY21, from a profit of ₹36 billion in the previous year.[1] In fact, the expected loss in FY21 was the first instance of the firm incurring a loss since its formation in 1995.

Fourth, despite the huge investment outlay for the sector, access to long-term capital—both debt and equity continue to be a challenge. Over the past couple of decades, one of the most important transformations has been the increased interest by the private sector in both managing and financing the infrastructure sector. The increasing focus on the private sector in infrastructure investment has resulted in investment capital flows from Private Equity (PE) investors for infrastructure projects. PE investment in infrastructure can take two routes: Dedicated PE funds for infrastructure or general-purpose PE funds that also invest in infrastructure.

Unlike the banks, PE investors more often than not play a very active role in the entities that they invest in. Infrastructure is no different. After the investment is made, PE investors work with the investee companies in a variety of ways. The project developers need to be aware that the PE investors are unlikely to be passive investors. Apart from monitoring the progress of the investment by asking for regular MIS reports, PE investors bring to the table the strengths of their network that can significantly benefit their portfolio companies. In this chapter, we describe the following:

1. The nature of involvement of PE investors in the lifecycle of an infrastructure project
2. The impact created by PE funding on investee companies at different stages of the project development
3. The relevance of PE as a source of funding for infrastructure projects

---

[1] Covid-19 impact: AAI likely to slip into red for first time in FY21. https://www.business-standard.com/article/companies/covid-19-impact-aai-to-slip-into-losses-for-the-first-time-in-fy21-120091801258_1.html, Accessed July 24, 2021.

To get answers to these questions, we interviewed diverse members, both the investors and the senior management from the portfolio companies.

The choice of interviewees was based on the following criteria:

- **Investors**
  - A broad spectrum of investors comprising both single country and multi-country PE investors. While single country funds have a better understanding of the local political and economic context, global investors had a larger multi-country perspective.
  - The investors should have also made PE investments in infrastructure projects. In some cases, more than one respondent was interviewed from the same fund to understand different perspectives related to different infrastructure assets.
- **Investee Companies**
  - Companies that had received investments in the past from PE funds.
  - Companies from multiple geographical locations were selected to increase the generalizability of the findings.
  - Companies engaged in developing and managing different infrastructure assets were chosen to understand investment characteristics in different cases.
  - Small-sized, mid-sized and large-sized companies were selected to analyze how value addition was different in each case.

Content analysis of the interviews indicated the following dimensions of value addition by PE investors.

9.2 Value Addition by PE Investors

9.2.1 Source of Capital

In most cases, the primary stimulus to take PE monies for an infrastructure company was the need for equity capital. Infrastructure developers usually need equity capital in two instances. The first case is when capital is needed to expand operations and realize greater growth objectives.

Most private infrastructure developers were erstwhile Engineering, Procurement and Construction (EPC) contractors, who have been engaged in a contracting arrangement for large infrastructure projects. EPC contractors do site surveys, get approvals and clearances and design the engineering work for a project to start. Thereafter, the contract may or may not be subcontracted to other companies. Nevertheless, EPC contractors are the backbone of infrastructure projects. While the EPC business required investment in working capital, they did not have to make investments in asset creation. EPC contractors receive milestone payments from the government or concessioning agency during the project construction phase and would therefore require capital only to bridge the time differences in cash flows, i.e., between expenses and milestone payments.

However, when the EPC contractors sought to become infrastructure developers, they were required to bring in the equity contribution for the project. The capital requirement was significantly higher when compared to being an EPC developer. An EPC contractor may not find it easy to mobilize the large amounts of capital needed from an infrastructure developer.

Infrastructure has traditionally witnessed large investments by the government, public sector corporations and large business houses. The need for high capital and complexities of the sector had kept individual entrepreneurs away from this sector. However, with the advent of PE, small entrepreneurs and EPC contractors were able to participate in the bidding for development of infrastructure projects. PE has enabled the adoption of entrepreneurship approaches in the infrastructure sector. Infrastructure projects are significantly financed by debt capital. However, lenders need the commitment from equity investors before they can advance debt. This is when PE emerges as an attractive source of capital, because it augments the equity capital for the project and enables developers to get more debt. As an India based investee respondent put,

> The presence of equity certainly incentivises banks to give out debt, since the debt-equity ratio can be expanded with more equity.

PE capital also helps to reduce the debt burden of highly leveraged and troubled infrastructure developers. In the first decade of the millennium, many infrastructure developers, particularly in emerging countries, were finding it difficult to access new capital for different reasons. One of the main reasons was the presence of a highly leveraged balance sheet and presence of distressed assets which prevented de-leveraging the same. Rapid growth of infrastructure in the economy resulted in delayed clearances from the regulatory authorities and incorrect demand forecasts by the developers. This caused setbacks in project completion and the consequent poor performance led to unviable projects. As a BOT developer put,

> Delays in land acquisitions or in getting environmental clearances after 2 years were not expected by most of the private sector developers. Bidding was conducted without having these linkages in place. This was not foreseen by the private developers and the positive assumptions were proved wrong. As a result, many projects became unviable.

The need to raise capital and also provide exits to existing PE investors in many cases prompted developers to sell some of these distressed assets to raise capital for new assets. There were different types of PE funds which were interested in buying existing assets. Most distressed assets are sold at a discount to such buy-out funds, whose long-term objective was usually to aggregate such assets, make them profitable and come out with a public offering of such assets. Such class of private equity funds became popular, as it helped companies to reduce their debt burden to a large extent.

In addition to sale of distressed assets, operating assets were also sold to raise capital. PE investment facilitates creation of new assets by releasing equity to the sponsors. PE investors bring in capital, either as a primary investment or as a secondary funding to buy out the promoter's stake. As the availability of capital to the promoter helps in the creation of new assets, the regulators too supported PE investment. In the words of investors,

> Primarily, when we give liquidity to the current developer or owner, he will use that money to create new projects. That is why bodies like NHAI are quite keen to support proposals to change the concession agreements. In the initial years, the concession agreement might have said that the original owner had to remain for 20 years. However by 2010, the government felt that the change in control can be allowed if the assets have been in operation. So the role of the financial investor like a PE investor is different in infrastructure.. Our role supports takeout equity structures.

> The asset itself becomes more saleable to the next set of investors who are looking for yield. As far as the existing promoter is concerned, it frees cash as well as guarantees given to banks. So even from a contingent liability point of view on their books, they become de-levered, thus helping the sector as a whole.

PE investments thus help in making available new sources of capital to the sector. The Limited Partners (LPs) who invest in PE funds more often than not, include investors who cannot directly take equity positions in infrastructure projects. Apart from banks and insurance companies, PE investors are also able to attract other investors such as pension funds to invest in infrastructure PE funds. As a global investor said.

> These is evidence that the a PE fund structure helps in bringing in new sources of capital to the sector, which was otherwise not available. For example, the institutional investors who we tapped were from North America and Europe would not have been able to directly invest in infrastructure projects. PE investors have been able to get newer investors to provide equity capital for infrastructure.

Not only does PE infusion help in meeting the capital shortfall of the infrastructure developers, it also helps in raising further capital. A global investor explained,

> We did some follow on investments in two or our investee companies. One of the companies needed short term debt, and as we were a large fund, we were able to meet this requirement.

Other investors agree that PE can help in raising further rounds of finance or for a strategic sale by positioning the company correctly,

> We help the company raise capital through our global connections and network in the industry.

> Preparing the company for a strategic sale, by getting all the systems in place for an incoming buyer and positioning the company right is something we do as investors.

9.3 Benefits of PE

While receiving investment capital is a critical benefit, PE investors also provide significant inputs during the monitoring phase to improve the regulatory, compliance and governance standards of the projects.

(i) **Project Structure**

First, PE investment helps in improving a corporate governance by regulating inter-company transactions. Private infrastructure developers usually adopt a holding company—subsidiary company structure. Large infrastructure businesses use this structure to define legal and governing relationships between the different entities—at the level of the holding company level or the infrastructure project company. The preference to invest at the holding company level or SPV level would be based on the investment thesis followed by the fund. Investors who prefer to invest close to the asset generally invest directly in the project subsidiary. When an individual project may be too small to invest in, a portfolio of projects could be considered by many investors and investments are done in the holding company. Sometimes, investments do happen at both the holding company and the project subsidiary.

Investment at the SPV level is often termed as development equity. This is because the investment is used toward creating the asset and is required when the asset is under development. Once the asset has been completed and starts earning cash flows, there is generally no requirement for a large amount of funding. The appreciation of equity also tends to plateau out at this stage, and the asset is considered as an yield investment to a large extent. Some investors would then look at investing in the holding company, which his often equivalent to growth equity and the portfolio of assets is looked at in totality. With the help of different structures, PE investors help the investee company to structure the organization and carve out efficient structures to improve corporate governance systems and, of course, also to maximize their returns! In the words of a specialist investor in infrastructure assets,

> In most PE funded companies, there is clarity in terms of organizing the business. Capital is taken where it is exactly needed and equity at the holding company level is not diluted.

PE investors are primarily financial investors unlike the sponsors of an infrastructure project, which means they do not have recourse to other cash flows from the project. For example, it is common for the parent company to acquire construction or other contracts from the project company. It may or may not be an arms length transaction, given the role of the sponsors. Having such contracts for equipment supply, construction or maintenance makes it easy for them to recover their equity investment made in the project.

However, for a PE investor, the investment made is the only relationship with the infrastructure project. Unless the project succeeds, they would incur an investment loss. Therefore, as pure financial investors, PE investors drive the operations to ensure success of the investment, thereby bringing in better levels of efficiency and corporate governance. PE investors investing at the development stage face an issue when infrastructure companies use the investment to award construction contracts to group companies. Therefore, they put in place checks and balances to deal with potential conflicts of interest. As a PE investor respondent opined,

> If we come into an under-construction project, we would look very closely at the contract for construction. We prefer to evaluate the risk and if it is not acceptable, then we won't do it. A typical way to cover that is by having fixed price and fixed time construction contracts.

While investors may not be concerned about promoters doing a construction contract per se, they might insist that the contract be awarded on an arms' length basis. In reality, that might not always be possible. When the promoter makes a higher margin through the EPC contract, the capital cost of the project goes up. This can impact the project in two ways. As one of the investor put,

> if the capital cost goes awry, two things can happen – one is the promoter has realized the returns beyond what he should have made, so there is no economic interest. Second, if the capital cost goes up, the project has to recover more through tariff or toll. This may not always be possible, leading to non-viability of the project.

Investee companies are also cognizant of this investor concern and try to work in a manner where there are enough safeguards built in so that the capital cost is not compromised. As an investee said,

> Typically investors don't like people having both project development and EPC in one company. Either they want only EPC or they want only developmental business. We create different structures within the parent company, and this gives different alternatives to raise money. Since PE investors will definitely see this as a conflict of interest, we structure contracts in such a way that this concern is addressed.

(ii) **Implementing Best Practices in Health and Safety**

The second aspect of regulatory and compliance measures generally involve implementing best practices in the areas of health and safety of the laborers. Safety of workmen is given a lot of importance, and this largely follows global practices. Investors stress on workmen condition on where they stay, how they stay and proper working condition for those workers. Any fatality or major injury is generally taken very seriously. Third, anticorruption policies are also insisted on in business transactions.

Investee companies are required to implement such compliance measures with utmost seriousness. These practices are unique to infrastructure projects and are usually not relevant in other sectors. Fourth, investors usually conduct a due diligence on the existing standards of environment practices of the company before making the investment. Best practices adopted in environment policies are usually insisted on by the PE investors. Any lapses found are incorporated as a part of the shareholder's agreement. A rectification plan with timeliness for actions are drawn up and agreed upon. Once the investment is made, progress on Environmental Health and Safety (EHS) matters would need to be updated, similar to other Management Information System (MIS) reports on a regular basis, investors opine that although adopting such changes is challenging, promoters have begun to realize that it is important in order to receive funding. A global investor responded,

> This may look difficult in emerging countries, where there is a tendency for taking short cuts. But if you put discipline and incentivize people, we have seen that there is tremendous improvement at the working sites where we have invested vis-à-vis where we have not invested.

An investee project agreed,

> Promoters have certainly begun to understand and respect the value of the input given by investors.

Adopting best practices in various areas of EHS, anticorruption in labor laws result in an improvement in the compliance, reporting and governance standards of the investee company. This improves credibility of the company in the eyes of various stakeholders. As some of the investor respondents opined,

> Normally the governance standards of the investors would be pretty high with very strict guidelines about anticorruption, environment, health, safety, and so on. We would spend money on making sure that the company follows good practices.

> We show promoters that they can do business the way it is globally done – by being compliant and following robust processes. It is not that they are incurring huge additional costs because of this. We demonstrate that compliance can go hand in hand, along with the business success.

The biggest difference brought in this aspect by PE investors would be the effective implementation of these practices. While implementing robust governance standards was by and large a voluntary practice in the past, PE investors have played a major role in making such practices mandatory and more institutionalized. There would a separate compliance manager appointed in the project companies who would be in charge of various compliance measures. As all the steps are followed meticulously to achieve compliance, the business becomes more sustainable, as the company greatly reduces chances of facing litigations. On the other hand, the developer may still achieve the end result, but may not follow all the requirements to achieve this. An investor said,

> A developer may cut short some steps to achieve a goal. He may not comply with all the processes, although he may achieve the end result. As a result, it may not be very sustainable.

(iii) **Focus on sustainable development**

The success of any infrastructure project depends on its sustainability—in terms of economic sustainability, social sustainability and environmental sustainability. While privately funded projects are naturally concerned about economic sustainability, PE investors also exhort their investee companies to achieve social and environmental sustainability. Not for a moment should the PE investors be considered as altruistic. Hardnosed financial investors, as they are, they realize that harmonizing social and environmental sustainability would actually improve business sustainability. Implementing best practices, better compliance and reporting and better corporate governance policies results in all-rounded sustainable development. Sustainable development helps in achieving better performance standards in the sector. In the words of some global investors,

> One of the cornerstones of our thinking is sustainable development. By sustainable development I mean all the elements of sustainability such as environmental, economics, as well as social development.
>
> As an example, in infrastructure companies where we have invested, we make sure that workers have good working conditions and there is safety.

Adopting sound governance practices also helps in gaining recognition for the company. As a domestic investor explained,

> Governance is something which most PE funds do not compromise on. In a country like India (for example), governance has a healthy premium attached to it. It is a well-recognized factor and gives comfort to all stakeholders.

While implementing better governance is desirable, this comes at an additional cost to the management and involves more time and efforts as well. This can affect project timelines and can also make infrastructure more expensive. Nevertheless, over the long term, regulatory and compliance measures help not only in the development of the sector but also the way companies operate in the sector as well.

(iv) **Better risk management and monitoring**

An improvement in the systems and processes followed in the investee company is one of the important areas of value addition of PE. The investors of many infrastructure PE funds are foreign LPs who have their own requirements of compliance and reporting. Further, many infrastructure PE funds are a part of a larger international group which specializes in infrastructure with a large pool of experienced human resource pool available. Therefore, funds implement the same global standards and best practices in their local investee companies also, thus helping in improving performance parameters. As one of the respondents from a global fund said,

> The global performance templates, global governance templates, risk management templates and the expertise that is available within the team are some areas where PE investors are effective.

PE investors also gain experience from their investments in other portfolio companies. These experiences can be used for the benefits of all their investments. In the words of an investor,

> We give value-add in the company because of our experience in one of our other investee companies in the same asset class.

Investee companies also acknowledged this experience. As a large-sized investee company respondent put,

> PE investors are more market savvy, they have more information as a result of various investments in their portfolio companies. In many companies they invest in, they are either part of the Board, or have an observer status. So they have a ring side view. They are able to use these experiences to benefit their other portfolio companies.

Following robust systems and processes would also be useful in bringing discipline in the organization. A respondent from a global fund explained,

> Most of the woes of the infrastructure sector are because of irrational bidding in the past. When we invest in infrastructure companies, we bring lot of process and discipline in terms of how the bidding process is done. There is a bid committee formed, where several assumptions are stress tested by the team and a lot of pre-work is done before the actual bidding. This value addition is unique to an infrastructure asset.

Regular monitoring and reporting after the investment is another cornerstone of PE investments. Unlike the banks and other lenders, who adopt a more hands-off approach to monitoring, PE investors follow a hands on approach when it comes to monitoring their investee companies. This not only helps in efficient operations, but also facilitates improvements and strategic decisions. Investors have safeguards to check the maintenance of the asset has been done properly and operations are being handled efficiently. They also demand regular MIS reports about the asset operations. In case of any shortcoming in reports of studies conducted by some regulatory authorities, like NHAI, the PE investor generally has the right to bring in third parties to fix the problem if the same are not done by the promoter. Any contractual default can affect all the equity investors, and more so the PE investors, since they do not have recourse to any other cash flows from the project. They make sure that systems are in place to ensure that there is no slippage in revenue. For example, in toll collection projects, video cameras and sensors are installed to control the leakage in revenues collected. In fact, PE investors begin monitoring the investee company's systems and processes even before the actual investment takes place. They do this in the form of a detailed due diligence. Any shortcomings are identified and the company/promoter is asked to improve these areas. In many cases where the PE investor buys a majority stake in the company, an external third-party agency is appointed to streamline processes. As one of the investors explained,

> Before we go in, as part of the negotiations, we define the total framework with respect to how the companies would run, what would be our participation, our representation on the board and all sub committees and the critical components in terms of governance. All this is laid down in the documentation at the same time of investment.

PE funds actively monitor their portfolio companies as long as they stay invested in the company. Most fund managers spend significant time on managing the asset once the investment has been made. While achieving operational efficiency would be the primary aim of any PE investor, the precursor to this would be to ensure that the existing systems and processes are proficient enough to reach the next level of improvement. Tighter monitoring can also be done keeping the end goal of the PE investor in mind, i.e.: to exit the investment with a profit. Unlike traditional PE where listing of the company or promoter buy-back are popular exit routes, infrastructure investors have other strategies also in place to exit their investment like securitization of assets or swaps into the holding company which may get listed.

Risk management is central to PE investing. As infrastructure projects are fraught with financing and implementation risks, it becomes imperative for the PE investor to adopt frameworks which help in managing the risks. An investor faces several risks such as market risk, operation risk, human rights risk, environmental risks, commercial risks and construction risks. An investee company said,

> A professional investor usually tends to take lesser risks than what a promoter will take.

Literature talks of syndication and staging as two popular risk management techniques. Syndication refers to group of investors jointly making an investment in a single round. While syndication by itself may not reduce risk, the risk appraisal techniques are perceived to be better when different investors bring in their expertise while evaluating the transaction. Moreover, syndication is also used when the size of funding deal is too large for a single fund to invest. Staging is a practice wherein the investor makes the investment in different tranches as the project progresses. As the investment is made only when the project moves forward, the line of thought is that this can reduce the risk. These techniques therefore help in risk management.

An objective approach with the adoption of best practices results in greater efficiencies in project implementation. One of the investors said,

> For example, typically promoter driven companies do not have that science going behind new acquisitions decisions. If there is an infrastructure investor on board, he is asked many questions about the acquisition, how it is value accretive and how this will benefit the investor and the organization. Structured thinking behind analyzing a project in a certain way and the discipline behind such investments is something which you will find in PE funded companies.

The requirements of PE investors also benefit the company's processes. In the words of a an investee company,

> Their (PE investors') investment came with riders like independent directors, the use of Big 4 firms as auditors and so on. This helped the Board to become very professional. Independent directors give unbiased, third party perspectives to issues. Also, when we are sitting in our own office we may not know where others fail, but an independent director who is experienced can definitely guide better. Similarly, a Big 4 auditor is highly process driven and structured, which helps us improve. So this was how we improved our audit processes, internal control processes and corporate governance.

Achieving structured business functioning and discipline in operations leads to an improvement in business efficiency. Over the long term, this helps in taking the company to the next level of growth. Some investors cite examples of achieving efficiencies in their investee companies,

> In the case of toll collections, in many cases, there are very long queues to pay the toll. So we could come up with systems which shorten the waiting time for the traveller.
>
> If there are higher collection of toll charges, we do not just keep these extra amounts collected. We follow the right procedures of informing the Government and depositing it in the designated account. The cash transactions are carefully accounted and monitored.

Following world-class processes not only helps in improving asset efficiencies, but also helps in controlling costs and improving financial metrics. This is because PE brings order and there is a greater control on the activities in the business. Investment decisions are questioned, analyzed and evaluated more thoroughly. The higher discipline in cash flow management and related party transactions results in improved efficiency in the use of capital. Further, it is a virtuous loop. A good-quality investor may bring in diligent lenders which in turn may ensure better cost of lending, leading to lower Interest During Construction (IDC) component. PE investors could also help in rationalizing finance costs. An investee company explained,

> As they (PE investors) have various investments, they know what is going on at other places and what interest rates have been given to other projects. This information is useful and PE investors pass it on to the investment company.

(v) **Management of costs and efficient capital structuring**

Cost overruns are a common occurrence in infrastructure projects. Keeping the project cost in control is one of the cornerstones of a successful infrastructure project. As one of the investors said,

> Projects invariably suffer from time and cost overruns. But if you have higher discipline on project management control on related party cash flows and do a regular review of the operations, soft costs can be controlled.

Another investor concurred, although with a caveat that Capital Expenditure (CAPEX) decisions once taken cannot be easily changed even by the PE investor.

> The decision making is not impulsive because it will go to the Board, the PE investor will think about it and ask several questions such as comparisons with other projects. So that brings some sort of discipline in governance which may contribute to lower costs. But if the CAPEX decision has already been made at the time of investment, the PE investor would not be able to change that CAPEX decision.

Financial processes and financial discipline lead to other important outcomes—efficient capital structuring and financial engineering. This value addition was summarized by many investors as follows,

> Once the project is in the operations phase then there would be a need to amend the financing terms. It might be possible to get lower cost debt or higher quantum debt. Normally in a project every 2-3 years one has to review the capital structure and see what is appropriate at the point in time.

> PE funds refinance the debt in many cases. In one of our listed investee companies, we did a rights issue to infuse more funds into the company. The cost of funds which had gone up to 16 percent redued to 13 percent due to a healthier balance sheet. So bringing in the right structure at the right time and at the right price is one of the important contributions ofthe PE investor.
>
> A smart financier can add a lot of value to an infrastructure project. It is not that promoters cannot do financial engineering, but many of them have not reached that level of sophistication. It also depends on the level of sophistications and ingenuity of the investor on how he could potentially structure a debt.
>
> Refinancing not just for the sake of refinancing, but to boost the equity IRR while at the same time meeting the requirement of the debt provider, the bond subscriber or the lending bank can be facilitated by the PE investor.
>
> We do project level analysis and not just at the corporate level. For example, when a project is being constructed, say the debt is at a 12 percent interest rate. But after-commissioning, the loans can be refinanced at a lower interest which brings down the cost of financing. It would also be possible to in yield seeking investors at a project level and replace equity. Such capital structuring can boost IRRs.
>
> There may be instances where the promoters may not even be aware of the option for the company to raise foreign debt at a lower cost., However, since we are global investors, we can help the investee company with such an option.

However, there is another viewpoint as well from the investor community that financial engineering is more appropriate only for well-developed capital markets. This is because India is still a growth market as far as infrastructure financing is concerned. While financial engineering could be employed to boost equity IRRs, it may not be possible in growth assets. In the words of an investor,

> We know the benefits of levering up and increasing equity IRR but this is more relevant in mature assets, mature sectors and mature geographies. Normally the debt for growth will be more difficult to find than debt for mature projects. So financial engineering would be relevant when there are matured assets with limited growth potential.

While the benefits of financial engineering are debatable even among the investor community, it was agreed by most respondents that smart financial techniques and robust systems and processes go a long way in strengthening PE-funded companies compared to those that did not have a PE investment.

(vi) **Network support and access**

An important contribution of PE investors is to help in networking with relevant people and organizations. When an external investor makes an investments, the promoters could also get access to the wider network of the investors. Building professional networks helps in building the customer base, sourcing better deals from suppliers, attracting talented employees and getting better terms of debt from banks. Therefore, networking not only refers to connecting with other investors, but also to other stakeholders like lenders, prospective employees, suppliers, customers and so on.

As a result of better networking, PE funding contributes to enhancing the credibility of the investee company in the marketplace. Building visibility and reliability is an important requirement for infrastructure companies. Further, investment from PEs also helps in authenticating an unproven business model in some cases. Banks are the largest contributors of capital in an infrastructure project, with a majority of debt capital coming from bank funding. The biggest comfort factor that banks get when a PE investor is a strong commitment for equity capital.

An investor said,

> PE funding helps the bank get the comfort that the balance sheet is fully funded on the equity side. One of the challenges that banks face in some countries is that equity is never fully funded. It is always left to the promoters to figure out equity as the project progresses. In PE funded companies, these things get sorted very quickly.
>
> With the commitment of equity investors in place, banks get the confidence to advance debt. Further, the project does not get delayed due to the inability of the promoters to bring in equity capital at the required stages. It brings more credibility to the project.

An investee company agreed,

> Banks have comfort that the company will be run more professionally with the presence of a PE investor. They are sure that the equity committed for the project will definitely come and will be tied in.

However, while the presence of equity is comforting for the banks, a majority of investors think there is no added incentive to welcome PE investors to the companies they lend to. This is because banks also have their own engineers who evaluate the project at different stages before releasing the funds, although the extent of monitoring may be less stringent when compared to a PE investor. Some investors, however, think that there is no difference in the monitoring levels between banks and PE investors. One investor opined,

> While PE monitoring of the projects that they invest in is intense, it doesn't mean that the banks scrutiny need to be less intense

In general, PE investors felt that the banks have not fully acknowledged yet the benefits that an external investor in the company provide. Some investors felt that foreign PE did not give banks the comfort that they need from local sponsors and promoter guarantees. This was also agreed by the investee community, as one of the renewable energy respondents explained,

> This is counter-intuitive, but in some instances banks actually feel safer with promoter backing than compared to foreign institutional backing. Some Indian banks are more comfortable having an Indian promoter to deal with, compared to a foreign PE investor, as it becomes an institution driven company rather than a promoter driven company.

On many occasions, PE investors may not have the leverage to manage the local microenvironment and that the developer may be better at operating the asset or in managing the political machinery, because of their familiarity with the local milieu. However, to overcome this challenge, most PE investors have started constituting expert teams to develop their own expertise and oversee the technical aspects of the project. With the importance of PE in infrastructure increasing since 2010, banks have started getting used to having a PE investor in infrastructure projects.

Enhanced credibility as a result of PE investment also helps the projects in talent acquisition. Recruiting better quality employees and retraining employees are important components of talent management process. With the presence of reputed PE investors, the process of talent acquisition also becomes easier.

The infrastructure sector is characterized by a continuous need for funds. It therefore becomes important to plan the funding process, both for the short term and the long term. Improving credibility becomes critical for securing further rounds of investment. The presence of PE investor in the company gives comfort to other potential equity investors, both in the case of private placement and in an Initial Public Offering (IPO). As an investee company respondent explained,

> The presence of a PE investor is a great value addition to equity holders post the listing, If the PE investor continues to be a shareholder in the company and has nominee directors, there is a lot of comfort that the company is monitored properly and run in a proper manner.

A global investor agreed,

> If the company plans to raise funds through an IPO, having a large PE fund automatically increases credibility, and thus the reception from potential IPO investors will also be good, because of the confidence that the presence of PE investors provide during the IPO process.

9.4 Limitations of PE

PE investment is certainly not a magic pill for the capital starved infrastructure sector. It has its own drawbacks and limitations. While we outline some of the prominent limitations here, the benefits outweigh the disadvantages in several instances.

An important requirement of the infrastructure sector is that funding should be made available for the long term, as the projects are also long term in nature. Availability of reliable long-term finance is one of the major challenges faced by the private infrastructure sector, particularly in those countries where long-term debt capital markets are not deep. PE therefore becomes an option for long-term equity capital. The presence of long-term equity also reduces cash outflows required to regularly service interest. Although a majority of investors interviewed were of the opinion that investing equity at the development stage was not preferred, the stage of entry largely depends on the investment objectives of PE funds. There are some investors who invest at the development stage, while others prefer the operations phase. Often, the infrastructure portfolio of PE investors could consist of investments in diverse stages. The tenure of investment would depend on the investment thesis of the fund and the life of the fund. Irrespective of the investment philosophy, infrastructure PE investors are long-term investors (may not be as long as long-term debt funds or promoters, for sure) and invest for a longer time frame when compared to generic PE. A global investor opined,

> ...most infrastructure investors would want to invest for at least 8-10 years.

However, the life of an infrastructure project is much longer than the average investment duration of a PE fund. This could potentially result in conflict of interests between the developer and PE investor. In the words of an investor,

> PE investors have an investment horizon. While certain decisions might be beneficial for the investors, it may not be beneficial in the long run for the company. So there may be misaligned interests in some cases, in terms of the timeline.

Further, some respondents are of the view that infrastructure as an asset class is best built by the government, due to its unique characteristic of delivering lower returns compared to conventional PE. The investor continues,

> Worldwide, using equity to develop infrastructure has been minimal. Majority of the infrastructure investment is made by the government. This is because the returns are so long drawn and will never justify the returns PE should conventionally make, unless it is a leveraged significantly, which then increases the project risk.

Another limitation of PE has been cited as the cost of funding. Equity is always more expensive than debt, and PE investors expect IRRs of about 25 percent to justify an investment. This in turn puts pressure on the cost of using the asset to the end users. A global investor respondent agreed,

> The high cost of capital poses a burden on the users of infrastructure. However, in emerging countries, the cost of capital is high. Also, there is a dearth of capital. Therefore, in some instances, the end users are made to pay the cost indirectly. However, it is generally felt that the benefits from the project overshadow the higher costs of equity capital.

Although the cost of PE is more, infrastructure developers have felt that PE is essential to meet the shortfall in long-term equity capital availability. PE investments help in making available new sources of capital to the sector. Many of the Limited Partners (LPs) who invest in PE funds are usually from developed countries. Some funds have a mix of both emerging and developed country LPs. Emerging country LPs have been typically banks and insurance companies. But commercial banks are restricted from doing large amounts of equity as they are governed by capital market exposure norms and also face asset–liability mismatch issues. Insurance companies on the other hand are ideal LPs as they have access to long-term funds. Since insurance companies directly cannot make equity investments in infrastructure projects because of prudential norms, PE firms act as a conduit to get equity capital from infrastructure companies.

As a global investor said,

> There is evidence that the PE fund structure helps in bringing in new source of capital to the sector, which was otherwise not available. For example, the institutional investors who we tapped were from North America and Europe. Now we are seeing newer and newer investors. There are several first-time institutional investors who have invested with us.

9.5 Summary and Conclusions

This chapter provides answers to three important questions relating to the involvement of PE investors during the lifecycle of an infrastructure project and the appropriateness of PE as a funding source for the infrastructure sector.

There are three distinct stages in an infrastructure project development—development phase (pre-financial closure and construction stage), construction phase and operational phase. The capital for development phase is usually provided by the developers, and entry of PE funds is usually after the financial closure takes place. The stage of investment varies depending on the investment thesis of the fund. Many funds prefer to invest at the operational stage, while some others with a higher risk taking ability invest during the construction phase. The nature of involvement of the PE funds can either be purely financial or it could also include non-financial aspects. During the construction phase, PE capital takes the form of long-term risk capital. Investors put in place financial controls and cash flow discipline. There is assistance provided during the initial stages of project construction in various aspects—rational bidding, risk estimation, building the core team and so on.

During the operational phase, developmental risk is eliminated from the business model, and as a result, the actions are focused more on improving efficiencies. On the financial side, PE involvement relates to assisting in further rounds of investment. Capital structuring and use of financial engineering techniques are other areas that PE investors contribute. On the non-financial side, there has been greater focus on monitoring, regular reporting and compliance, adoption of global frameworks and introduction of risk management techniques. PE investors are also actively involved in providing connections using their network and industry connect and in helping the infrastructure developer to build business connections.

This chapter also highlights the impact created by PE funding on the infrastructure companies. As the nature of involvement differs during the construction and operational stage, the impact created also changes across the two stages. PE makes available large amounts of equity capital, which is of paramount importance during the developmental stage. Availability of risk capital in this stage also helps in fostering entrepreneurship in the sector, as EPC contractors are able to take up projects as developers. When adequate equity is tied in, banks also gain comfort to grant higher debt for the project.

On the non-financial side, bidding rationally helps in reducing failures due to incorrect estimation. The involvement of PE investors also leads to improvements in efficiencies and corporate governance practices as well. When PE investors invest during the operations phase, they buy-out the equity from the promoters, which enables them to reinvest in other projects by releasing their equity capital. A significant non-financial impact created on entry at the operational stage is to improve visibility and credibility of the investee company. This helps the company raise further capital from the markets, either from strategic investors or through a public offering. Better governance standards also result in sustainable development, which

Involvement and Impact Analysis of Private Equity Investment during the Lifecycle of an Infrastructure Project				
Parameter		Development Phase	Construction Phase	Operational Stage
Involvement	Financial aspects	Development Capital primarily contributed by development institutions or project sponsors. Entry of private equity investors is usually at the end of development stage and thereafter	Provision of long term risk capital Financial controls and cash flow discipline	Assistance in further rounds of investment Optimise capital structuring Financial controls and cash flow discipline Financial engineering techniques
Involvement	Non-Financial aspects		Assistance in rational bidding Assistance in risk estimation Motivation and support throughout initial stages Assistance in recruiting and building a strong team Safety measures and policies for workforce Setting up anti-corruption policies	Assistance in structuring the organization Quality checks and regular monitoring Adoption of risk management techniques Regular reporting and compliance Networking support to build business connections Adoption of global frameworks
Impact	Financial aspects		Availability of new capital sources for the sector Large pools of capital for long time frames Comfort to banks Innovation and entrepreneurship fostered	Free up of capital to create new assets Cost controls in the business Better IRRs Improvement in financial metrics and performance
Impact	Non-Financial aspects		Rational bidding reduces incorrect estimations Improvement in efficiencies Better quality employees and Board of Directors Better corporate governance	Scaling of the company and preparedness for IPO Discipline in operations Improved credibility and visibility Sustainable development Improvement of performance standards in the sector

Fig. 9.1 Conceptual mapping of the involvement and impact of private equity during the lifecycle of an infrastructure project

is critical for the success of any infrastructure project. Such project-level improvements also contribute to the improvement of performance standards in the sector as a whole.

Figure 9.1 maps the involvement and impact of PE investment during the lifecycle of an infrastructure project.

It is expected that the infrastructure sector will be one of the main growth themes for many developing economies in the years to come. Apart from directly contributing to improvement in the quality of life, capital spending in infrastructure creation would also catalyze economic growth.

As the infrastructure sector matures and evolves, there will be greater need for capital and innovative structures to come into play. PE infrastructure is one such innovative financing mechanism which can help in further development of the sector.

However, the increased compliance levels, the systems and checks required by a PE investor could cause increase in timelines and costs. An investor respondent said,

> A balance is needed between compliance and the cost of compliance.

Nevertheless, over time, project developers have realized that systems and processes are necessary for sustainable growth and future funding. Unless there is an external impetus, many of these initiatives brought in by the PE investors would not have been implemented by the developers. An investor said,

> Governance requirements do result in high timelines. But investors prefer investing in a promoter who is open to accepting this. Such measures also benefit the promoter in the long run. Initially, there may be resistance, but over time, promoters have realized the importance of organizational systems and process. It makes the company ready for further foreign funding. Large investors will not invest unless the company is ready with these requirements.

As the infrastructure sector is one of the most complex sectors, it is vital that capital sources should bring more value than mere contribution of funds. PE as a financing mechanism provides this value addition in a significant way as compared to other forms of external investment in infrastructure projects.

Chapter 10
Value Addition by Private Equity Investors: Real Estate

I would give a thousand furlongs of sea for an acre of barren ground.
—Shakespeare

10.1 Introduction

Tracing the history of funding in the real estate sector becomes important to understand how the financing needs of the sector have evolved. While most of the observations in this chapter has been based on the characteristics real estate market in India, it would be widely applicable to most emerging markets. Prior to 2005, bank lending and private lending were the predominant sources of funding for the real estate sector, in addition to relying on cash flows from the advance sale of units. However, bank credit was insufficient to meet the growing demand from the real estate sector. Informal private sources were predominantly used to fund land acquisition, i.e., before the construction began. The projects developed were not of large size, and as approvals did not take long, there were no undue delays in construction. The informal investors were either allotted units or repaid using sales proceeds.

Post 2005, when the Government of India (and also many other emerging country governments) opened the sector to FDI, there was significant amount of investment in real estate from foreign investors. The sudden flow of capital from foreign sources led to considerable changes in the way the sector operated. From 2005 to 2008, the real estate sector witnessed its highest growth, also supported by the growth in equity markets. As a result, raising funds from domestic equity markets and offshore listing was also an attractive option, in addition to other sources such as PE, bank loans and private lending. Therefore, during this period, the characteristics of the sector as well as the funding mechanisms underwent a significant transformation.

This changed in 2008, when equity markets across the world collapsed. Raising funds through public markets became unviable due to the meltdown. Bank loans and private loans continued to fund the sector, albeit at a lower proportion. On the

J. Gemson and Thillai Rajan A., *Private Equity Financing in Infrastructure and Real Estate*, https://doi.org/10.1007/978-981-16-1634-1_10

operations front, developers were finding it increasingly difficult to manage large projects. While approvals were getting delayed, developers started failing on delivery mechanisms and on timelines as well. The delays not only hurt returns to the PE funds because of the time factor, but also resulted in escalated construction costs and labor costs. However, the sale prices of real estate did not increase at the same pace. As a result, majority of PE funds did not get the returns that they had originally envisaged.

Over time, the structure of the PE investment changed from being purely equity based to being structured. Structured instruments in the form of Compulsorily Convertible Debentures (CCDs) or Non-Convertible Debentures (NCDs) offered a higher guarantee of returns to the investor, where there was a regular payment of interest by the developer. Majority of investors preferred mezzanine and structured formats while investing since it resulted in more risk sharing with the investor. The real estate sector has for long been viewed as a family-run sector, characterized by opaque practices. The advent of PE in real estate changed this, with Board managed companies, better reporting and increased transparency. Therefore, similar to PE investments in other sectors, real estate PE investment was also subject to stringent due diligence before making the investment and continuous monitoring after making the investment.

PE investments in real estate are predominantly in residential assets and commercial assets, especially office assets. In many cases, the funds are targeted at specific classes. Residential projects are less capital intensive, and there is no need for high leverage, due to sale realizations, sometimes even before the project was formally launched. The project was also self-liquidating for the PE investor, making it easier to exit. Commercial projects on the other hand were more capital intensive and riskier, as leverage rose. There was no concept of selling the units as the property is leased to tenants only on completion of construction.

The real estate sector is unique in several respects, and this brings about a complexity in the funding requirements. While the sector's growth prospects largely depend on the growth of the economy, understanding of the micromarket cycles are equally important.

This chapter highlights the impact created on investee companies (specifically the real estate investments) by PE funding in addition to analyzing other important aspects such the investment patterns and alignment of interest between the investor and the investee. Specifically, this chapter highlights the following using the experience of the real estate industry in India:

(i) The suitability and appropriateness of PE to address the funding needs of the real estate sector.
(ii) Alignment of interests and incentives between the PE investors and the investee companies.
(iii) Value addition to their portfolio by the PE investors.

The findings in this chapter are based on in-depth interviews with real estate companies and PE funds that invested in the real estate sector.

10.2 PE as Source of Capital

Equity capital is usually constrained for the developers as the size of the projects has become larger over the years and the timeframe for approvals has also become longer. Moreover, developers also wish to invest in multiple projects. The need for capital is usually the first trigger which starts a PE investment discussion, with capital being viewed as the most important contribution of the PE investor. In addition, PE investment is sought when the project is in the development phase where conventional funding (say bank term loans or advances from customers) is not available. Therefore, PE investment is also considered as adding value to the project development. Both investors and investees agree that adequate and timely availability of both debt and equity capital is critical for the success for a real estate project development. In the words of an real estate PE investor,

> There will always be the need for PE in real estate projects, as developers cannot undertake such huge capital costs themselves and banks in India do not finance the land acquisition.

The investor also indicated that even large developers with adequate capital backing go for PE, as a de-risking strategy. In his words,

> Even if a developer has sufficient growth capital, if deployed in a large project, he would be able to deliver only one project in 3 years. Augmenting investment from PE helps to diversify his sales risk by investing in projects in different locations. He de-risks his cash flows by diversifying in different markets and PE funding helps in this.

PE capital is very different in its characteristics when compared to conventional bank funding. PE investors may be willing to invest at locations and stages of development where the conventional banking funding may not be available. An investee company respondent observed,

> Banks have certain specified norms as a policy and they would not want to fund real estate developments in specified geographical locations. But PE investors may see the same location as potential opportunities over the next 4 or 5 years. The ability to take risks makes this an attractive source of risk capital.

Even when bank funding is available, there may be certain conditions or stipulations attached to loans given to risky projects. However, PE investors may be willing to relax the conditions if they see future potential in the investment and developer. In the words of a domestic investor respondent,

> Banks have standard terms and do not take equity risk in a loan. But in PE, there can be a lot of flexibility in the structuring and the terms. In a mezzanine structure, PE investors take equity risk.

A South India-based real estate company said,

> Bank funding for construction stage comes with different conditions and usually banks do not make significant customization or deviation from their standard terms and moratoriums. However, PE investors can customize the terms and conditions even for a structured debt transaction.

Banks are not allowed to fund the real estate sector for the purpose of land acquisition. However, this is the stage when companies are in most need of funds. The unavailability of bank loans to purchase land results in a significant increase in demand for equity capital. This restricts the capacity of the developer to grow and scale. Many small developers thus resort to other forms of private capital sources, such as borrowing from small individual investors. This can limit the growth because of the unorganized nature of such individual investor market. PE, on the other hand, gives access to large pools of capital for longer timeframes. As an investee that had received PE funding said,

> Money raised from private financiers can be used for fund small projects. The maximum the can be raised is ₹200 – 250 million. But if there is a need capital that is 10 times the above amount for a large project, PE is the best option.

This view was supported by two other investor respondents as well,

> Informal money normally does not come from one person. It also does not officially come into the bank account. But with PE, the developer can talk to one person and get all the funding required. More importantly informal money typically is short term money with 2-3 year timeframes. But with PE, the developer gets long term money from one source and for large quantity.

> Land prices have moved up and constitute a significant portion of capital cost. Informal sources cannot fund such huge land costs.

> The ability to raise further funding increases with PE investments. They managed to open doors to several investors at the time of IPO. Getting associated with a global PE brand gives an edge when a company goes out for further funding.

PE also helps in authenticating the developer and the business model. The investment helps in setting a benchmark valuation, which can be very relevant during the IPO. Not only does the PE investor help in garnering investor interest, but the process of raising funds from public markets also becomes easier. The investee respondent shared,

> We had governance principles in place, had independent directors on board and were doing quarterly closings much before we got listed and these things became mandatory This was because of the presence of a PE investor. So when we got listed, these things were not new and became very easy.

Further fund infusion from other PE investors also becomes easier if there is an existing PE investor in the company. The real estate business is capital intensive and requires adequate debt capital in addition to equity capital. The presence of a PE investor helps the investee company to secure debt from banks and NBFCs since, like an investor stated,

> Banks gain comfort as the presence of PE increases the corporate credibility of the builder.

The PE investors insist on better cash flow discipline, and their portfolio companies have healthy financials at the time of their investment as compared to firms that do not have PE investment. This automatically gives greater comfort to the lender, resulting in better terms.

Despite the importance of PE as a source of capital, it is not without limitation. PE capital is an expensive source of finance. Equity is always costlier than debt. Even in the case of structured deals, which involve minimum or no equity, the rate of interest on the debt line is much more expensive than bank loans. As a result, the cost of the project increases. This can in turn increase the prices of PE funded projects when compared to prices of projects which do not have PE investment. As investee respondents puts it,

> PE increases the project cost substantially because the cost of that money that comes in from private equity is quite high.

> When a lot of PE money goes into larger projects with high tenure, the holding cost keeps piling up. However, prices do not move at the same rate. Also, the cost of construction is growing at a higher pace than price increase. This can make it counterproductive.

PE funding in real estate companies can be during different stages of the project—prior to commencement of construction or after construction. While the purpose and magnitude of funding can vary during each phase of construction, it is apparent that the sector needs capital across all stages. Capital required before the construction of the project is typically for the purposes of land acquisition and obtaining approvals. Land acquisition is usually the most capital intensive among all the stages of project development. However, banks in India are not allowed to fund land acquisition, and they can only fund the construction stage of the project. As a respondent from an investee company puts it,

> Banks will only fund projects which are approved and are ready for construction. The construction finance is also based on the construction progress and other conditions.

As a result, PE is a popular funding source for purchase of land and for expenditure associated with various project approvals. In the words of an investor,

> As the need (for funding) is more at the time of land acquisition or for the initial approval stage, investments are mostly at this stage.

PE funding during the construction stage of the development is primarily to finance the erection of the building and project. Fund infusion after the completion of the construction is for the purposes of improving the façade or structural improvements being made in the project.

Typically, in the case of residential projects, PE funding usually occurs before the construction commences. This is because in residential projects, developers fund the construction with the monies raised from the buyers. In some cases, PE capital is also raised during the construction stage, to meet the shortfall in capital. However, residential projects rarely need capital after the construction is complete. In the case of commercial assets, PE investors usually prefer to invest during the later stage of construction or after the completion of construction. This is because investing during the initial phases of commercial asset development is highly risky, and in most cases, developers finance this from their own sources or from bank or NBFC funding. A domestic investor respondent explained his fund's investment philosophy,

> For residential projects, investment is both at land acquisition stage as well at construction stage, depending on the requirement. Therefore, this would typically be growth capital when construction is yet to commence. However, for commercial assets, investments are mostly in completed assets. We invest in properties which are at least 70 – 80 percent leased to tenants.

Investments made before construction of the project have the highest risk for the investor. The risk levels gradually reduce as the construction progresses. This is because there is no uncertainty in the development when the construction nears completion. Investments made in projects after the completion of construction (typically in commercial assets) do not carry any development risk. The only risk which can arise to such investments is on the tenancy levels. However, PE funds usually opt for projects that have been significantly leased to tenants. This automatically brings down risk levels. Corresponding to the level of risk, the potential of returns to the investor is also high when investments are made in the initial stages of the development and becomes lower as the construction advances. In the words of one of the global investor,

> If funds have to deliver a high IRR, they have to come in at an early stage – land acquisition or close to approvals.

Another investor agreed,

> When the construction is complete, the investment is low risk in nature with expected rental yields as low as 9-10 percent. This is because most of the risk is already priced in. Also, if one enters at 100 percent tenancy level, there is no upside to the rental yields. 60 – 70 percent occupation level implies an upside to the potential rental yields. When the investment is in development stage, the expected rental yields are much higher.

This is because when an investor enters after the construction is complete, all risks are priced in. This changes the nature of returns from being growth based (on entry before commencement of construction) to being purely yield based (on entry after completion of construction). Some funds have specific allocations to such assets, wherein they can earn a regular yield in the form of rental income, which carries low risk and are more predictable. While any investment by PE involves intensive due diligence, the focus of the diligence varies depending on the stage of investment. For example, an investment made before the commencement of construction or during the initial stages of development will entail a due diligence done on the developer and on the legal aspects. However, if an investment is done when the construction is nearing completion, due diligence is done on the quality of the tenants and the potential of the project location. As an investor in commercial assets opines,

> When one enters after the construction is complete, the credit quality of the tenants is closely studied. Technical due diligence is done to verify the quality of the building, the potential of the location, the leasable area and on other legal compliances.

10.3 Investor Selection as a Strategic Choice

Although the primary purpose of securing PE monies is to increase the available equity capital, the success of the investor–investee relationship is paramount for the success of the PE investment. Unlike bank loans which are passive in nature, PE capital is more active in nature, with investors being involved in all important decisions of the company. Therefore, the strategic choice of the investor is of significant importance while opting for this mode of funding.

First, the investee company must gain comfort from the presence of an external investor. Managing expectations of the developer by limiting interventions and at the same time influencing the company positively is the cornerstone of any PE investment. Many investors have also recognized this requirement. As a domestic investor puts it,

> It (the relationship) will not work if the investor tries to encroach the business decision making of the promoters. A collaborative approach should be adopted.

This was affirmed by another foreign investor.

> The investor must let the developer sit in the driver's seat, sit next to him and help him steer the wheel. , Only then would the developers appreciate and understand that both parties' money is in the business and decisions will be value assertive to all the shareholders.

The comfort with the PE investor is usually gained over a period of time, after the investor had stayed invested for few years. In many cases, the investee company prefers to receive investment from the same investor for multiple projects or in different funding rounds, as there is high familiarity with the working style of the investor and vice versa. A real estate developer who had received PE investment summarized this as follows:

> It is very important that the PE fund we partnered with has same levels of transparency and integrity as us. Also, it is crucial for the mental wavelength to match. We look at the investor more as a strategic partner than as a financial partner. As these attributes matched our requirements, we went ahead with the same investor to fund multiple projects.

The choice of the investor also depends on the type of project undertaken by the developer and the investment philosophy of the fund. Many funds are asset-agnostic and invest across different classes of real estate assets. However, there are other funds which are specific to investing only in residential assets or only in commercial assets. A developer who specializes in residential assets would prefer an investor with the same specialization, as this usually helps in better synchronization of interests and greater value addition.

10.4 Investment Structuring and Alignment of Interests

The alignment of interests between the investor and investee determines the success of the relationship. In the case of PE funding, the investor–investee relationship is usually for a longer time frame as compared to other funding sources. As a result, it becomes critical to align interests at the beginning of the relationship, to avoid potential conflicts at a later date. A common mode of aligning the interest of the investor and the investee is by adopting the appropriate investment structure.

Unlike bank loans or NBFC debt, PE fund infusion can be modeled in different ways. The most common and basic investment structure is by way of common equity shares, wherein the PE investor receives equity shares in exchange for the investment amount, based on the valuation of the investee company. Another popular structure is in preference shares which can be converted to equity shares at the option of the investor. Such preference shares usually carry a built in dividend. Yet another structure would be in the form of a structured instrument, usually mezzanine financing. This involves infusion of funds in the form of debt which carries an equity kicker. This debt financing can further be modeled into two forms which may or may not be converted into equity shares at the option of the investor. Occasionally, there may be no equity component involved, and the investment would be only in the form of debt capital, which may or may not be converted into equity shares at a future date. When an investment is made using structured instruments, the investor receives regular cash flow, which is modeled based on the IRR requirements specified in the investment agreement. A global investor explained,

> Structured instruments are effectively IRR driven. The document gives adequate protection and specifies that CCD (Cumulative Convertible Debenture) or NCD (Non Convertible Debenture) will carry an IRR of say, 19 percent. They are secured, in the sense that the cash flows are senior to the developers' cash flow rights.

Real estate PE financing in India has been usually by way of straight equity or in the form of structured instruments. In the initial years of PE investment in real estate, it was mostly in the form of straight equity. However, over time, the trend has gradually changed in the sector, with a higher incidence of structured finance deals. At times of uncertainty, investors generally tend to use structured investments. Investors decide the structure of the investment based on the pedigree of the investee company and also the relationship dynamics. The investor continued,

> Although in today's markets we prefer structured deals, we also do pure equity deals with selective clients – large companies which are reliable.

The stage of entry into a project is another factor which can be determine the basis of the investment structure. When an investor makes an investment at an advanced stage of development, the risk and uncertainty is significantly lower when compared to an investment made during the beginning of the project. In such cases, straight equity may be used instead of structured instruments.

Structured instruments carry lower risk to the investor, as there is regular cash flow which is received periodically by the investor. As compared to this, the risk is much higher in a straight equity, where investors do not receive an interest payment regularly.

While straight equity entails receipt of dividend, it is dependent on the financial performance of the investee company. As the risk is lower in a structured investment, returns are also correspondingly lower to the investor compared to straight equity deals. In structured investment deals, the investee company agrees on a predetermined IRR to be paid to the investor. Any profit earned above this goes to the investee and need not be shared with the investor. However, in the case of straight equity, the entire project returns will need to be shared depending on the shareholding pattern. As one investor respondent explained,

> In structured deals, if the upside is more, promoters can earn even more. However, if it is a straight equity deal, they would have to share the entire profits with investors. Thus promoters are happy to go ahead with structured instruments.

As the risk is higher in straight equity deals, the due diligence and monitoring is more stringent and proactive when compared to structured instrument deals. An investee respondent from a midsized real estate company said,

> Both in the case of straight equity and structured finance, there is extensive amount of due diligence which happens. This was probably not the case 3 – 4 years back. However, an equity investor has a great involvement when compared to a structured debt investor, because the latter has a certain form of income. Therefore, the due diligence done by an equity investor will be more rigorous than what a structured debt investor does.

However, for structured instrument deals, the investors generally do not interfere with the company's functioning unless there is a disruption in servicing the interest payment. Another small investee agreed,

> Even after entering the project, the straight equity investor is more involved than a structured finance investor. For example, if they see the project slowing down in terms of sales, they will definitely get involved and make recommendations in terms of how sales can be improved. But in a structured debt unless there is a default in payment, there is no interference. However, any kind of investor regularly monitor sales as well as construction.

The tax treatment of the two forms of investment structures is also an important consideration while deciding the form of investment. A structured instrument entails payment of interest either at a monthly or quarterly frequency. This interest payment is a tax deductible expense and hence can lower the taxable income of the SPV, which in turn reduces tax outflow. However, straight equity gives no such benefit, as there is no interest payment. Straight equity involves payment of annual dividend which does not reduce the tax liability. Hence from a taxation point of view, structured instrument is more tax efficient than straight equity for the SPV because of the tax deduction available for interest payments.

The developer also prefers a structured investment as the cost of structured debt is comparatively lower than the cost of equity. Although structured debt by PE is more expensive than project loans by banks or NBFCs, companies with PE infusion accept this form of funding due to other aspects of value addition in addition to the capital. In the words of an investor respondent,

Promoters understand that that they have to pay a premium to get the money, not just for the capital per se, but also for the other advantages a PE investor brings to the table.

However, as structured investments require regular payment of interest, this can lead to operational cash flow crunch, if not planned properly. This is not the case with straight equity investments. A respondent of an investee company which opted for straight equity investment explained,

We had opted for straight equity and had received an upfront investment of ₹1200 million for land acquisition. There was no need for us to regularly service this money, as it was equity and not debt. Even if one takes a conservative interest rate of 10 percent per annum, there will be a cash outflow of ₹120 -130 million per year or approximately ₹ 10 million per month if this amount was given as debt. This can put an additional squeeze on operational cash flows during poor market conditions.

Structured instruments are also a way to avoid disagreements on valuation discussions at the time of investment.

Investing in the form of straight equity instruments require arriving at a valuation of the investee company, which decides the shareholding percentage. However, in many cases, the PE deal falls apart due to disagreements on valuation. This discussion does not feature in the case of structured instrument transactions, since it brings in element of performance in the returns.

Another way of structuring the investment to ensure greater alignment of interests is to take the investment at the appropriate level in the company. PE investments can take place in two levels in a company—(a) in the parent company or at the holding company (HoldCo) level and (b) directly into projects or at the SPV level. Investments at the holding company level follow the traditional corporate finance structure, while investments in the SPV adopt a project finance arrangement. While both the forms of investment prevail, the preference for a majority of PE investors in real estate is to invest in the SPV and not at the level of the holding company.

From the investor's viewpoint, investing at the SPV level brings in higher transparency. The investment is easier to monitor, with checks and controls being more effective. One of the investor respondents explained,

Holding companies hold land parcels which are in different stages of development. Some are under development, some are under approval and some are under litigation. Having such a portfolio is impossible to monitor. We always prefer project specific investments, which are relatively much easier to monitor.

However, when the investor invests at the holding company level, there is diversification of risk to some extent, as there are various types of projects at the HoldCo level. Comparatively, a SPV-level investment results in risk concentration, as the returns are solely dependent on the success of the project(s) within that SPV. Nevertheless, despite the risk concentration, investors prefer to invest at the SPV level due to greater control over the cash flows of the specific project. In the words of a real estate investor,

Although there is reliance on cash flows from only a single project (in the SPV), the higher control and stringent due diligence at the time of the investment offsets this risk. Further with escrow accounting, it is easier to monitor the cash flows of the project.

Investor can also invest only in projects which suit specific interests, rather than be a part of all projects at the HoldCo level. The investor continued,

> Generally developers would have some residential projects, some commercial projects and some land accumulated at the holding company. Everything may not interest us. Also, investing in HoldCo would mean frequent disagreements with developer, if the latter wants to invest in land or property which does not interest the PE fund.

Exits are another important factor for the investor. When the investment is at the holding company level, the common forms of exit for PE investors are either in the form of an IPO, promoter buy back or strategic sale. When equity markets are bad, this becomes extremely difficult, as witnessed in the recent past. In the words of an investor from a large-sized PE fund,

> Exits become a challenge at the HoldCo level. Ultimately, the company will need to get listed or the developer has to buy back the shares. But when the equity markets are unfavorable, it is not possible to go for an IPO. Therefore, the preference is always to invest at the SPV level, where is it relatively easier to exit.

Investing in the SPV offers a wider set of exit options for the investor. While strategic sale is an exit option, in many cases of structured debt investments, the exit takes place when it is refinanced by a bank loan. Residential projects are usually self-liquidating, and investors are paid off from the sale proceeds. In the case of commercial assets, Real Estate Investment Trusts (REITs) can be an attractive exit option in the coming years. Many PE funds focused on commercial real estate have accumulated asset pools which can be effectively bundled as REITs and exited. Commercial asset pools can also be sold to other investors in the form of a strategic scale.

From the investee viewpoint, investments received at the holding company level gives a lot of flexibility in the utilization of funds. Despite this, developers prefer to take investments at the SPV level in order to avoid sharing the returns from other projects to the PE investors.

Another benefit of taking investment at the SPV level as perceived by the investee companies is to avoid investor oversight at the holding company level. When an investment takes place at a holding company, investors take a keen interest on all projects. This increased level of interference may or may not be acceptable to the investee companies. A real estate developer explained,

> At the holding company level, we work on several projects. We may sometimes want to move the cash flows of one project to another based on market conditions. But the investor may not be comfortable with this arrangement. This is why SPV level investment is the most preferred method for us, as there is more freedom. This method will also be easy for the investors to exit.

PE results in stringent monitoring, financial controls and cash flows discipline in the investee company. This not only ensures that the investor's interests are aligned with the investee, but also brings about best practices which help the investee company. PE funds are very organized and structured in their functioning. A South India-based investee said,

> PE investors are very process oriented, structured and organized. They have specific processes defined for every activity which helps us in many ways.

The effects of monitoring and process-driven practices are elaborated by a domestic fund respondent,

> The biggest value addition of a private equity investment is in terms of the cash flow discipline in the investee company. As the growth of the company affects the investor as well, cash inflows, cash outflows, pricing, configuration and so on are closely monitored.

There is close monitoring of the project development, construction and sales progress, monthly cash flows and MIS statements. In addition to cash flow management and escrow, PE funding also results in clean title papers. Earlier, the developer may appoint a local lawyer who may not even have the right knowledge to go through the title papers and establish its veracity. However, companies seeking PE investment appoint top lawyers proactively to clear all legal disputes. All this brings about a greater discipline in the investee company leading to higher efficiency in operations.

There is a result-driven approach, reducing delays and cost over-runs. PE investors bring about discipline in operations, insist on regular reporting and closely monitor all activities of the development process. In the words of an investor,

> We are no passive investors. We take active involvement in the activities of the investee company and bring in global standards in their processes and operations.

As a result of using best in class practices and more stringent monitoring, there is higher efficiency in processes and systems as compared to similar companies that does not have PE investment.

10.5 PE Certification

The presence of PE investment increases the visibility and credibility of the investee company. As the developer becomes a part of the broader PE fraternity, there is access to professional network which can help his business grow. The better-quality governance and management practices help in validating the integrity of the investee company and its promoters.

As a result, various stakeholders are more confident to do business with the company. First, banks and other lenders have greater comfort on the financial stability of the company. As mentioned earlier, in some cases, this could get translated to better terms of loans granted. In the words of an investor,

> Banks view PE positively, as this form of funding brings in financial discipline, has stringent monitoring and increases accountability. Effectively, the investor is monitoring on behalf of the bank. A lot of pricing gets driven by this

PE has been an important reason for the popularity and widespread use of the escrow mechanism. As a Mumbai-based real estate investor said,

> The concept of escrow accounts in real estate was not no commonplace before the advent of PE funding.

This means that all receipts and cash inflows to the investee company will be deposited in a separate escrow account for this purpose. The PE investor will then authorize the disbursements from this account, thereby preventing any form of siphoning of cash by the developer. This automatically ensures that the project is not unduly delayed and also gives comfort to the buyer. The investor continues,

> Based on agreed cash flows, we release the money from the escrow account to a working fund account. From here, the developer pays the various suppliers. The escrow mechanism ensures that the developer does not have surplus liquidity. When there is a surplus liquidity, the developer could indulge in actions that can divert cash.

Project contractors are confident of receiving payments promptly for the work done. This helps in timely work, thus avoiding undue delays in construction and development. The investor continues,

> Contractors are confident that there will not be delays in payment. As a partner, we are also able to negotiate better rates with contractors, which help the developer.

PE also helps in attracting better-quality employees. Simultaneously, customers also gain confidence about the quality of the project and timely delivery when there is a PE investment. Sales channel partners gain comfort from PE and are confident of receiving sales commission on time from the investee company. As an investor explained,

> Developers engage channel partners to help in selling the residential units. Earlier, channel partners always used to have a problem of realizing their commissions, especially from small builders. Now, in a PE funded company, channel partners are assured of their payment and this increases the comfort factor.

PE helps in attracting better-quality tenants and increased lease rentals as there are new innovations which increase brand value. The investor continued,

> The pride of being associated with a large PE brand is significant for the investee company. Tenants recognize the value of institutional holding in a project and are ready to pay some premium just to be in that project. This is because of the services that are offered, the amenities that we invest in.

Another investor agreed,

> An institutional owned property always commands premium in terms of rentals and also capital gains. The presence of the PE brand helps in attracting good quality tenants as well.

10.6 Value Addition by PE Investors

The discussion and analysis thus far set the context to discuss about the value addition from PE investment in a more direct way. While the need for capital is usually the single most common reason for a real estate company to think of PE investment, this form of funding usually goes beyond mere contribution of capital. The non-financial areas of contribution can be across different functional areas of an enterprise, with many aspects unique to the project type (residential or commercial assets). In the words of a Bangalore-based investee respondent,

> Private equity comes with a lot of intangible value.

The real estate sector has for long been considered to have opaque practices. PE investment has changed this scenario, as there is a greater insistence on transparency and regular reporting of financials. In the words of an investor,

> Compliance starts figuring very high on the agenda and books out of accounts are regularly scrutinized. A PE funded company starts looking at results on a more regular basis rather than just an annual basis.

PE investors bring about better governance in their investee companies. Usually, the investor is represented on the Board of Directors of the company as a nominee director and also on the different board committees. Other funding forms like bank debt do not usually have such representation on the company's board. This helps in better corporate governance, improves transparency and also aids strategic decision-making process in the company. This was supported by an investor's observations,

> With PE investment, the entire set of governance practices comes into place. The company moves from a promoter driven entity to a Board driven entity.

One of the biggest advantages of PE investment is access to market intelligence. Funds would have invested in multiple companies in various geographies with different business models. Moreover, most PE funds have a global presence. The benefits and experiences gained from one investment can be shared across all their investments, thus helping the investee company gain from the global experience of the investors leading to better processes and efficiencies. An important aspect of market intelligence is to understand real estate cycles and market movement. This was agreed by different investee respondents,

> At the time of finalizing the business plan and budgeting, they (investors) give us a lot of inputs based on their expertise. Some of the ideas may be new to our geography but might have been tried and tested in other investments. Such inputs and ideas have been of great help for us in our projects.

> Market inputs are also useful when the developer wants to enter a new segment. For example, a low cost residential developer who wants to enter the premium segment or vice versa. Another example is when investors give inputs on the growth potential of land banks, based on their location.

> Investors bring in knowledge about real estate cycles. As the fund has a real estate team they also become good bouncing boards for our management, as they are specialists who understand the real estate market very well from different perspectives.

Sharing of inputs sometimes helps in value engineering in the investee company. Inputs help in reducing costs, improving the product quality and reducing wastage. In the words of real estate developers:

> The investors have shared ideas on some of the best practices used in other parts of India and the world. For example, some of their inputs helped us to control costs in our project.

In the case of residential projects, PE investors usually enter before the construction commences or during the initial stages of construction. During this stage, the technical team of the PE fund help the investee company in planning and designing the unit sizes, the layout and the pricing of such units. An investor explained,

> We are not just passive investors and play a proactive role in the development process. We not only sit on the Board but also participate in various committees with regard to planning, designing and pricing of units. For example, if a developer has bought a piece of land in a location based on a future potential we use our intelligence and data to share information on the ideal size of units in that location, the demand scenario, the value of these units, the specifications and so on. Using such information, we participate in the designing and pricing and add value.

PE investors also help in designing marketing communication, preparing sales pitches and adopting marketing ideas. No other financial investor contributes toward the development of the project to such an extent. Inputs relating to designing, pricing and marketing are based on their in-house experiences as well as market intelligence gained from other investments. As a domestic investor explained,

> We sit with the developers to help in designing the market agenda, the communication material and advice on the best type of unit that can be sold. We help the developer get better rates on advertising. We have relationships with banks and distributors who can help in selling the units.

Another area which can benefit the investee company is guidance on phasing sales. The real estate market in general appreciates over time, although this is subject to market conditions. Almost all real estate developers in residential segment phase their sales, selling the inventory over a period of time. This helps them to get a higher price on the units sold toward the latter part of the construction. However, this technique can result in a financial problem if the cash flows are not planned properly. The presence of PE investment gives sufficient funds to the developer to phase the sales and maximize realizations. PE investors also give inputs on the timing of the sales. In times where the markets are bad and sales velocity is low, PE investors give innovative marketing ideas for the unsold units. They help the investee company in tapping their networks and bank connections to sell the unsold units.

In commercial projects, PE investors help in bringing about product-level improvements, both in terms of structural enhancement as well as terms of facilities provided. Commercial complexes and office spaces have today developed beyond being mere places of work. A better work environment is extremely important to attract and retain talent. This has been recognized by tenants, who prefer office spaces that meet the conveniences of the modern workforce. An investor who specialized in commercial assets investment explained,

> As investors, there has always been the urge to push the envelope and bring about innovations at all levels. For example, offices are not just a place to work. Open park spaces, cafeteria, gyms, sports and cultural events and so on are offered to employees. Standalone buildings have now given way to integrated business complexes. As a PE investor, we facilitate these innovations to draw quality tenants.

Almost all PE funds which hold a majority stake in commercial projects have a specialized asset management team which manages the asset professionally. This results in better operations management, better control and enhanced monitoring mechanisms. In the words of a commercial asset investor,

> Technical assistance is given based on the investor's need. But in almost all our investments, there is an asset management team which specializes in project management. These professionals have cross functional experience and help in improving the design and construction.

The purpose of a dedicated asset management team is summarized by commercial investors as follows,

> The asset management professionals have cross functional experience and help the developer by contributing ideas, saving money and avoiding pitfalls in the project. There is some resistance from the promoter initially; but on realizing the benefits over the long term, this gets accepted eventually.

In some cases, the asset management team suggests ideas and contributes to the project development, rather than just implementing the project. In the words of a real estate developer,

> Investors typically bring in a project management team. We do consider their ideas on costs, budgets and designs. However, they do not insist and just provide recommendations. But we will take the final call.

The asset management team also strives to bridge the layer between the top management and frontline construction workers. This team is also allowed to move across investments and geographies in many funds. This helps in cross-pollinating ideas across different investment sites. As put forth by different investor respondents,

> We bring in a layer where our asset management team interacts with the project personnel as well as the top management. They bridge the gap and the developer is really happy with the asset management capability that we have brought. Everything becomes a lot more streamlined than it used to be.

> Asset managers are usually rotated across projects. The best practices from one project could be implemented in another. This helps in sharing skill sets, reducing costs, improving deliverables and so on.

In commercial assets, maintenance of the property is of high importance to the PE fund. In many cases, the building is constructed and leased out to tenants, but it is usually not managed properly afterward. This results in loss of good-quality tenants. PE investors stress on continuous and active asset management. A Mumbai-based investor explained,

> Usually developers build and then forget about the maintenance. For example, one of our assets was a great building leased out to a large number of tenants before our entry. But somewhere down the line, the property became completely mismanaged. When we invested, we spent less than half million dollars and we pushed up the quality of the asset by making basic changes like fixing the landscaping, changing the project team, hiring external resources and giving tenants better facilities. We vacated non performing tenants and this was automatically replaced by better tenants because of the facelift we gave the building.

Similar opinions were also expressed by other commercial asset investors.

> A PE investor will not hold back on expenses for maintenance of the asset. Periodic large maintenance activity once in 3 or 5 years is a must for a large commercial property. When the property is owned by a PE fund, this is done on time, whereas chances that a developer does this once he completes the construction are low.

> In a commercial asset, property management is very important. Property management has different aspects such as facility management, security management, leasing management, and so on. We have in-house teams to perform all these functions, give out assessments to do the right thing and to continuously monitor and manage the asset to get the right yields.

Value addition is of significance only if it results in taking the company to the next level over the long term, in addition to improving short-term performance. Therefore, it becomes very important that the value addition is sustained. Moreover, the value added by the PE investor is considered to be of relevance only if it would be perceived as "true value" by the investee company as well. Else, the various actions and endeavors of the investor community may not be accepted by the investee companies. Therefore, the key to value addition in a PE transaction is to make sure that the perception of value addition is the same for both the investor as well as the investee. In some cases, it was witnessed that although the investor perceived himself to be giving valuable inputs to the company, the latter considered the investor to be reporting authority, to which monthly reports need to be sent. In the words of a real estate developer,

> There was no interference in any of our operations. We were required to send them the monthly statements. As long as everything went right and we paid the interest every month, the investors did not get in the way.

Another developer agreed,

> Only during initial stages of freezing the budgets and preparing the business plan, the investors gave inputs, which were valuable. But after this, there was minimal interference with the project.

While minimal interference was one way of avoiding conflicts, this should not be at the cost of contributing meaningfully to the growth of the company. The success of PE funding lies beyond capital and other inputs; it lies in seeking to reduce differences in perception of value addition between the two parties.

10.7 Discussion

This chapter analyzes three important features pertaining to PE investment in real estate, the alignment of interests and the value addition by PE investors.

PE as a source of capital is very important to the real estate sector for four reasons. (1) It is risk capital which is available for locations and stages of development for which alternate sources of funding are not available, (2) it is available for longer timeframes and in larger quantities than conventional capital, (3) there is higher flexibility and customization from PE investors, and (4) it helps in scalability of projects and facilitates fund raising from other sources such as banks.

PE can be infused at different stages of the project development. Monies infused before the commencement of construction are usually to purchase land and for other expenditures related to obtain approvals. PE funding toward the end of construction is more relevant in commercial assets than residential assets. Despite the usefulness of PE capital in the project development, it is an expensive mode of finance. As the success of a real estate project in India is directly dependent on the expertise of local rules and legal systems, the promoter's role does not reduce even with the infusion of PE capital. However, PE investment can add value in various aspects of the business. Figure 10.1 highlights the various parameters of PE involvement in different stages of project development and Figure 10.2) provides an illustration of alignment of interests in PE investments in real estate.

Parameter	Before Construction	During Construction	After Construction
Purpose of Funding	Land acquisition & approvals ↔	Construction Funding ↔	Improvements in property
Project Type	Residential ↔		Commercial
Risk Involved to Investor	High ↔		Low
Returns to investor	Growth based ↔		Purely Yield based
Level of Due diligence	On developer ↔		On tenants and location potential

Fig. 10.1 Conceptual mapping assessing suitability of PE in real estate

Criteria		Parameters						
		Risk	Returns	Valuation Mismatch	Cost of Capital	Tax Efficiency	Monitoring	Exits
Investment structure	Straight Equity	High	High	High	High	Low	More intensive	
	Structured Instrument	Moderate	Moderate	Nil	Moderate	High	Less intensive	
Level of Investment	HoldCo Level	Diversified	Unrestricted				Lower ability	Complicated
	SPV Level	Concentrated	Restricted				Higher ability	

Fig. 10.2 Conceptual mapping assessing alignment of interests in PE in real estate

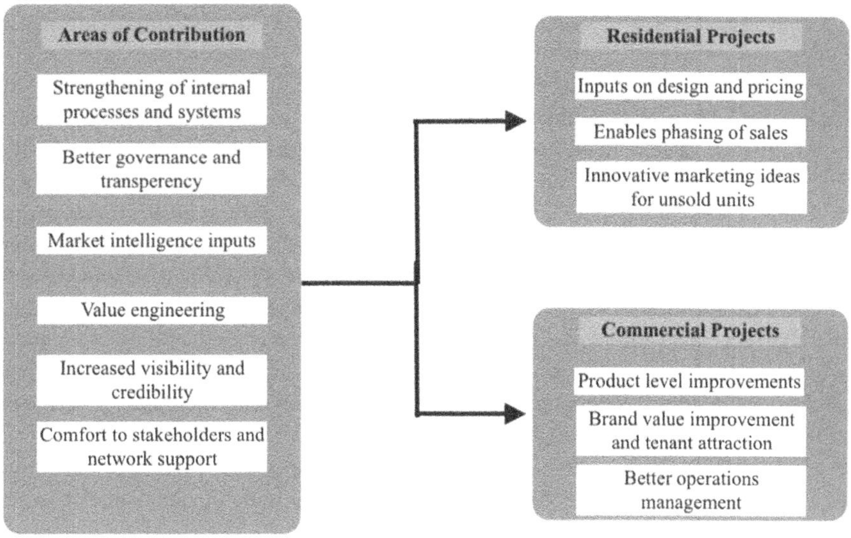

Fig. 10.3 Conceptual mapping of the value addition by PE in real estate

Value addition by PE investors in real estate companies has several noteworthy features. Improved levels of transparency and corporate governance, access to market intelligence and global best practices, value engineering, contribution with respect to planning and designing of projects and asset management assistance are some important areas of value addition which are unique to the real estate sector. Additionally, PE capital improves the credibility of the investee company. This results in improved confidence among the different stakeholders of the business, viz., lenders, contractors, employees, prospective customers and tenants and channel partners. While value addition is in itself very important, what is more significant is that the inputs given by the investors must be perceived as "true value" by the investee company as well (Fig. 10.3).

10.8 Summary and Implications

Globally, the real estate sector had attracted significant amount of PE investments since 2010. The advent of this form of funding has brought about changes in the functioning as well as funding in the sector.

Over time, investments in the SPV level have increased rather than in holding company levels. This is because of the need for transparency and control for the investor, which is better available in the SPV as compared to the holding company. The use of structured instruments has also become more popular as compared to straight equity. Structured instruments help investors to align expectations on returns and exit. Mezzanine and structured instruments also help in achieving flexibility in tenure.

PE as a funding source has many implications to the sector from a policy perspective as well. Despite the higher cost of funding and increased reporting requirements, PE can be beneficial because of the value addition and contributions by the investors. PE investors play an active role in their investee company and contribute more than mere capital. The non-financial areas of contribution by PE investors are quite significant, as they take a keen interest on the different business areas. Further, the certification effect to the company as a result of PE investment is considerable from the perspective of the lenders, customers, employees and other stakeholders. PE helps real estate companies to achieve scale and expand considerably. Developers have over time realized that these are necessary for sustainable growth and funding. Investee companies have also started to appreciate the need for increased governance and reporting requirements of PE capital.

From a policy perspective, studying the implications of PE helps in designing the right policies to improve the effectiveness of this funding mechanism. Measures such as the introduction of Real Estate Investment Trusts (REITs) have catalyzed the development of the stagnant real estate sector. REITs are essentially real estate companies managing income producing properties and which offer the interest in these properties as common stock to the public. REITs can play a significant role in providing easy exit mechanism to PE investors. Many large PE funds have begun to accumulate commercial assets, which can effectively be aggregated as REITs.

Rapid urbanization and changing demographics have resulted in a strong demand for residential and commercial properties. This has increased the requirement for larger projects, posing a challenge to the highly capital-intensive, capital-starved real estate sector. PE has emerged as an important source to meet these capital requirements. However, time is of the essence for PE investors. As the lengthy approval process is an important reason for long timelines, it would be useful for the government to bring policies which can effectively reduce the approval timelines. As a domestic investor respondent said,

> An importance concern in the real estate sector is the lengthy approval process which is complex and lacks transparency. Unless the approval process becomes transparent, housing prices will not come down easily.

Reduction in approval timelines not only quickens project completion and makes real estate affordable but also improves returns to the PE investors. This can help in attracting private capital to the sector.

PE has been an important contributor in shaping the real estate sector. The developer community has also started realizing the value of this form of funding, which contribute both on the financial as well as non-financial aspects.

Chapter 11
Appendix: Data Sources and Methodologies

By a small sample, we may judge of the whole piece.
—Miguel de Cervantes

This note presents details on the data sources and methodology used for conducting the various financial and statistical analysis in this book. Analysis of PE in infrastructure used infrastructure deals and projects, whereas analysis of PE in real estate used real estate deals and projects.

11.1 Analysis of PE in Infrastructure

Analysis of PE investments in infrastructure used project-level data and deal-level data.

Project-level data was sourced from the Global Project Finance Database provided by Venture Xpert. An infrastructure project was considered as the unit of analysis. A project represented a completed transaction between an infrastructure company and an investee company—one that infused capital into the infrastructure company through a project finance transaction.

Deal-level data was obtained from Securities Data Corporation provided by Venture Xpert. The infrastructure deal was taken as the unit of analysis. An infrastructure deal represents the transaction between the infrastructure company and an investee firm(s) at a particular time. If the investee firm(s) was a PE firm, it corresponded to a PE investment into the infrastructure deal. Such a deal was also known as an investment round or financing round (Lerner, 1994).

Infrastructure deals include data about the parties in the transaction, financial arrangements, structural arrangements and external conditions that existed when the parties entered into the transaction. Details of parties in the transaction include name of the investor, country of origin, inception date/year of investor, name of the investee, country of origin and date of financing the deal. Financing arrangements include the amount of capital forwarded by the investor to the investee and capital available to the

J. Gemson and Thillai Rajan A., *Private Equity Financing in Infrastructure and Real Estate*, https://doi.org/10.1007/978-981-16-1634-1_11

investor, while structural arrangements include round details. External conditions that existed when the parties entered into the transaction include economic and financial conditions such as the level of development of the economy, prevailing interest rates and the robustness of its stock market.

11.2 Data Sources

11.2.1 The Global Project Finance Database

The Global Project Finance database was provided by Venture Xpert. This database contains detailed historical information on project finance deals. Information about the various characteristics of the project such as project sector, project cost, gearing ratio and project sponsors is available. The sample period chosen for the study was from 1990 to 2009. 1990 was taken as the start year because significant private sector investment into infrastructure started at that time. The database provided 3001 infrastructure projects from 1990 to 2009, which were designed on project finance basis, of which 365 had PE funding. While information is available in all sectors where deals have been designed on a project finance basis; only oil and gas, power, transport and water sectors have been considered for this analysis.

Investment data from January 1990 to December 2009 across 83 developing countries and 34 developed countries was used to examine the impact of PE investments in the infrastructure sector. To ensure the analysis was adequate and comprehensive, it was also required that the project cost (size of the project in US$ millions) be available. Thus, a total of 2821 infrastructure projects were examined, of which 349 projects financed by private equity (PE). The total value of the sample considered in the analysis is US$1.43 trillion in nominal values.

Data obtained from Securities Data Corporation, Venture Xpert used worldwide PE investments in the infrastructure sector from 1990 to 2009. This database included dates of venture financings, the details of investors and portfolio companies in each round, and the amount of funds available and disbursed. It included firms that did and did not go public. The data was divided into three company industry classes—“Information Technology,” “Medical/Health/Life Sciences” and “Non-high Technology.” “Non-high Technology” industry class, from which the sample of infrastructure deals was sourced, provided data on investments in agriculture/forestry/fisheries, business services, construction, consumer related, financial services, industrial/energy, manufacturing, transportation and utilities investments.

The scope of infrastructure projects covered in this study was limited to the industrial/energy sector, the transport sector and the water and utilities sector. The industrial/energy sector included deals on energy deals, alternate energy, geothermal energy, solar energy, wind energy, oil and gas projects including oil and gas exploration. The transport sector included deals on transport, airfield and other transport and railways. The water utilities sector included deals on water and utilities.

The infrastructure deals were extracted from the "Non-high Technology" Industry sector in the database. The initial list obtained from the database had 1098 deals. Deals with "Undisclosed Company" names and critical data missing such as investment size, fund size and round number were removed from the sample. To ensure that all the deals indeed pertained to the scope of infrastructure projects considered in this study, each portfolio company name was researched in the Internet and eliminated if they did not relate to the infrastructure sector. Eleven deals were eliminated this way because they were not infrastructure deals or did not have enough information available on the Internet to suggest that they pertained to our scope of infrastructure projects.

Historical venture investments usually contained over-reporting of rounds (Gompers and Lerner, 1999). Round or round number was the numerical value of the financing round when investment into the investee company took place. To account for correctness of round data in this study, all deals were examined to remove duplications. Any deal that had round date which fell within 6 months of the earlier round and which contained the same details of the previous round was considered a duplicate. This exhaustive checking ensured that the final sample did not contain any duplication of rounds. Finally, efforts were taken in securing missing data in data points such as "Age of the infrastructure company at the time of PE financing" by researching for the company's inception date in the company's website online. The final sample for the study consisted of 358 infrastructure deals where PE firms invested approximately US$9.743 billion.

Data relating to the level of development of countries was sourced from UNCTAD (United Nations Conference on Trade and Development) Handbook of Statistics, 2010. The CPI Index for the various countries was obtained from the World Bank Web site www.worldbank.org.

11.2.2 Adjusting Variables to Ensure Comparability

The Venture Xpert database provides details of investment sizes/round sizes and fund sizes in thousand US$. In order to account for inflation and make these values uniform, the real values of these investments were computed based on the nominal amounts present in the database. These real values were used in the various econometric analyses in the study. The real values known as "Round amount controlled for inflation" were computed as follows:

$$\text{Real Value} = \text{Nominal Value} * \text{Factor},$$

where

Real value	Investment size or fund size controlled for inflation (Calculated Value)
Nominal Value	Round amount available in the database
Factor	Country CPI Index[1] factored to US dollar 2009 values.

[1] The CPI Index values for the various countries were obtained from the World Bank website - http://data.worldbank.org/indicator/FP.CPI.TOTL.ZG - accessed on 31.10.2011.

11.3 Analysis of PE in Real Estate

Analysis of PE investments in real estate used project-level data and deal-level data.

A real estate deal was considered as the unit of analysis. A real estate deal represents the transaction between a company in the "Real Estate" industry and an investee firm(s) at a particular time. If the investee firm(s) was a PE firm, it corresponded to a PE investment into the real estate deal. Such deals include data about the company, inception year, diversity, Pan India presence, project name, parties in the transaction, financial arrangements and other variables. Details of parties in the transaction include name of the investor, origin, investor type, stake, inception date/year of investor, name of the investee, city and date of financing the deal.

11.3.1 Data Sources

Data for investments in the real estate sector was obtained from multiple sources: the Emerging Market Information Services (EMIS) database, the CRISIL database and Venture Intelligence. PE investment data for deals in the real estate has been obtained from Venture Intelligence.

The Emerging Market Information Services (EMIS)[2] database provides information on emerging market companies and industry sectors in over 197 companies. The CRISIL database (an S&P Global Company)[3] is India's largest independent integrated research house and provides details on the Indian economy, industry, capital markets and companies. The Venture Intelligence Service[4] was established in 2002 and provides information on private equity and venture capital transactions in India. This database is the leading source of information on PE and VC investments in India and contains details on PE investments, promoter and project details, demographics and details on the project. DealCurry (www.dealcurry.com) is a vertical social network-based business analytics platform in multimedia format, tracking financial and corporate markets for events, interpret, and integrate the information in its platform and provide a device and network independent cloud-based solution. Its integrated research product tracks, prospects, and prepares quick pitches for the whole range of transaction markets in India. DealCurry's suite of products includes DataBoard, Startup, and PitchBoard along with Mobile or Tab Apps that binds the community into marketplace (https://www.crunchbase.com/organization/dealcurry). A comprehensive dataset was then created by integrating PE investment data with non-PE investment data in real estate. This data was cross-checked to ensure there were no duplicates.

The scope of projects in this study was limited to residential real estate projects in India. Our final sample consisted of a total of 453 projects in the residential real

---

[2] https://www.emis.com/about.

[3] https://www.crisil.com/en/home/our-businesses/india-research.html.

[4] https://www.ventureintelligence.com/index.htm.

Table 11.1 Indian states distributed region-wise

Region	Indian state
North	Delhi
North	Haryana
North	Himachal Pradesh
North	Jammu and Kashmir
North	Punjab
North	Uttar Pradesh
South	Andhra Pradesh
South	Goa
South	Karnataka
South	Kerala
South	Puducherry
South	Tamil Nadu
East	Andaman and Nicobar Islands
East	Arunachal Pradesh
East	Assam
East	Bihar
East	Manipur
East	Meghalaya
East	Mizoram
East	Nagalan
East	Sikkim
East	Tripura
East	West Bengal
West	Dadra and Nagar Haveli
West	Daman and Diu
West	Gujara
West	Lakshadweep
West	Maharashtra
West	Rajasthan

estate sector in India. A total land area of 621.8 million sqft was developed with a construction area of 537.579 million sqft.

Demographics:

1) Projects are classified based on geographical location using 5 main regions – North, South, East, West, and Central depending on the where the project is situated in India. Table 11.1 indicates the regions in India and the corresponding states belonging to them.
2) Metro status: Projects are classified as metro (dummy variable 1) if they were situated in a metro city. The metro cities taken in this analysis include Bangalore, Chennai, Mumbai, Kolkata, Delhi and Hyderabad. All other cities were considered non-metro cities and assigned the value '0'.
3) Luxury status: Residential projects which include any one of the following amenities are termed 'luxury' status and assigned the value '1': swimming pool, jogging track, gymnasium, restaurant, departmental store, health care facility and ATM. All other projects are termed 'non-luxury' and assigned the value '0'.

11.4 Methodology

This study used multiple methodologies to answer the objectives and sub-objectives. The empirical analysis used various statistical tests that were used by past studies and that were relevant in this study. The data analysis methods used in this study are described briefly below.

11.4.1 Comparative Analysis

Comparative analysis was used to explore differences in infrastructure/real estate deals: Deals which due to PE investments may have perhaps shown significant statistical differences in various deal parameters as compared to deals which did not have PE investments in them. For example: comparative analysis compared infrastructure projects that had PE funding against those projects that did not have PE funding were compared across parameters such as project size, debt ratio and number of sponsors.[5]

The independent sample *t*-test or Mann–Whitney *U*-test have been used in the comparative analysis.

The *t*-test is a parametric test and is used to test a hypothesis stating that the mean scores on a variable will be significantly different for two independent samples or groups. It is used when the number of observations (sample size) was small, and the population standard deviation was unknown. The null hypothesis about differences between groups normally states as $\mu_1 = \mu_2$ or $\mu_1 - \mu_2 = 0$. In most cases, comparisons are between two sample means.

When the difference in the location of two populations is to be compared based on observations from two independent samples, the Mann–Whitney *U*-test is used. This

[5] See comparative analysis in chapter titled "The Case of Global Infrastructure".

test corresponds to the two independent sample t-tests for interval scale variables, when the variances of the two populations are assumed equal. In the Mann–Whitney U-test, the two samples are combined and cases are ranked in order of increasing size. The test statistic, U, is computed as the number of times a score from sample 1 or group 1 precedes a score from group 2. If the samples are from the same population, the distribution of scored from the two groups in the rank list should be random. For larger samples (>30), U is transformed into a normally distributed z statistic. This z can be corrected for ties within ranks.

Comparative deal analysis also facilitated the creation of initial hypothesis which in turn warranted in-depth analysis. In the comparative analysis for both the independent sample t-test and the Mann–Whitney U-test, the null hypothesis and the alternate hypothesis were formulated as follows:

Null hypothesis (H_0)—the difference between the two medians/means was insignificant.
Alternate hypothesis (H_1)—the difference between the two medians/means was not insignificant.

If, probability value <0.01, 99 percent—Significance that the alternate hypothesis is true, which is indicated with *** next to the variables of interest in the various figures.

0.01< probability value <0.05, 95 percent—Significance that the alternate hypothesis is true, which is indicated with ** next to the variables of interest in the various figures.

0.05< probability value <0.1, 90 percent—Significance that the alternate hypothesis is true, which is indicated with * next to the variables of interest in the various figures.

0.1< probability value, then the null hypothesis is not rejected (for want of more evidence) and the difference is not significant. (Variables which do not emerge significant are left blank in the figures).

11.4.2 Regression Analysis

Comparative analysis of deals was followed by regression analysis. "Regression analysis is concerned with the study of dependence of one variable on one or more other explanatory variables with a view to estimating and predicting the population mean of the former in terms of the latter" (Gujarati and Sangeetha, 2007). The objective of a regression is to use variable(s) whose values are known or observed in an effort to determine another predicted variable. The variable(s) whose values are known or observed are known as independent variables, and the variable which is predicted is known as the dependent variable. The independent variables are weighted to ensure that there is a maximal prediction from the set of independent variables. These weights denote the relative contribution of the independent variable to the overall prediction and can facilitate interpretation of the influence of each variable in making the prediction (Hair et al., 2016). When one independent variable is used in the regression, it is known as a simple regression. A simple regression model can be stated as:

$$X = a_0 + a_1 Y_1 + \varepsilon_1 \tag{11.1}$$

In Eq. 11.1, X is the dependent variable, and Y_1 is the independent variable. a_0 is the intercept term while a_1 is the regression coefficient, i.e., the amount of change in the dependant variable due to the independent variable. a_0 and a_1 are known as the parameters of the equation and ε_1 is the error term.

When more than one independent variables are used in the regression, it is known as a multiple regression. A multiple regression model can be stated as:

$$X = a_0 + a_1 Y_1 + a_2 Y_2 + \cdots + a_n Y_n + \varepsilon_1 \tag{11.2}$$

In Eq. 11.2, X is the dependent variable, and Y_1, Y_2, ... Y_n are the independent variables. a_0 is the intercept term while $a_1, a_2, \ldots a_n$ are the regression coefficient, i.e., the amount of change in the dependant variable due to the independent variables Y_1, Y_2, ... Y_n respectively. $a_0, a_1, \ldots a_n$ are known as the parameters of the equation and ε_1 is the error term.

In our study, various types of multiple regressions were used.

11.4.3 OLS or Ordinary Least Squares Regression

The OLS regression is the most common type of linear regression which uses a least squares method for estimating the relationship between the independent variables and the dependent variables. The OLS aims at minimizing the sum of the squared differences between the independent or observed variables and the dependent or predicted variable.

When Eqs. 11.1 or 11.2 are considered, the OLS attempts finding those parameters $a_0, a_1, \ldots a_n$ for which the error term is minimized.

11.4.4 Logistic Regression

This statistical technique is a specialized form of regression that was formulated when the dependent variable was a categorical (nominal or nonmetric) variable and the independent variables were metric variables. Logistic regression is also known as logit analysis, and the form of the logistic regression variate was similar to the variate in multiple regression. It is less affected when basic assumptions such as normality of variables are not met and could accommodate nonmetric variables through dummy variable coding, just as multiple regression can. Logistic regression differs from multiple regression, however, in being specifically designed to predict the probability of an event occurring. Because the binary dependent variable has only the values of "0" and "1", the predicted value (probability) must be bound to fall within the same range. To define a relationship bounded by 0 and 1, logistic regression uses the logistic curve, the typical s-shaped curve, to represent the relationship between the independent and dependent variables. At very low levels of the independent variable, the probability approaches 0, but never reaches 0. Likewise, as the independent variable increases, the predicted values increase up the curve, but then the slope starts decreasing so that at any level of the independent variable, the probability will approach 1 but never exceed it. The estimated coefficients for the independent variables are estimated using either the logit value of the odds value as the dependent measure. Each of these model formulations are shown below:

$$\text{LOGIT}_i = \ln\left(\frac{\text{prob}_{\text{event}}}{1 - \text{prob}_{\text{event}}}\right) = b_0 + b_1 X_1 + \cdots + b_n X_n \tag{11.3}$$

$$\text{Odds}_i = \frac{\text{prob}_{\text{event}}}{1 - \text{prob}_{\text{event}}} = e^{b_0 + b_1 X_1 + \cdots + b_n X_n} \tag{11.4}$$

In addition to the regression analysis, correlation tests and multicollinearity tests were also run to ensure validity of results.

11.4.5 Endogeneity

Endogeneity refers to the fact that an independent variable included in a model is potentially a choice variable, which may be correlated with other independent variables or variables that are not included in the analysis. Endogeneity can arise as a result of measurement error, autoregression with autocorrelated errors, simultaneity, omitted variables and sample selection errors. Endogeneity occurs when there was a feedback relationship between one or more of the independent variables and the dependent variable. It causes the OLS-estimated coefficients and standard errors to biased.

Endogeneity in an independent variable can be handled by making the endogeneous independent variable exogeneous, that is, make it independent of the disturbance term that influences the dependent variable. This can be achieved by creating a new independent variable which was formed by regressing all the exogeneous variables on it, and taking the fitted value as the new variable. The individual exogeneous variables (as well as the new fitted value) are called instrumental variables or instruments. Since the new variable is created from exogeneous variables, it was not and should not be correlated with the disturbance term, and can be considered exogeneous. The regression was run next in which the residual left over when the new (exogeneous) variable created is included. The *t*-statistic on the residual's coefficient indicated the presence of endogeneity with the null hypothesis stating that there is no endogeneity.

Endogeneity testing was performed to ensure that independent variables were not being affected by other independent variables and variables not included in the study. The Hausman specification test, the most commonly used test to control for endogeneity was used to test the variable and make it exogeneous.

11.4.6 Duration Analysis

Duration analysis is referred to as survival analysis or event history analysis.[6] Duration data is generated by what is called a "failure time process." A failure time process consists of units that were observed at some starting point in time. These units are observed when they are in a particular state and then again observed over time. At any given point in time, these units are "at risk" of experiencing some event, where the "event" essentially represented a change or transition to another state.

In the case of this study, the "risk" was being funded and the "event" was receiving the funding. After this event, the unit was either no longer observed or it was at risk of experiencing another kind of event (in this study, receiving the subsequent round of funding). In some circumstances, units were not observed experiencing an event; that is, no transition is made from one state to another while the unit was being observed (there is no staging of investment). This process was called a "failure time process" because (a) units were observed at an initial point in time, (b) the unit survived for some length in time and (c) then the unit "failed."

The risk in this process was captured in the following formula:

$$\text{Risk} = (\text{Chance that something happens})/(\text{Chance that it has not happened yet}) \tag{11.5}$$

A different way to depicting this was

$$\text{Risk} = P\,(\text{Failure})/P(\text{Survival}), \tag{11.6}$$

where

Failure	The unconditional probability that an event will occur
Survival	The probability that up until now the event has not yet occurred

The risk was the conditional failure rate—given that the event had not yet occurred, what were the chances that it will occur and risk ratio was called the hazard ratio and was at the center of duration analysis.

[6] http://jdemeritt.weebly.com/uploads/2/2/7/7/22771764/introduction.pdf.

Duration analysis was used because the data was right censored; and this methodology overcame the drawbacks of conventional Ordinary Least Squares (OLS) regression in this regard.

References

Gompers, P., & Lerner, J. (1999). *The venture capital cycle*. MIT press.
Gujarati, D., & Sangeetha, N. (2007). *Basic Econometrics* (4th ed.). Tata McGraw-Hill.
Hair, J.F., Black, W.C., Babin, B.J., & Anderson, R.E. (2016). Multivariate Data Analysis (7th ed.). Pearson
http://jdemeritt.weebly.com/uploads/2/2/7/7/22771764/introduction.pdf
Lerner, J. (1994). The syndication of venture capital investments. *Financial Management Association, 23*(3), 293–316.

The manufacturer's authorised representative in the EU is Springer Nature Customer Service Centre GmbH, Europaplatz 3, 69115 Heidelberg, Germany. If you have any concerns regarding our products, please contact ProductSafety@springernature.com

Printed and bound by CPI Group (UK) Ltd, Croydon, CR0 4YY
30/09/2026
02225303-0004